The Complete Handbook of Gardening

Edited by Roger Grounds
Based on the German text by Martin Stangl

Consultant Editor George Elbert

The
Complete
Handbook of
Gardening

WARD LOCK LIMITED · LONDON

Stangl/MEIN HOBBY—DER GARTEN
© BLV Verlagsgesellschaft mbH, München

English text © Ward Lock Limited 1975

ISBN 0 7063 1856 0

First published in Great Britain 1975
by Ward Lock Limited, 116 Baker Street,
London, W1M 2BB

Layout by Sheila Sherwen

Text filmset in Ehrhardt by
Servis Filmsetting Ltd, Manchester

Printed in Hong Kong by
Lee Fung Asco, Printers

Contents

Foreword

Gardening and gardeners have changed a lot over the last couple of decades.

There was a time when anyone with any claims to being a gardener would call in a jobbing gardener and tell him he wanted a garden. The jobbing gardener would then go to work (sustained by innumerable cups of tea from your kitchen, whose floor he would cover with the mud from his boots and your garden), dig the whole area with a spade, lay trails of grit which he would tell you were the gravel paths, leave dead twigs sticking out of the ground in various places, which he would tell you were the shrubs, and leave a levelled area of earth covered in seeds which he would tell you was the lawn. He would then go away, telling you that if you watered everything at the right time you would have a garden by spring.

Those days have gone. Today most home owners have to be their own gardeners. To get any satisfaction out of a garden it needs to be as carefully thought out and planned as the living room: to stay looking good it needs almost as much loving attention to keep it neat and tidy.

It is, of course, possible to design a garden which, once planted and established, will maintain itself without further attention for five to ten years. But gardens, unlike living rooms, keep growing. You may move the sofa in the living room because you get bored with it always being in the same place, but the usual reason for moving a shrub is that it has outgrown the space allocated to it. Fortunately sofas seldom grow.

The most satisfying gardens are those in which, while the majority of the plantings can be regarded as permanent, there is room for movement and expansion. A garden, unlike a living room, is a complex of interrelated living things, and the gardener's aim is usually to arrange these elements in as pleasing a manner as possible.

Whichever sort of garden you want, a minimum-maintenance garden or a gardener's garden, this book sets out to tell you all you need to achieve either ambition, and it does so in a simple, straightforward way, taking you step by step from first principles through the flower garden all the way to the complexities of growing fruit and vegetables to keep the larder full.

Roger Grounds

1 From Wasteland to Garden

Most gardeners have to start from scratch, usually with the mud and rubble the builder left behind. And that can be as daunting as confronting a child with a large sheet of white paper and telling him to draw something—anything—on it.

Faced with this situation most people do one of two things. They either shirk making a start until tempted out by warm weather, when they begin to pick away at the weeds and broken bricks, or else, fired with blind enthusiasm, set about digging frantically, only to regret it later, often leaving themselves with a legacy of problems.

Even if you buy a house where the previous owner tried to make a garden you are relatively little better off. You probably won't like what he did, just as you probably won't like the wallpaper he had in the sitting room. And creating a garden is very like furnishing a living room. The choices you make will be highly subjective, and the end result a projection of your own personality.

Whether starting on a fresh garden or transforming an established one, the first thing to do is to decide just what sort of garden you want.

Are you going to have a minimum labour garden, laid down to lawn, shrubs and ground-cover? In which case you will get most of your colour between March and June and little after that. Or are you going to go for bedding plants and a riot of colour from April till October? In which case you will have a completely barren garden all winter. Or might you go for spring bulbs and hardy herbaceous plants? Do you want a woodland garden of rhododendrons and camellias (in which case you need to have the right soil) or a hot patio of sub-tropical plants? Do you want a vegetable garden? Do you want to grow fruit? Do you want the enchantment of a myriad of summer roses, and the impossible dream of flowers in profusion tumbling everywhere? Do you want a garden of indolence, to laze in while the birds sing and the bees hum in the flowers around you? Or do you want a bit of everything—a rose bed here, a rock garden there, a pool on the patio with a fountain playing, some lawn and the vegetable patch hidden by a trellis of giant-flowered clematis? Are you going to go for the sort of tidy well-designed garden your neighbours can admire—or are you going to go for its opposite, a plantsman's garden, full of frames and pots and rarities so rare they don't impress your neighbours because they don't even know what they are?

Your garden is yours: and the choice is yours. The only problem is which to choose.

If you are furnishing your house what do you do? You probably look through innumerable magazines, and you go on countless window-shopping trips. And you probably keep notes of things you like and where to get them.

You do just the same for your garden—look through magazines, catalogues, books—but most of all go out and look at real gardens. Look most closely at the gardens in your own neighbourhood: they will show you most quickly what plants are likely to do well in your own garden. And look at gardens wherever you go for ideas. Ideas are what make a garden really interesting. Keep notes of interesting plants and make sketches of features that really please you.

Garden of a detached house

1 Herbaceous border: erigeron, white summer Marguerite, phlox, *Achillea filipendula* 'Gold Plate', low, single-flowered dahlias, chrysanthe-mums, and so on, in combination with tufted perennials.

2 Rambling rose 'Coral Dawn' (double pink).

3 Border of low ground-coverers like stonecrop *Sedum hybrida* 'Little Evergreen', red-leaved bugle *Ajuga reptans* 'Atropurpurea', together with taller plants like rodgersia, *Bergenia cordifolia* 'Dawn', and the plantain lily *Hosta sieboldii*.

4 Dutchman's pipe *Aristolochia macrophylla* (= *durior*) at the house entrance.

5 Floribunda rose 'Meteor' (vermilion).

6 Stony bed with a few grasses —*Festuca glauca*, striped zebra grass *Miscanthus sinensis* 'Zebrinus'; some perennials—foxtail lilies

Eremurus robustus, stonecrop *Sedum telephium* 'Autumn Joy'; and some suitable low annuals such as gazania and creeping, red-flowered *Verbena peruvianum*.

7 Dwarf trees and shrubs, deciduous and coniferous, such as red-leaved Japanese maple *Acer palmatum dissec-tum atropurpureum*, cinquefoil *Potentilla fruticosa* 'Arbuscula', and so on. As ground cover plants: alpine forest heath *Erica carnea*, *Dianthus gratianopolitanus*, and low grasses such as sheep's fescue and creeping red fescue.

8 Staghorn sumach *Rhus typhina* Laciniata'.

9 Close-to-nature planting— hardy plant growth around the house, including grasses, ground-cover plants, wild flowers and small trees.

10 *Spiraea nipponica* or bridal wreath (*Spirea arguta*).

11 Three *Stephanandra incisa* shrubs.

12 Japanese Autumn cherry *Prunus subhirtella* 'Fukubana' and so on.

13 *Kolkwitzia amabilis*

14 Flowering purple leaf plum *Prunus cerasifera* 'Nigra'.

15 Two shrubs of *Kerria japonica* 'Flore-Pleno'.

16 Dawn redwood *Metasequoia glyptostroboides*.

17 Mock orange *Philadelphus virginalis*.

18. Gold rose *Rosa hugonis*.

19 In front of this shrubbery, as a border to the lawn, a row of floribunda roses 'Irish Wonder' (from a distance, an amazing blaze of blood-orange colour) together with tulips, and other spring bulbs.

20 The June or service berry *Amelanchier canadensis*.

21 Rock spray *Cotoneaster dielsianus* with elegantly overhanging branches.

22 Three Scots firs *Pinus sylvestris*.

23 Three rhododendrons.

24 Two purple hazels *Corylus maxima* 'Purpurea'.

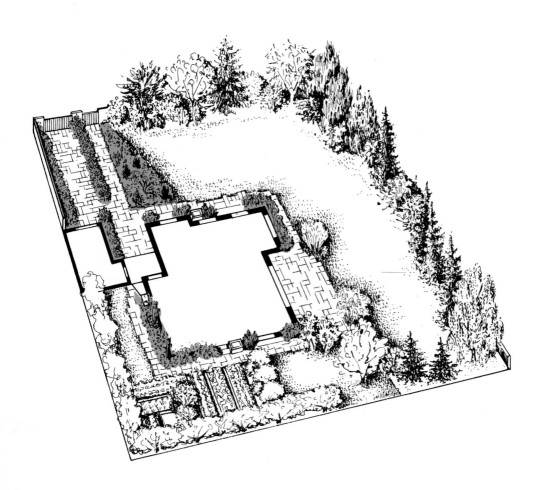

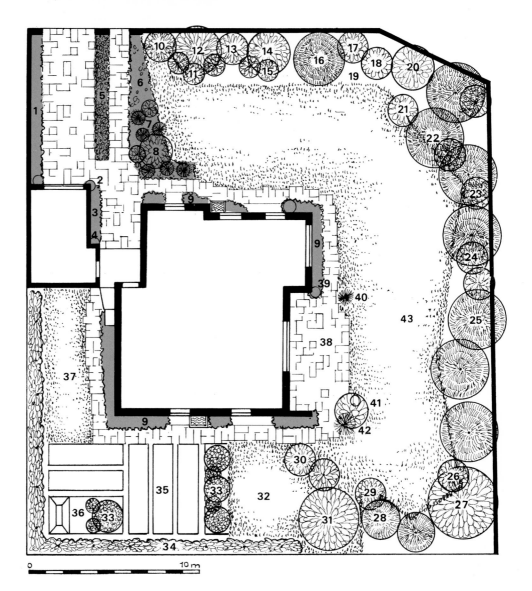

25 Four larches *Larix decidua.*
With pruning, these can be
kept to about 4·5 metres or
15 feet tall. By restricting
their growth, an illusion of
greater size is given to the
garden, and in later years
the terrace will still get plenty
of sunshine. Under the
larches grow ground-cover
plants like woodruff, wild
ginger, ivy, and so on and a
few taller shade-loving plants
like ferns.
26 *Forsythia intermedia*
'Lynwood Gold'.
27 Weeping birch *Betula
verrucosa* 'Youngii'.
28 Two serbian spruces *Picea
omorica.*
29 A dogwood shrub with white-

edged foliage *Cornus alba
albomarginata elegans.*
30 Dwarf plum.
31 Two lilacs ('Souvenir de Louis
Spath' dark purple; 'Madame
Lemoine', double, white; or
'James MacFarlane').
32 Small play area for young
children, with sandpit and
combined swing and
climbing-frame.
33 Four red currant and four
gooseberry bushes in all two
different sites.
34 Fruit hedge (apples, pears,
morello cherries).
35 Vegetable garden.
36 Compost heap.
37 Grass plot (and place for
hanging out washing).
38 Terrace.

39 Climbing plant e.g.
Wistera sinensis.
40 Tall ornamental grasses (e.g.
Pampas grass, or *Miscanthus
sinensis* 'Silver Feather').
41 *Aralia elata.*
42 Golden prairie grass
Spartina michauxiana
'Aureomarginata'.
43 Lawns.

Dwarf evergreens, diminutive trees and shrubs which brighten the winter garden with their varying tones of green, are becoming increasingly popular. They require little space and therefore are suitable for both courtyard and terraced-house gardens, as well as for patio. Nurseries and garden centres offer a wide choice of dwarf pines, spruce, false cypresses, and so on. They look most effective when grown together with tufted perennials.

Most important when creating a new garden: don't overcrowd it! Trees and shrubs may look charming while they are still small, but bear in mind they will require a lot of space later in order to develop into their full beauty. A garden which looks rather spartan in its early years will look better in years to come than one that starts overcrowded. During the early years the gaps can be filled with annuals.

If you see a garden that really delights you don't be afraid to knock on the door and ask the owner to show you round. Most gardeners are friendly people, only too pleased to show someone round their garden. They may even give you a few plants, and advice on the best nurseryman to go to.

Take the best ideas from several people's gardens, and then try to blend them into something completely new and wholly your own.

Alternatively you can opt out of this type of decision-making and put the design of your garden into the hands of a firm of landscape gardeners. But even then you need to give them some general, broad outline of the sort of garden you want, otherwise you may take a strong dislike to what they give you.

In most districts there are local garden clubs or societies. Don't be shy of joining yours just because you are a beginner; all the other members were beginners too, once. These societies are usually unpretentious and ask only a very modest annual subscription. The great advantage you will gain by joining is that all the members garden in the same district as you, with the same weather and usually the same soil. Get them to tell you the problems they had when they made their gardens: it'll save you making the same mistakes.

Once you have made up your mind about the sort of garden you want in general terms—and before you set your heart too firmly on it—remember that other members of the family have a right to have a say too. Like the house, the garden is something for the whole family to enjoy. Women usually have strong ideas about the ways colours combine; they may also want an area set aside for flowers to cut or plant materials to dry, not to mention free vegetables and fruit for their deep freeze. They may want a herb garden near the kitchen, and somewhere for the clothes line: also a compost heap for vegetable peelings just where you wanted to put the tool shed.

Then there are the children. They need the largest possible lawn you can give them, a climbing frame, a sandpit, swings and a paddling or swimming pool (preferably heated and covered—according to them!).

Put all these needs together, along with your own ideas, and what you have is a number of elements which somehow you now have to fit together in the space available, in as pleasing a way as you can. Your problem is very similar to that of an architect. You need a vegetable garden (the kitchen if you like), a children's area (the playroom), a greenhouse (the study) a patio (the living room) and various other elements. All you have to do now is link these things together logically and harmoniously. You may find, as architects sometimes do, that there is not enough room for everything. So make a priorities list and plan first for those things you know you must have.

The next step is to sketch-plan the garden. Make a colour key (lawn—green, vegetable garden—brown, shrubs—red, patio—purple and so on) and just draw these roughly on a piece of paper, fitting together squares and circles, triangles, curves and swirls until you feel happy with the shapes you have made and their relationship to each other, both functionally and visually.

Garden-lovers who are not satisfied by 'common' shrubs and are looking for something out of the ordinary should consult specialist nurserymen. Garden centres seldom have rarities. However these very special plants should only be used very sparingly, and be positioned with great care. Leave it to the well-known and unassuming ornamental shrubs to form the basic structure of the garden.

A garden is never quite completed. It is a living thing, constantly changing. No matter how well planned or well planted, there is always work to be done with shears, saw or spade. But this should be unobtrusive: the loveliest gardens are those where everything seems to be growing of its own accord.

Then transfer the whole thing to a scale plan. If you don't work to scale you'll find your garden has grown to four or five times its real size in your imagination. Use paper with squares already on it. You don't have to stick to one square to the foot or yard. Use four squares to the yard if you want. For a general plan a scale of 1:100 is usually satisfactory. When you want to fill the details in, redraw the plan to a scale of 1:50, or 1:25 if you really want the fine details.

First, mark in all known measurements on the plan—those of the house or other buildings, the entrance, any pool or existing trees, and so on. These can often be copied from the builder's plans. There is no need to do any actual measuring, except to mark the position of trees already growing on the property.

Next mark any paths or terraces on your plan, remembering that paths are not ornaments: they should really only be laid when their function is to link different parts of the garden.

Next, the position of ornamental shrubs, and, in the kitchen garden, fruit trees and vegetable beds should be marked. The beds should be about 1 metre (say 3–4 ft) wide, with narrow walks, about 50 cm/18 in. wide, between them. The appropriate distances for planting ornamental shrubs, fruit trees and bushes are discussed later in the book.

An important and often overlooked essential in the kitchen garden is a water-tank. This can be a conventional water butt, or a circular structure of concrete, about 1 metre 20/4 ft in diameter, 30–60 cm/1–2 ft deep and with a concrete base. This is large enough to hold an abundant store of water for the garden, and also to provide a substitute bathing-pool, something children particularly appreciate. There should also be enough room for a compost-heap.

Similar details should be filled in for the rest of the garden. Don't try to get too much into the garden: if you do it will look a mess. If the plan looks overcrowded, harden your heart and drop something. Check your priorities list to see what can go. It is easier to drop ideas when they are on paper than when you have actually created them in the garden.

When, after various calculations and corrections, the overall plan is ready, the details can be tackled. Drawings for the herbaceous borders, terrace, pond, pergola, and so on should be to a scale of 1:10 or 1:20. Using this scale the details can be defined on paper. You can transfer them to the garden either by eye or if you really want to be accurate, by marking the garden out in squares marked with lime or peat and corresponding to the lines on your plan.

THE HOME GARDEN

A garden is not a painting, not just something to be looked at from the sitting room window. Nor is it there merely to excite the admiration of your neighbours. It is an extension of the house, an integral part of the home, meant for everyday living and enjoyment, for healthy exercise, games and relaxation.

Most people do all their gardening themselves,

so it is important that the garden should be planned from the start to be self-maintaining to some degree otherwise you will find your garden all work and no fun, and that is just what you don't want. This is particularly true of gardens of over quarter of an acre.

If you are lucky enough to buy your plot of land before the house is built you start with a tremendous advantage. You can plan, with the architect, the best possible place for the house so that you do not only get the house you want but also an interesting shape for the garden.

The larger part of the garden, together with the patio, should be on the south side of the house. Between the house and the road, you only want a small garden—just enough to give you quiet and privacy. The areas on either side of the house are more interesting if they are not of equal size. This will improve the all-round design of the garden.

Before any building starts have the builders move the topsoil—that is the upper layer of earth usually 13–15 cm/5–6 in. deep—and push it into two or three big heaps on the fringe of the site, before the foundations are dug out. If you are lucky enough to have established trees already standing on your land, be sure to include these in the garden plan, unless they stand too close to-gether. Above all, if there is only one valuable tree, make every effort to position the house so that this tree can be saved. With thoughtful planning, this tree might perhaps form a strikingly attractive corner-feature of the patio. While the work of building is going on, protect the trunks of existing trees with boards, rush-matting, and similar

materials. Their roots too must be left undis-turbed.

A further point: if at all possible, have two stands for water-taps on opposite sides of the house included in the building plan. This will save the need for long water-hoses later on. Sufficient power-points should also be provided outside the house, so that an electric lawn-mower, hedge-cutters or electric lamps can be connected later. If the builder knows you want these things before building starts, they can be supplied easily and cheaply.

Once the house is finished, the builders pack gravel, building-rubble or any other coarse material round the foundations. These must be firmly rammed down, especially where the terrace and any paths are to go, otherwise it will subside in years to come, which will mean relaying the paving stones.

The next step is to have the subsoil for the whole garden—except the terrace and path areas—broken up by a rotovator or rototiller—which you can hire. This will thoroughly loosen the subsoil which has been compressed and hardened by the wheels of the builders' trucks. Only when this has been done should the topsoil from the heaps be distributed over the garden. Before moving any soil take into account what features you want, whether you want a level garden, a sunken garden, a hole dug for a pond or a mound made for a rock garden.

PATH AND TERRACE

If there is to be a path leading from garden gate

A roof garden with a wood floor and wooden railings. The plant containers are also made of impregnated wooden beams. This creates a light, airy garden atmosphere.

The bare concrete wall of this terraced-house garden is draped with Virginia creeper. The border in front contains blue lavender, yellow marigolds, and a red-leaved Japanese maple.

▼

to the front or back door it should be at least 1–1.5 m/4 ft wide. That is wide enough to allow two people to walk side by side along it in comfort. If the drive runs directly alongside this footpath—and this is often the case—a border of plants, about 60 cm/2 ft wide, should be made between them. If the whole area were put down to uninterrupted tarmac or concrete it would look very dull indeed.

Another solution is to pave only a narrow track for the car, turfing the rest of the drive. Paths leading from the front or back door across the patio to the kitchen garden need not be more than 1 m/3 ft wide, and in smaller gardens 75 cm/2 ft 6 in is usually sufficient.

The patio itself should always be of generous proportions—ideally the full width of the house and at least 240 cm/8 ft deep, with plenty of room for people to sit on it, sunbathe or have a barbecue.

Paths should never be built right against the house. The nearness of walls can make one feel hemmed in. Besides, the walls of a house are one of a gardener's greatest assets where he can grow some of his most beautiful plants. So always make a flower-bed at least 60 cm/2 ft wide between the ally path and the house. Since these are separated from the lawn by the path they are very easy to look after.

A SECOND SITTING AREA

In addition to the patio, which should if possible be on a level with the living room, you may also want to set aside a second place for sitting out.

This could, for example, be under an arbour or scented roses or clematis which would provide welcome shade on hot summer days. It could be sited among the flowers and shrubs, well away from the house, perhaps beside a pool containing water plants, or by a decorative wall. This gives you the advantage of being able to see the house and garden from an entirely different angle.

For the most part, ornamental shrubs will form a green screen round the property, with a few taller shrubs or trees here and there. A good screen of vegetation is particularly desirable round the patio. When planting the screen it is worth considering conifers. These enliven the garden in winter with a variety of green tones as well as blues and yellows. In smaller gardens the green screen may be just a hedge. Once the screen or hedge is planted, make a start on the lawn and then the rose beds and flower beds.

THE KITCHEN GARDEN

If you have room for a kitchen garden, have one. Shrubs, roses, bushes or a hedge can, to a certain extent, screen the vegetables from the rest of the garden although there is no need to hide the vegetables, fruit trees and bushes. They have a beauty of their own.

THE FRONT GARDEN

This can, in a detached house where there is enough space between the front door and the road, continue the style of the rest of the garden. If, however, space is severely limited, then a different approach will have to be adopted. A climbing plant looks very attractive round the front door, and brings the whole house into harmony with the surrounding garden. Since front doors are often on the north or east side of the house, plants such as Dutchman's Pipe *Aristolochia macrophylla* (=*durior*) a hardy honeysuckle like *Lonicera henryi*, the May-blooming *Clematis montana rubens*, or an ivy, will do particularly well.

Clothes-lines and a courtyard   When planning the garden, make sure to provide a place for the washing to be hung out, preferably fairly close to the house. All too often it tends to be tucked away somewhere in the region of the kitchen garden, which may fit very neatly into the plan, but will seldom get used.

The children's climbing-frame or swing should be placed to one side of the terrace, not directly in front. The sand-pit should be in view of the kitchen window, but not in full sunlight. Children seldom like playing for very long in really hot surroundings and since sand attracts the sun's heat, sandpits can become extremely hot.

Something else you should include in the garden if you can is an inner courtyard, within easy reach of the kitchen. It should be paved, and can be enclosed by a wall, a hedge or ornamental shrubs. There should be a water tap and a sink—an old stone trough would be ideal—and also a sturdy work-bench at a practical height. A small courtyard like this, catching the early morning sun, makes an excellent place for doing a few normally indoor chores in the open—cleaning shoes, preparing vegetables or arranging flowers, and a variety of other tasks which are more pleasant in the fresh air.

THE COURTYARD GARDEN

This is a world apart from any other sort of garden. Surrounded on 4 sides by the house or on 3 sides by the house and on the fourth by a wall, it is completely private. Space is very limited so one has to dispense with the luxury of a lawn and settle for exciting paving, with a few containers for plants, and make the maximum use of the walls.

Suitable paving includes small granite setts or blocks, concrete paving slabs, hard-fired bricks (engineering bricks), or a floor of timber, similar to a wooden landing-stage. The advantage of a timbered surface is that children can sit and play on it in the sunshine from February to November, or even December, without risking catching a cold. To give the courtyard an illusion of greater size, keep the pattern of the flooring as small as possible.

Leave areas unpaved for planting with specially selected shrubs, roses, or small bushes. Decorative shrubs might include the slender, split-leaved stag's-horn sumach *Rhus typhina* 'Laciniata', the so-called Judas tree *Cercis siliquastrum*, or the tropical-looking *Aralia elata*, while among the conifers, the dwarf blue pine *Pinus procera glaucanana*, the hemlock fir *Tsuga canadensis*, together with various dwarf conifers, are highly decorative.

A courtyard garden, being enclosed by walls, holds something of the warm south in its atmosphere, so that it would also be possible to grow a variety of sun-loving plants in tubs. These might include *Cassia corymbosa*, the Oleander, the African blue lily *Agapanthus orientalis* or the Passion flower *Passiflora caerulea*, and many other tender plants. During the winter these must be brought into a cool, bright room.

What a courtyard garden needs above all is water. This can be in the form of a little spring, bubbling up from an old millstone and trickling across pebblestones into the ground, a small wall-fountain with a stone trough beneath it, or a simple basin made of concrete or plastic sheeting and containing water plants.

The furniture for a courtyard garden should be chosen very carefully. If it is light and slender, it will give width to the courtyard and enhance its air of comfort and intimacy.

What has been said about a courtyard garden also applies to some extent to a roof-garden. A roof-garden, however, has other problems such as accident prevention, water supply and assessing the load the roof itself can bear. These must be solved with the help of an architect and/or a garden designer with particular experience in this field. It is far too dangerous to try to solve these problems yourself.

THE GARDEN OF A TERRACED HOUSE

The piece of ground that goes with a terraced house is usually the shape of a narrow hand-towel. At best it may be 8–10 m/25–30 ft wide, at worst only 6–7 m/18–21 ft. It is very difficult to design a pleasing garden on such a site and indeed well-designed gardens are extremely rare on these sites. These hand-towel plots are either densely overcrowded with shrubs, or else they consist of a meagre lawn, a few concrete slabs, and some forlorn-looking roses.

The ideal solution—but only in theory From the landscape gardener's point of view, the best way of solving the problems of these narrow gardens would be if all the adjoining plots in a row of houses were designed to an overall plan, without partitions. The whole would then look like one single, well-proportioned and beautiful garden.

It has been tried. But—and it's a big but—this 'ideal solution' has its drawbacks. To begin with, who is supposed to look after this communal green belt? And how much freedom should children and dogs have to roam the whole area? In many cases and it has been tried, it's not long before some residents begin to hate the sight of one another, and up go the wire netting and hedges, defeating the whole idea.

Almost every house-holder in the row has not only dreamt of having his own four walls but also his own individual garden, and will therefore plan accordingly. If, however, various points of common interest are taken into account in the process, so much the better for all concerned.

The outside room To enjoy a garden as a place to live in, the first requirement is a sitting-area by the

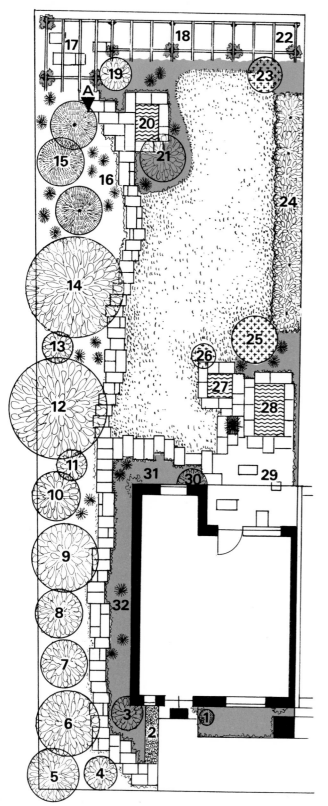

Garden of a corner-house in a terrace

1 Irish Yew *Taxus baccata fastigiata*; the rest of the front garden: ground-cover plants, ferns.
2 Beech hedge.
3 Holly *Ilex aquifolium*.
4 Scented snowball tree *Viburnum carlesii*.
5 Forsythia.
6 Japanese weeping cherry *Prunus serrulata* 'Shidare Sakura'.
7 *Spiraea arguta*.
8 *Kolkwitzia amabilis*.
9 Weeping lilac *Syringa reflexa* or *S. yamanensis rosea*.
10 Purple barberry *Berberis thunbergii* 'Atropurpurea'.
11 Yellow bush-rose 'Fruhlingsmargen' or 'Gold Bush'.
12 Mountain ash *Sorbus aucuparia*.
13 Red bush rose 'Crimson Glory'.
14 Birch.
15 Three Serbian spruces *Picea omorika* or *P. maxwellii* (together with the birch these screen the windows of a house across the street).

0   5 m

16 Floribunda roses 'Irish Wonder' or 'Montezuma' (effective against the green of the Serbian spruces) and low tufts of fescue grass.
17 A shaded sitting-area.
18 Pergola with various climbing-plants.
19 *Cotoneaster horizontalis*.
20 Pool with bog plants.
21 Staghorn sumach *Rhus typhina* 'Laciniata'.
22 Compost heap.
23 Giant cow parsley *Heracleum laciniatum*.
24 Fruit hedge apple, pear.
25 Evergreen bamboo *Sinarundinaria murieliae*.
26 Broad-leaved sunflower *Helianthus salicifolius*
27 Water-lily pool.
28 Small swimming pool.
29 Terrace.
30 Firethorn.
31 *Wistera sinensis*.
32 Between house and paved pathway and in front of shrubbery: ground-cover plants, grasses, wild flowers and small woody plants.

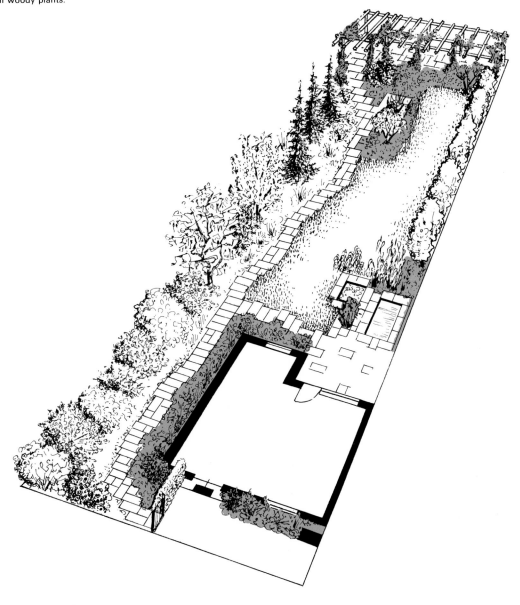

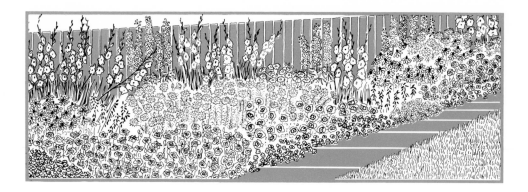

house, which should be screened as far as possible from the neighbours, even when one is on good terms with them. It should be possible to enjoy breakfast or supper on the terrace, to sunbathe or entertain guests, in short, to feel completely private and at ease.

A wall projecting about 3 m/10 ft from the house into the garden is the best way of ensuring privacy. If the house already happens to have a built-in, recessed sitting area, an awning can be fitted on above this so that, together with the side wall, quite a comfortable open-air room is formed.

It is even better if the individual terraced houses are staggered, in which case the protruding house-corner, with the addition of a wall, or perhaps a screen of wood or rush matting or even a hedge, will form a spacious sitting out area, sheltered both from view and noise.

The screen can be enlivened with rambler roses or other climbing plants. Under no circumstances should the terrace be cut off from the rest of the garden by a welter of plants, so that one sits in a kind of green prison. On the contrary, the terrace should open out on to the lawn without interruption, giving an illusion of greater size to the small garden.

The green frontier In small gardens of this sort the boundary between neighbouring houses is best marked by a low fence about 1 m/3 ft high. Avoid planting tall bushes or trees on either side of this fence, since this would turn the already narrow plot into a sort of green tunnel. You already have the privacy of the patio area; the openness of

the rest of the garden provides an interesting contrast. The best thing is for neighbours to talk over the matter of fences or hedges and come to an agreement. If one party plants a low-growing hedge along his side of the fence, it will serve the purpose for both gardens. A man who is fond of fruit-growing might train a hedge of fruit trees along the boundary with the help of taut wire (see Fruit-growing), or rambling roses could be grown. If, however, the plots are as wide as 7 m/20 ft or even 10 m/30 ft, then freestanding ornamental shrubs could be planted on one side of the fence. If the same procedure is repeated all along the row of gardens, the result will be attractive little areas of greenery screened from both sides, although the owner of each plot has had to bear only half the planting cost.

Along the fence which has been planted on the neighbour's side with a hedge or some ornamental shrubs, one could make a colourful bed of perennials or roses, separating it from the lawn by a paved path. This should be made of adjoining paving-slabs, not just stepping-stones, so that grass is prevented from growing into the flower-bed and one is saved the tedious job of cutting the edges. It also makes lawn-mowing easier.

A green backcloth If the garden facing the terrace ends in a wall (the back wall of a row of garages, for example) this could make a suitable place for putting up a little pergola in conjunction with a second sitting area. Shaded by climbing plants, this would make a delightfully cool retreat in summer. However, if there is another row of houses at the back of the garden, it would be best to screen the rear with trees and bushes that will grow quite tall. It looks particularly attractive when a planting of this kind is continued in the neighbouring garden.

A plot which is far too long for its width can be made to look better proportioned by dividing off roughly two-thirds of it with the help of a hedge or bushes, an espalier, or something of that sort. Behind this a little vegetable garden can be planted. There usually isn't much room to spare, but even so one can plant some herbs, lettuces and radish, a few tomatoes, and in particular a good bed of strawberries which will give several crops.

The front-garden The front garden is often rather neglected, though in some cases this may also mean it is over-loaded with plants. Yet it is most people's first impression of your home, and first impressions last. It should be treated with at least as much love and respect as the rest of the garden.

The front garden of a terraced house is generally as wide as the house itself and often only 240–300 cm/8–10 ft deep. It can only be given an appearance of distinction by a rational awareness of its limitations. Restrain yourself from copying the usual oval-shaped mound rising from the middle of a tiny lawn, on which a few forlorn roses try to charm visitors.

Even worse are those little front gardens squashed between the house and a hedge, so that they look even smaller than they really are. Worst of all is the planting of a blue pine or weeping willow behind the hedge. These trees look charming when young, but they grow into giants. Their branches rob both your house and your neighbours' of light, and their roots rob the soil of all goodness and can actually strangle drains and mains gas supplies. They are a menace and should never be planted in small gardens.

Such mistakes can easily be avoided by using only plants whose ultimate size will be what is wanted. Supposing the house entrance is on the north or east side, where there is not much sun, one could plant nearby for example an elegantly drooping, evergreen *Cotoneaster salicifolius* 'Floccosus', a dwarf form of the yew *Taxus baccata*, a slow-growing holly (one of the many named forms of *Ilex aquifolium*), a small hardy hybrid rhododendron, a few azaleas, or some similarly interesting plants which will not grow too large even in maturity. Mixed ground-cover plants like *Asarum europaeum* or *A. canadense* periwinkle, foam flower *Tiarella cordifolia*, Japanese spurge *Pachysandra terminalis,* or woodruff; or trailing shrubs such as *Cotoneaster dammeri, C. salicifolius* 'Park Carpet', and so on. All these are suitable for planting in a shady position, as are ivy or wild strawberries.

Very small areas should be planted with only one particular kind of ground-cover plant. Standing out from this green carpet there might be a few ferns, some Astilbe plants, bugwort, Japanese windflower *Anemone japonica,* or other taller perennials. In springtime you could have snowdrops, crocuses and tulips to catch the eye, so that the front garden could be tasteful and yet unpretentious throughout the year.

The house entrance can be given a personal note by using a climbing plant, an interesting shrub or a freely-growing perennial. Here a plume poppy, macleaya with a rodgersia grows beside an entrance facing north.

Ground-cover plants for shaded or partly-shaded spots: ivy, wild strawberry, *Asarum europaeum* with glossy leaves or the matt-leaved *A. canadense* or *A. caudatum*.

If you're lucky, the front garden may get full sunshine, in which case you can plant the entire area with low-growing polyantha or floribunda roses—it is best to stick to one particular sort. Another attractive idea is to have tufts of grey fescue grass springing up among a ground cover of *Erica carnea,* with a small group of perpetual-flowering bush-roses against the house wall. In a sunny situation, ground cover can be provided by low clumps of perennials.

Of the varieties already mentioned, the cotoneaster and ivy will also do quite well even in full sun. Other suitable plants include various kinds of stonecrop such as *Sedum kamtschaticum* or *S. sieboldii,* thyme *Thymus serpyllum* or *T. citriodorus* 'Golden Dwarf' with its yellow-green foliage, purple *Ajuga reptans* 'Atropurpurea', or a wormwood with silver-grey leaves on prostrate stems.

For somewhat larger areas, a pleasing ground cover can be made by making plantings of different groups of plants, so as to create attractive colour contrasts throughout the year. You could use, for example, the silver-white of snow-in-summer *Cerastium tomentosum,* red-brown bugle *Ajuga repens* 'Purpureum', yellow-green thyme and green tufted phlox. This carpet of low-growing plants can be enlivened with a few specimens of taller ornamental grasses such as *Avena sempervirens glauca, Pennisetum compressum, Stipa maxima S. gigantea* or *S. splendeus* (which are probably all the same plant masquerading under different names) or a few single-flowered roses. However, this sort of planting would be better left to the more advanced and experienced gardener.

In the case of larger front gardens, a green expanse of lawn is really a necessity. It provides the perfect foil for the flowers round it. In smaller gardens, however, the numerous corners and edges make lawn cultivation a tedious business, and for this reason it is best to concentrate on ground cover plants.

Flowers round the door   As already mentioned, climbing plants can do much to add charm to a porch or front door. If the porch door is on the south side, the sturdy wistera or the more delicate, large-flowered clematis hybrids are particularly suitable; on the west side, climbing roses; while on the north or east side there might be a Dutchman's pipe *Aristolochia macrophylla* (= *durior*) with its healthy, luxuriant foliage; a fragrant honeysuckle *Lonicera japonica,* for example, or *L. henryi,* which is an evergreen variety; or the elegant, single-flowered *Clematis montana rubens,* which in May surrounds the door with a profusion of small pink blossoms.

It is important that the colour of the flowers should go well with the colour of the house—for example, yellow climbing roses against a blue-grey housewall, dark violet clematis or red climbing roses against a whitewashed wall, and so on. Another way of giving the house entrance a very personal note is to choose one or just a few plants with attractive foliage, such as plume poppy or the showy-leaved rodgersia.

All that has been said so far about terraced house gardens also applies to the small gardens of semi-detached houses.

Basic soil cultivation   Before any soil cultivation is begun, paths and the area to become the patio, already marked on the garden plan, should be staked out. This is done by knocking in wooden pegs at each corner and connecting these with garden-line. The paths and patio sites should then be dug out to a depth of 45 cm/18 in., the rich soil excavated by this operation being distributed over the remaining garden area. In the case of a new private house one should already have ensured that, when all building was finished, the rich topsoil had been distributed only on the areas intended for cultivation, leaving the sites of terrace and pathways untouched as far as possible.

The first step in preparing soil for cultivation is to slice off any turves with a broad, strongly-made mattock or turfing spade and pile them up where the future compost heap is going to be. In order to speed up the process of decomposition, calcium nitrate (obtainable in plastic bags from garden shops and centres) can be sprinkled in between the individual layers. This turf will provide excellent soil later on. If you want a grass path and there is a vigorous growth of grass, you can save yourself a job by leaving the turf where it is (see Path building).

Preparation of the soil for cultivation is carried out in much the same way in all three types of garden under discussion. The entire garden area is dug over one spade deep. A spade is the best tool for tackling very heavy or very sandy soil, but a fork is often easier to use on lighter soils. Clods should be broken up at this stage, and not left for the frost to break them up as one would normally do. If the ground is infested with couch-grass, ground elder, bindweed or other persistent weeds, use the fork to dig deeply until every last piece of root has been removed. Roots of weeds should be shaken free of soil before being dropped into a nearby trug or wheelbarrow, and then taken to the compost heap. If you lay alternating layers of weeds and calcium nitrate in the compost heap, even these tough weeds will rot quickly. If you are a bit dubious about putting persistent weeds on the compost heap—and many people are—leave them on a path until the sun has baked them completely dry and dead before adding them to the compost.

It takes time to rid a piece of ground of couch-grass and other persistent weeds, for the soil must be free of every last little bit of root. Once you have got rid of all the ordinary weeds, leave the ground alone for a few weeks. Here and there some surviving couch-grass and ground elder may sprout up. These can easily be uprooted with a fork. If you still suspect there may be some roots left in the ground, leave the soil alone for a few more weeks, and then take out the weeds again. Only when you are satisfied that all the weeds are out should you move onto the next stages.

The areas intended for shrubs, fruit-bushes, roses or perennials should be dug two spades deep. The uppermost layer of living topsoil must always remain on top. How this is done is explained in the diagram. First a section of soil is dug out across one end of the plot, and the excavated topsoil put on one side (1). The layer beneath it (2) is then dug over with a spade or fork, or, in the case of heavy soil, with a mattock. After this, the topsoil from the

The site for the paths and terrace must be dug to a depth of about 20 cm/8 in. The excavated topsoil is spread over the rest of the garden. Particularly weedy areas should be well worked over with a garden fork until even the smallest piece of weed has gone. Early potatoes can be planted here if time is no object.

section (3) adjoining the first trench is thrown on top of this loosened under layer (2). This process is continued until the whole plot has been dug over, when the excavated topsoil from the first section (1) is wheeled round to fill up the end of the double-dug plot.

When at last the whole garden has been dug and the ground where shrubs and fruit trees and bushes are to be grown has been loosened to a depth of about 45 cm/18 in., the whole area should be given a liberal sprinkling with peat. This will vastly improve the quality of the soil. How much you use will depend on your purse, but ideally a layer 5–7 cm/2–3 in. thick will be needed to make an appreciable improvement.

Peat makes heavy soils lighter, and helps light soils to retain moisture. Its use is particularly important in places where permanent plantings are planned (ornamental shrubs, roses, and so on). If you cannot afford to be so extravagant with peat all at one go, then just treat the areas of permanent plantings, including the lawn, and do the rest of the garden later. The vegetable garden and beds for summer flowers can be left for the time being. You will have plenty of opportunity to improve their soil in the coming years.

In heavy soils, Krilium—a white, flaky product which remains effective for a long time—can be used instead of peat. On lighter soils, bone meal adds nourishment and helps water-retention. More information can be found in the section on Fertilizers.

After the peat, Krilium or bonemeal has been distributed, it should be dug in, preferably with a fork, but it should only be dug into the top 15 cm/ 6 in. Any remaining weeds can be picked out.

Your next problem is the stones in the soil, unless you've been lucky enough to find a stone-free piece of ground. One often sees gardeners passing every bit of soil through a fine sieve. They finish up with a really admirable pile of stones, and soil that looks delightfully fine. You've got to admire the hard work they've put in. The sad thing is it's all in vain.

The soil in this fine form cannot breathe properly and tends to become waterlogged in winter and bake done dry in summer. If you take all the stones out you must put coarse sand, grit or peat back in to keep the soil open. So it's far better to leave all the small stones in the ground. The larger stones—those roughly 4 cm or 1½ in. in diameter or bigger—can be picked out during cultivation and brought to the site of the pathway and terrace. These should already have been marked out and the stones make useful hardcore.

The sheer hard labour of this first stage of soil cultivation can be considerably lightened by getting a garden-contractor to do the job with a rotovator or rototiller, or by hiring one and doing the job yourself. This machine will first plough the ground with deep-digging coarse tines and then go over it a second time with a fine rotary hoe. Unless you happen to have an ideal piece of ground—which is seldom the case—it will need to be forked over manually once more to remove odd pieces of turf, persistent weeds and larger stones but this job will be much less back-breaking if the ground has been rotovated.

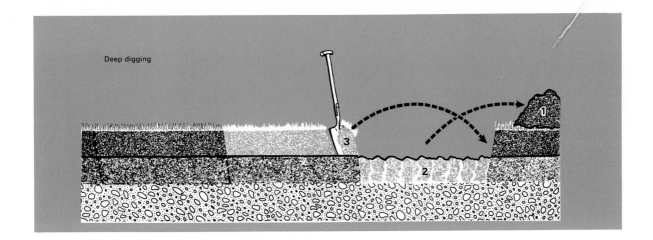

Deep digging

The peat or other materials used for loosening the soil can be worked in by the rotovator or rototiller when it goes over the ground the second time, or forked in by hand during the final weeding operation.

Path-making and Path-edging The main requirement of a path is that it should be usable in all seasons and in all weathers. It should also be easy to keep clean and tidy. There are several ways of making paths that measure up to these criteria.

The inexpensive gravel path A well made, laid and maintained gravel path can look really good. A neglected one, covered in weeds and moss can let the whole garden down. So if you make a gravel path, make it properly and look after it well. Make a start by ramming the subsoil of the excavated trench down really firmly. Then fill the trench with a layer of rough stones, broken bricks, cement rubble or coarse slag to a depth of about 15 cm/6 in. This layer in turn is rammed down really hard, working from the edges towards the middle. The surface should rise in a light curve of 2–5 cm/1–2 in. from sides to middle to form a 'crown', to allow rainwater to drain away. Next add a layer roughly 5 cm/2 in deep of good loamy material mixed with fine gravel, fine brick rubble or fine slag. This should be well-moistened and then rammed down from sides to middle, as before. Finally, spread a thin layer of split stone or gravel on the surface, rake it smooth and roll it hard.

It's a good idea to spread only half of the gravel or split stone on the path to begin with. Once this layer has been well trodden, add the rest little by little. It is important to keep weeds down, otherwise the path will just look a mess. The days of hand-weeding of paths have gone. You can do it quite simply and effectively with a good chemical weedkiller. Make sure the weedkiller you use is one of those that acts on the foliage of the weeds and is neutralised when it touches the gravel. If you use a total weedkiller it will seep into the surrounding soil and kill the lawn and flowers near the path.

The turf path Grass paths always look relaxing in a garden made on meadowland. All you have to do is leave the turf where paths are wanted, mow them and shape the edges.

Pleasant though such paths look when in good condition, they will not stand heavy wear, and they look dreadful when trodden bare down the middle.

The paved pathway Paved paths have two great advantages over either gravel or grass. They look good and if properly made, can last for a century or more. There are many materials available, so you can take your pick and create a path that expresses your individuality. Such a path can be a feature of a garden, not a mere utility. The only care and attention a well-made, paved path will need—and even then only if it is in shade—is an occasional watering with an algicide or moss-killer.

When you come to choose the paving, bear the following considerations in mind. Natural stone

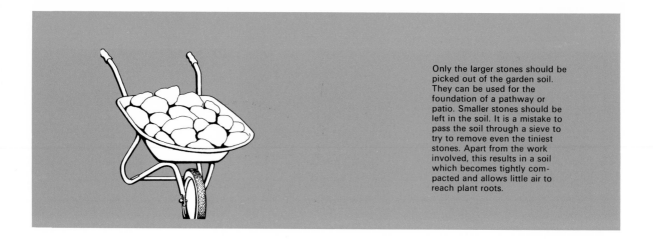

Only the larger stones should be picked out of the garden soil. They can be used for the foundation of a pathway or patio. Smaller stones should be left in the soil. It is a mistake to pass the soil through a sieve to try to remove even the tiniest stones. Apart from the work involved, this results in a soil which becomes tightly compacted and allows little air to reach plant roots.

probably looks best, but it is expensive to buy unless you happen to have a quarry on your back doorstep. The real cost of natural stone is the cost of transporting it, so the nearer home it is quarried the less it will cost you. Sometimes you can pick up second-hand stone locally from demolition contractors. Natural stone occurs in a variety of colours, but it is best to use most the mellow shades: bright colours look harsh and out of keeping with all but the most *avant-garde* of gardens.

Artificial stone slabs are durable and much less expensive. These are not the composition slabs used for town pavements, but artificial stones specially made for garden use. The best, most natural-looking of these are made of reconstituted stone, but many other types are just as useful; it all depends what you want to use them for and what design effect you want to create.

Most of these are made of concrete of one sort or another: there is more than one type of concrete. Some are as smooth as fine sandpaper and others peppered coarsely with fine grit; some have a surface covered with slightly raised dots, while others have a brushed finish. Some come in a variety of colours, made by adding a dye to the concrete mix. Beware of using too many coloured slabs: you may finish up with a patio looking like a nestful of Easter eggs. The best effect, if you want to use coloured slabs, is to strike a balance of about eighty per cent one colour and the remaining twenty per cent a shade which goes well with it. For example, the main colour could be a discreet sandstone red, and the remaining twenty per cent a pleasant light yellow.

Washed concrete slabs are popular. They are handy, good-looking, and brighten the garden scene without being obtrusive. They go equally well with flower-beds or lawns. Moreover, they can be combined with other materials such as pebbles, timber, and so on, to create various designs for footpaths and patios. These slabs, like most other artificial paving, are available in standard sizes.

Square paving slabs are preferable in a square courtyard, whereas in large patios slabs of different sizes can be combined to form a 'Roman bond'. Even here the square format can be very effective, especially when used in combination with blue engineering bricks, small paving-stones, or other contrasting materials.

Casting concrete   Concrete slabs are the handiman's delight, since he can make them himself. If you want to do this, the first thing to decide is the size of the slabs. If you can use the same size for both paths and patio, so much the better: you can soon· have a regular production line going. The easier slabs to handle are those 30 cm/1 ft square or 25 cm/9 in. square. They should be 5 cm/2 in. thick. The casting-frame can be made of wood or iron.

With an iron frame (see diagram) the job can be done in no time. To save expense, a whole group of you could get together to buy the frame, and it could be used by all of you in turn down the street or round the estate. All that has to be done when putting the two angle-irons together is to see that the eyelets at both ends meet. These are securely

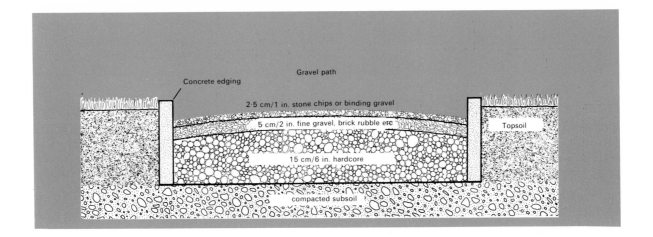

Gravel path

Concrete edging

2·5 cm/1 in. stone chips or binding gravel

5 cm/2 in. fine gravel, brick rubble etc

Topsoil

15 cm/6 in. hardcore

compacted subsoil

bolted together by means of a hook passed through the eyelet holes. The frame must be large enough to accommodate the largest of the slabs required. For smaller sizes the frame can be divided by means of a free-moving piece of angle-iron. If you work out a clever module you can cast 5 or 6 slabs at a time in a large frame.

The concrete mixture is prepared in a ratio of 1:3—one shovel of cement to three shovels of clean washed sand. The materials must be thoroughly mixed while dry with a shovel until the whole mass is the same colour. The mixture is then dampened with water and turned again. More water is added little by little and the mixture turned and turned until it is evenly damp throughout. When ready for use it will have the consistency of rather stiff paste. The frame must be greased to prevent the moulded concrete from sticking to it. Used motor oil serves the purpose very well.

If the empty frame is placed upon an already existing flat concrete base, an underlay of paper or —better still plastic sheeting—will be needed to prevent the mixture sticking to the base. Alternatively the frame can be set on an oil-coated metal sheet or piece of thin board.

After filling the frame, the mixture must be firmly tamped down with a wooden board to get rid of air bubbles and to level it. If you want a skid proof surface all you do is place a sheet of ribbed glass (well oiled) inside the frame before adding the mixture. Alternatively you can press the glass down on the concrete after the frame has been filled. A particularly attractive surface can be obtained if, immediately after filling the frame

with concrete, you sprinkle variously coloured pebbles over the top and press them in. The result is similar to the composition or washed concrete slabs you can buy, and makes a very attractive paving to contrast with plants growing nearby.

Once the concrete has set, pull the hooks out of the eyelets and take the frame apart. Remove your slabs and the empty frame is ready to be put together and used again.

Once the concrete starts to set, it must be protected from the drying action of sun and wind which could cause surface cracks. Keep it damp for two or three days by putting wet sacks over it. After two or three days, the concrete should have hardened enough to allow the slabs to be lifted off the underlay. Allow a few more days before laying the paving.

Bricks for paths and patios Brick is one of the most popular and versatile of paving materials. It is, however, important to use the right kind of bricks. The ones to avoid are interior bricks. These break up very quickly when exposed to frost, rain and sun. The ones to go for are exterior bricks, especially the ones used in older houses. The mellow red of these old bricks goes well with most plants, and particularly well with the green of the lawn. If you have the chance to get some when an old house near you is being demolished for redevelopment, don't miss it. Such bricks are already weathered and mellowed. You may have to clean the old mortar off the bricks, which can be hard work, but if you are prepared to do this you can often buy the bricks quite cheaply.

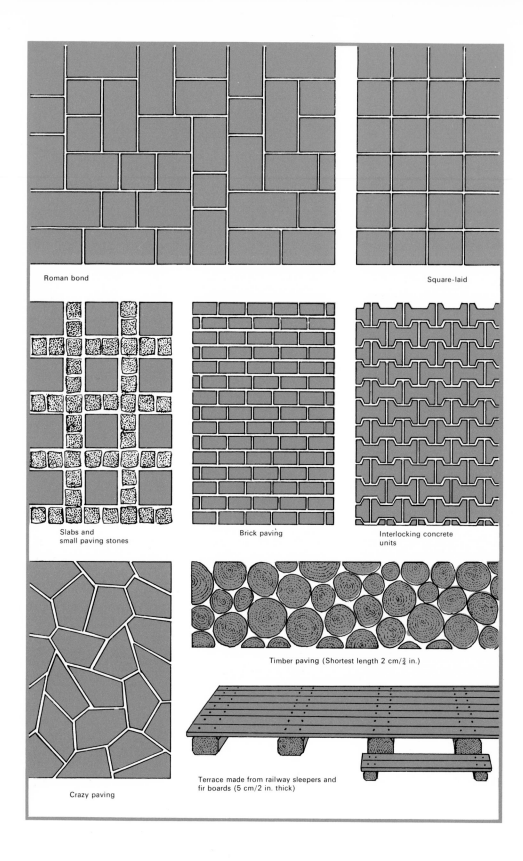

Roman bond

Square-laid

Slabs and
small paving stones

Brick paving

Interlocking concrete
units

Crazy paving

Timber paving (Shortest length 2 cm/¾ in.)

Terrace made from railway sleepers and
fir boards (5 cm/2 in. thick)

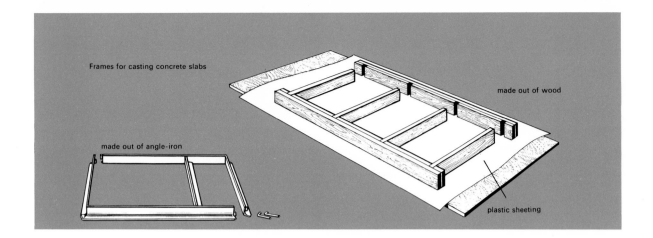

Frames for casting concrete slabs

made out of angle-iron

made out of wood

plastic sheeting

Old building bricks of this kind should only be used for paths or patios that will be in full sun. If you use them in the shade, not only will moss soon form between the joints—though this looks rather pretty at the time—but the surface of the bricks will acquire a green patina which makes them slippery and even dangerous to walk on in damp weather.

If you have the opportunity of obtaining granite setts or blocks when street-paving is being replaced, make the most of it. These provide a most original and decorative paving material, particularly if you have a large area such as a drive to pave. Once laid they will last for ever. You may, however, prefer to leave the job of laying these to a skilled man. Granite blocks are very heavy. A single granite block, measuring some 20 cm/8 in. by 10 cm/4 in. can weigh as much as one stone. Hard limestone cobbles are also well worth buying.

Laying the slabs There is nothing difficult about laying paving, and the method described here applies to all the materials mentioned so far. Garden paths and patios do not have to carry great weights, so the paving may perfectly adequately be bedded in sand. First you dig out the site of the path or patio to a depth of 20 cm/8 in. Then you fill it with about 10 cm/4 in. of hard core (shingle, slag, stone and concrete rubble, broken bricks and so on) and you ram this down. On light soils the bed need only be 10 cm/4 in. deep and will not need the hard core. Over this you place a layer of sand about 5 cm/2 in. thick, and on this you bed the slabs.

All the equipment you need is a line, a builder's or gardening trowel (for packing in the sand), a spirit-level, a wooden straight edge, a wooden mallet and a piece of square-cut timber to cushion the blows when knocking the slabs into place. If you need to cut a piece off a slab, do this with a mason's hammer and chisel.

The surface of the slabs must be level when laid, and the only way to be really sure that they are is to use a spirit-level. Test the slabs laterally, longitudinally and diagonally. If you find a slab is wobbly or off true, lift it and re-level the sand beneath it before relaying. Repeat the process until the level is correct. After the level of the slabs has been checked and corrected, they can be bedded firmly in the ground by tapping them with a masonry hammer cushioned by the piece of timber, or by using just the handle of the hammer. After this has been done, sweep wet sand into the joints until any tendency to rock is eliminated.

A path 150 cm/5 ft wide should have a drop of 1·5–2 cm/¾–1 in. from one side to the other, and this should be borne in mind when making a spirit-level test on the slabs. For a patio, the paving should drop about 2·5 cm/1 in. in every 1 m/3 ft, allowing surface water to drain away from the house.

There are some general rules to consider when paving paths and patios. If you are laying slabs of different sizes in the pattern known as 'Roman bond', on no account should there be any unbroken lines of jointing. The joints must be staggered, in a random fashion, otherwise the path may become something of an eyesore. This also applies to patios, where again the jointing lines should be broken.

When laying natural stone slabs, many people try to use up small left-overs. Such small pieces of stone are not only unsightly but are also unstable, and may tip when trodden on. A slab should be large enough for you to stand on with both feet.

If path or terrace borders on a lawn, the slabs should lie flush with the grass verge. If laid at a lower level they will collect water, while if higher they will damage the mower when you are cutting the lawn. Only when the path runs alongside planted areas should you lay it higher—preferably about 5 cm/2 in. higher—than the soil, thus preventing soil being washed away from the beds on to the paving.

In the garden of a terraced house there is no problem in laying the paving yourself or with the help of an experienced friend. In larger gardens the area to be covered could be much larger and you might prefer to get a contractor to do it. The important thing whether you do it yourself or not, is to ensure that when building has been completed, the loose rubble around the house and on the site of path and terrace is firmly compressed, preferably with a pneumatic rammer, before the slabs are laid. If this is not done, the ground will subside and the paving sink or slant in the coming years. This causes needless trouble, and you will either have to live with a ruined patio or take all the slabs up and relay them.

Path edgings, attractive and otherwise Here and there a path may run alongside a cultivated area (vegetable plot, fruit bushes, rose-beds, flower borders). A gravel path, unlike a paved walk or a grass path, will require some sort of edging to prevent gravel and soil getting mixed up. Tufted perennials can help to form a natural border here. Within a few years these tuffets will have closed their ranks, and soil will no longer get on to the path. This makes a very pleasant edging, softening the harsh lines of the path. Furthermore, plants suitable for this purpose (see section on 'Perennials') bloom for weeks on end and hardly require any attention.

However, such a simple and attractive solution is not always popular with gardeners. A 'proper' edging is built in the following way. Concrete kerbstones, usually 1 m/3 ft long are set up either before or during the construction of the path. To avoid any shifting during the surfacing of the path, the butt joints of the individual kerbstones should be bedded in mortar (cement and sand in a ratio of 1:2). For the best visual results the finished concrete edgings should not protrude more than 5 cm/2 in. above the path surface.

If concrete edgings of this kind border on lawns, they must be flush with the turf. If they are alongside a vegetable patch, the top of the path edging should be about 10 cm/4 in. higher than the soil level. Within a few years the continuous composting of the ground will level out this small difference in level.

Concrete kerbstones can either be bought ready-made or made at home.

Those with a smooth flat top or with a very slight slant in the direction of the path generally

In the foreground to the left is a
red-leaved Japanese maple
Acer palmatum dissectum. In
the wall corner grows a giant
Provence reed *Arundo donax*.

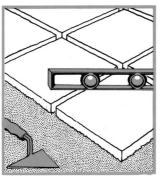 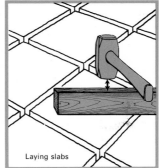 

Laying slabs

look smarter than those with rounded or moulded tops.

If you want to make the kerbstones at home, cast them in lengths of 1 m/3 ft since this produces a kerbstone that is easy to handle. You will need a detachable frame (mould) just as for casting paving slabs, but designed to case the kerbstones.

Apart from concrete kerbstones, an excellent edging can be made with bricks set upright in the ground. These must not protrude more than 5 cm/2 in above the path surface, otherwise they will wobble. They can either be placed with all the tops level or obliquely to create a dog-tooth pattern. The following should never be used for path-edging: timber boards (they soon rot), beer or wine bottles, or corrugated iron, which causes very nasty cuts if you fall on it.

Paved paths should never be given edging. These are completely unnecessary, a waste of money and usually unattractive into the bargain. They are impractical, too, since the lawn is then no longer flush with the paving and mowing becomes far more difficult.

Walls and steps A garden on a sloping site is a challenge and a half. It has far more potential than a level site, but it takes skilful planning, time, hard work and money to make the most of it.

The first problem to be overcome is that of changing levels. This is most practically done by means of walls and steps. The function of walls in such a garden is to retain soil at various levels and protect the house if it is situated lower than the surrounding gardens. Avoid, if possible, plain grey concrete walls: they make the place look like a fortress.

Walls of exposed aggregate or washed concrete look handsome and modern. For these, clean pebbles of various sizes are added to the concrete mix, or pressed evenly into the outer layer of concrete. Within seven to twelve hours when the concrete is half set but not completely hardened, the shuttering can be removed. The concrete is then washed down with a stiff brush and a hose, so that the wet film of mortar comes off and the interesting, lively colour-pattern of the pebbles comes to light. Its appearance will be further enhanced if furnished with trailing shrubs such as *Genista sagittalis* and other suitable plants.

More traditional retaining walls can be built of natural or reconstituted stones. So-called dry walls can look very handsome. As their name implies, they are built without mortar. Natural stone makes an excellent material for such a wall. For low dry walls up to about 1 m/3 ft in height, a concrete foundation approximately 20 cm/8 in. deep is recommended. For higher dry walls the foundations must be laid deeper, about 45 cm/ 18 in. below the surface otherwise frost will damage it. The thickness of a dry wall should be about one-third of its height, and never less than 30 cm/1 ft.

A dry wall should always be battered, that is, it should lean back against the soil it is supporting. If you build it vertical the weight of soil behind it will push it over. The wall should tilt back about 30 cm/1 ft for every 1 m/3 ft it rises. This also

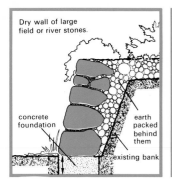

Dry wall of large field or river stones.

concrete foundation

earth packed behind them

existing bank

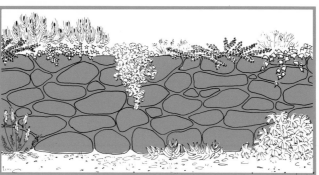

enables plants growing between the stones to catch enough rainwater to survive. The first course of stones should be set on the foundation with cement mortar, but the other courses should be bedded in good loamy earth. Plants must be put in while the wall is being constructed. It is very difficult to push the plants in afterwards. Each stone should be pressed firmly into the loamy soil with a piece of wood or a hammer handle to make it firm and safe.

When building the wall, take care to see that the vertical joints do not run in a straight line from top to bottom: if they do the wall not be very strong. Stones set on edge have a disturbing effect: each stone should be laid on its 'lazy' side: any other position looks unnatural. Extra long and heavy stones should be put at the corners, thrusting upwards and closely bonded with adjacent stones.

Walls on slopes must have some form of drainage otherwise water will collect behind them and cause the walls to collapse. The best way of providing this is to put a layer of coarse gravel or similar material behind the stones and to leave a few 'weep-holes' at intervals along the lowest course.

Natural stone is not the only material suitable for building dry walls. Large pieces of concrete from old foundations or demolished concrete walls can be used. Though most people may throw their hands up in horror at this suggestion, concrete chunks can be used very effectively when the joints are so crammed with plants that they completely hide the concrete. This provides an attractive stone wall at a low cost.

Railway sleepers also make good walls. Your local railway station can tell you where you can buy old sleepers. They are very heavy and you will need help moving them. Place the sleepers upright or sloping slightly back in a trench about 1 m/3 ft deep, then ram the soil back in really firmly round them. Since the sleepers are just over 2 m/6 ft long, this will make a good retaining wall about 1 m/3 ft high.

Another possible material, and a very modern one at that, is the Karlaruher 'garden-stone'. As the illustrations on pages 44 and 45 show, this is basically an U-shaped concrete unit. The unit is simplicity itself, which is probably why it is so versatile. Like paving slabs, its something you can make yourself. These units can be used for a variety of purposes. Retaining walls, wall seats and steps can all be constructed quickly and easily. They can also be used for troughs for growing plants in.

If you want to use these units for building a retaining wall, there are two ways this can be done. The first is to set the units one upon another, the side-pieces penetrating the bank, the open side filled in behind so that each unit is firmly embedded in the earth. The next layer is fitted closely to the preceding one, so that there is no danger of the stones shifting later on. This makes a smooth wall where plants can grow in the continuous horizontal joints. The second is to set the pieces one upon another in a 'step' arrangement, creating small graduated planting areas, particularly suitable for growing perennials, ground-cover plants and dwarf shrubs.

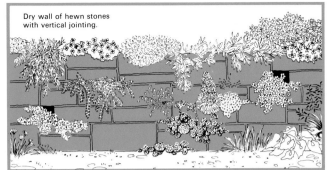

Dry wall of hewn stones with vertical jointing.

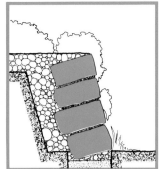

Steps This is one other structured feature you are going to need in any garden on a sloping site. Steps can be expensive to build, and they can be hard work, but if well designed they can make a really attractive feature in the garden. The important thing is that they should not just be a point-to-point short cut. If one side of a curving flight of steps borders a lawn, for example, while the other side is planted with perennials, dwarf shrubs and annuals, it adds movement and interest to the garden.

Steps do, however, have a function to serve and that is something you should never loose sight of, no matter how pleasing you want them to look. Their function is to be walked up and down, so try to plan them to fit in with a normal walking stride. This is about 60 cm/2 ft uphill, which gives you the depth of the tread. The riser should be about 13–15 cm/5–6 in. for comfort. If fairly high steps are needed, the treads should not be too wide, whereas with low steps the treads ought to be wide in comparison. If space is short and the steps have to rise sharply up a bank, the height of the risers has to be increased to about 18–20 cm/7–8 in.

In a long flight of steps, landings provide welcome rests. If possible, the number of steps between the different landings should vary. Provided there is enough room, have flights of three, five or seven steps between the different landings.

Now to the building of the steps. Start with a spirit level and a foot rule, and calculate the difference in height between the upper and lower levels. Then work out the amount of ground they can cover. Then calculate the number of steps with

risers of 13 cm/5 in. you would need to give you the required rise, and after that the length of ground covered assuming treads 60 cm/2 ft deep. Say there is a rise in level of 270 cm/9 ft over a distance of 12·60 m/42 ft. It would take 18 steps to overcome the 270 cm/9 ft rise. If the steps are 60 cm/2 ft deep, the 18 steps would occupy only 10 m/36 ft of the 12·60 m/42 ft allowed, leaving 180 cm/6 ft for landings.

However, as a general rule the landings should be twice as deep as the steps—120 cm/4 ft instead of 60 cm/2 ft. You are therefore faced with the problem of having to decide whether to make one 120 cm/4 ft landing and use less land than you allowed, two 120 cm/4 ft landings taking more land than you allowed, or compromising on two 90 cm/3 ft landings. Probably the compromise is the best solution. Alternatively, you could increase the height of the risers on each step, which would mean you would need fewer steps and so have more room for the landings. An increase of 2·5 cm/1 in. on the height of each riser would give you 15 steps instead of 18 and save you 180 cm/6 ft on distance.

Once you have worked out these calculations, you can start building. A simple flight of steps which would look good in any garden can be made with logs of impregnated timber. Untreated pine logs, with the bark left on, can also be used, but they will need renewing every five to ten years. Depending on the required height of the risers, two or three logs are superimposed horizontally and held in place by two strong wooden pickets driven into the ground immediately in front of them. The treads are made by ramming down the

U-shaped garden units

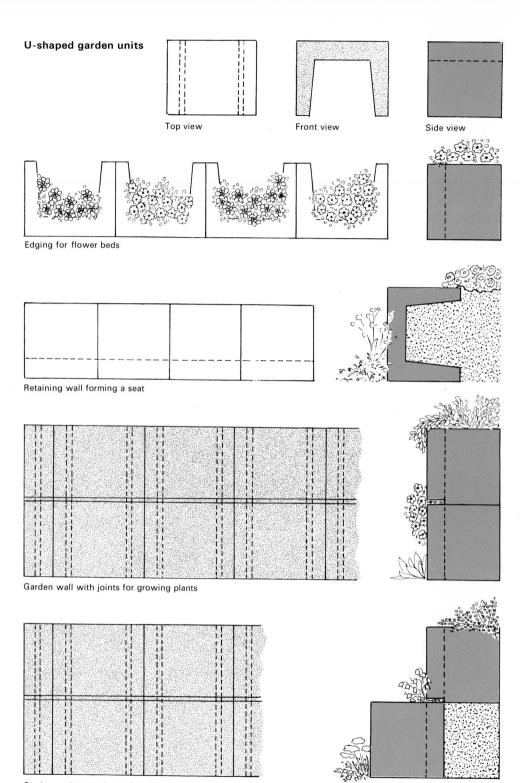

Top view   Front view   Side view

Edging for flower beds

Retaining wall forming a seat

Garden wall with joints for growing plants

Garden wall in the form of steps

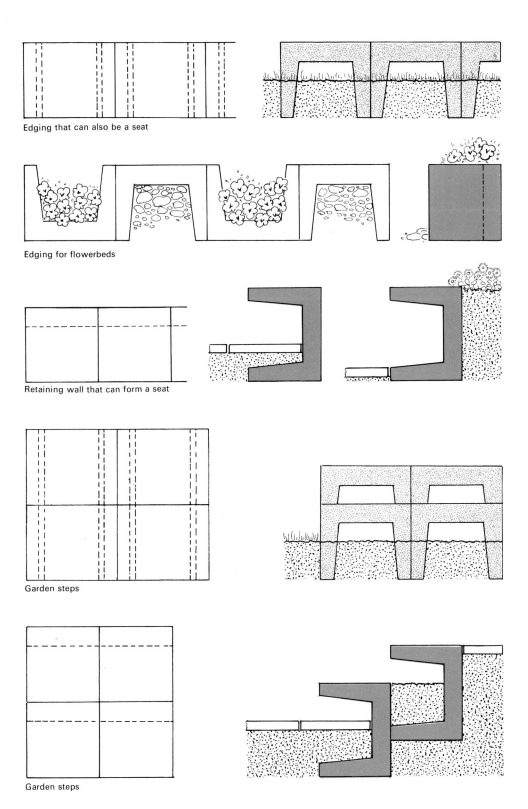

Edging that can also be a seat

Edging for flowerbeds

Retaining wall that can form a seat

Garden steps

Garden steps

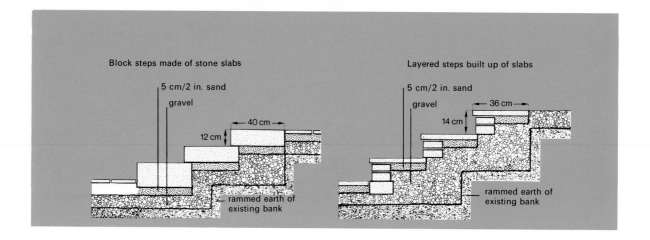

Block steps made of stone slabs

5 cm/2 in. sand
gravel
40 cm
12 cm
rammed earth of
existing bank

Layered steps built up of slabs

5 cm/2 in. sand
gravel
36 cm
14 cm
rammed earth of
existing bank

earth at the back of the logs and then filling in with coarse stones, followed by rubble and finally by fine gravel.

Steps that are going to be used a lot must be made of more durable materials. Here again, as with walls, natural stone is stylish but costly. Concrete or washed concrete is more practical. Steps made of concrete slabs on layered risers are also excellent, but make sure that the edges of the slabs forming the treads overhang the risers by about 3 cm/1½ in. Steps should have a slight downward slant so that rainwater can drain off. This really is important: in winter any lying surface water could freeze. Your steps would then be absolutely lethal. The bottom step, which gets the greatest pressure, should be set in concrete. The remaining steps can simply be set in a thin layer of gravel on the shaped earth of the existing bank. Apart from concrete, railway sleepers can also be used for steps.

The U-shaped units mentioned before for wall-building are also excellent for making steps. There are attractive possibilities here. Small steps can be formed by pushing the shanks of the U-piece vertically into the earth bank, each piece leaving a rather cheerful-looking opening visible as it rises above the next. A more formal, closer step formation can be created by building up the pieces on their sides. Here, the treads project, unsupported by risers. The heavy appearance of concrete is overcome by the U-form of this pre-cast element; everything about it is light and friendly.

Trelliswork and pergolas Structures for grow-ing creepers and climbing plants up and over sel-dom look good standing on their own. Generally they need something to lean on—a house, a wall, a garden shed, though they can look very effective when used as partitions, for example dividing the vegetable plot from the ornamental garden. They can also be used for creating a secluded sitting area.

Trelliswork or pergolas can be built of wood or metal. Since they are exposed to all weathers, they should be thoroughly treated with preservatives. For wood a colourless preservative is usually best, unless you deliberately want to darken the timber. Metal parts should be treated with a rust preventa-tive paint before use. Once erected, the metal parts can be given an undercoat and finally a top-coat of weatherproof paint of any colour you want. Paint them shocking pink if you like but generally the traditional garden colours—black, white or green look best. After all, the idea is to show off the plants on the pergola, or trellis, not the pergola itself.

Rustproof screws and nails should be used for fastening latticework. Square-cut or rounded timbers can be used for the pillars of a trellis or pergola, and in a small garden lightweight metal tubing is more in scale. Single waterpipes of about 3 cm/1¼ in. in diameter are suitable. Flat iron struts, about 20 cm/8 in. long, can be welded at right angles on either side of these pillars at the top, and the horizontal wooden beams screwed edgewise on to them.

The metal should be tubes set about 50 cm/20 in. deep in the ground in concrete. Wooden pillars should not be buried in the ground: they will

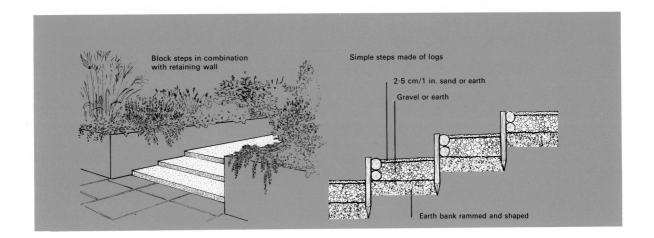

Block steps in combination with retaining wall

Simple steps made of logs

2·5 cm/1 in. sand or earth

Gravel or earth

Earth bank rammed and shaped

simply rot. They last much longer if screwed to flat iron bases set in concrete, then air can circulate all round them.

The scale of pergolas and trellises depends mainly on the size and layout of the garden. It is also a matter of taste. The height of a pergola affects the appearance of a garden just as much as, say, the size of a pool or the design of a terrace. For best results, proportions of a pergola or trellis should relate to the length and bulkiness of the materials used in its construction. If it is under 210 cm/7 ft you'll probably bump your head, if not on the pergola itself, then on the branches of the climber going over it. If it is more than 300 cm/ 10 ft tall your friends will ask you why you put it on stilts. The pillars should be 10 cm/4 in. square, 10 cm/4 × 15 cm/6 or 15 cm/6 × 15 cm/6 in. thick, which are also roughly the dimensions for rounded pillars. The thickness of the horizontal beams depends on the thickness of the pillars. Beams 10 cm/4 × 10 cm/4, 10 cm/4 × 12 cm/5, 10 cm/4 × 15 cm/6, or 10 cm/4 × 20 cm/8 in. are suitable. The cross-beams are generally 5 cm/2 × 10 cm/4, 7 cm/3 × 15 cm/6 or 10 cm/4 × 20 cm/8 in.

You can leave the construction work to a carpenter or metal-worker if you like, but you'll get far more satisfaction by making it yourself. Start by making a plan to a scale of 1 : 10. You will certainly need this if you are going to do the work yourself. If you are going to pay someone else to do it you may finish up with a rude surprise unless you give him a detailed drawing—a massive structure which looks as though it will last forever, more like a gallows than a decorative element in the garden.

Most people know how to use a hammer and nails, and usually a power drill and a saw as well. For the finer details of how to fit the different parts together borrow a good carpentry or metal-working manual from your public library.

Another idea worth considering is growing an espalier fruit tree against one of the house or garage walls—a peach, perhaps or a morello cherry, a pear or perhaps a grape vine? This would add greatly to the attractiveness of an otherwise dull and empty-looking wall.

Espalier trellis-work is easy to make and expensive to buy. Start with wooden slats about 5 cm/2 in. wide and 2 cm/¾ in. thick and treat these with wood preservative. You'll also need some wedges, about 5 cm/2 in. thick and 15 cm/6 in. long, to put under the corners of the trellis to keep it away from the house-wall: if it fitted flush you wouldn't be able to tie the shoots back onto it. The finished trellis will be nailed to the wall at the cross-joints with long galvanized nails or pegs.

But before you buy a single wooden lath or even a galvanized nail make a sketch of the trellis at a scale of 1 : 10. Draw the whole area of the wall to be occupied by the trellis, not just the trellis itself. If you do this you will often find the trellis looks best with its top level with the top of the windows —just the sort of detail that if overlooked can mar the whole effect—and you could easily overlook it if you didn't draw the whole wall area.

The laths should always be evenly spaced on the wall, usually 30 cm/1 ft apart, but as much as 60 cm/2 ft apart if you want. Keep the verticals the same distance apart as the horizontals. The

Left: Fence of vertical boards.
Squared posts: 10 cm/4 in. ×
10 cm/4 in.
Horizontal beams: 15 cm/
6 in × 5 cm/2 in.
Vertical boards: 10 cm/4 in ×
10 cm/4 in.

Right: Fixed screen of reed
hurdles.

trellis can be made either 4-square or with the laths running obliquely, creating a diamond pattern. Like most decorative things in the garden, a trellis has a function to serve as well, and that function is to provide something to tie twigs to. Do bear this in mind whatever pattern you choose to make.

For smaller wall areas where you want to grow espalier fruit or climbing roses or other climbers, extruded plastic meshes make the best trellises. Though more expensive than galvanised wire, these meshes are usually an unobtrusive green or brown, and never rust or rot. The only thing you have to be careful about is not cutting through them when pruning the plant trained against the mesh.

Garden fences, garden gates Garden fences are purely utilitarian objects and should look attractive. They should only be erected when really needed and then every attempt should be made to make them as original and as good-looking as possible. Basically they should be used merely as stop-gaps while green fences—ornamental shrubs, small-growing fruit trees, spindle-bushes, or hedges—grow up.

The smaller the garden, the more a fence makes it feel even smaller. If all you want to do is mark the boundary between your garden and the one next door, a couple of strands of plain wire drawn tight between posts 60 cm/2 ft apart is all you need.

If what you want is privacy, a good hedge is infinitely to be preferred every time. Start with a fence for instant seclusion if you wish, but replace it later with a good evergreen hedge such as *Chamaecyparis x lawsoniana* which becomes denser year by year. Once it reaches maturity it offers much more protection and privacy than any fence. To keep out unwanted visitors of any kind, wind a few rows of barbed wire into the hedge as an additional safeguard.

The best sort of fence to keep unwanted visitors out of the garden until the hedge grows up is a simple wire mesh one. The wooden posts need not be treated with preservative since the hedge will have grown up round the wire netting before the posts have rotted in the ground. The wire fencing will eventually disappear inside the hedge, but it will still be there, camouflaged, to protect your garden against dogs and game. Galvanised rabbit wire is cheap but longlasting.

As a fence substitute, and in place of a trimmed hedge, uncut ornamental shrubs can be used. These will take up more room than a hedge but on the other hand need no trimming and have the additional advantage of bearing flowers and fruit.

Wooden fencing This is still the most popular means of enclosing a garden today. You can take your choice from a wide range of types, but interlocking pine fencing is probably the most popular. It can be bought in two or three standard heights and in standard runs. The posts usually come with the panels. All you have to do is plant the posts and fix the panels to them. The timber posts should be well treated with a wood preservative and ideally should be set in concrete. Such a fence should then last for at least 20 years.

For an appearance of stability a pergola should be linked with the house, a wall, or a large group of trees.

Ranch fencing, made of horizontal boards fixed to hardwood posts or T-irons set in concrete, looks smart and modern. In rural districts, rough-cut boards with the bark still on the edges can be used for a fence of this kind, giving it an appropriately rustic air. The horizontal boards should be about 5 cm/2 in. thick, and the uprights 240–270 cm/ 8–9 ft apart. Ranch fencing looks best kept rather low, no more than about 1 m/3 ft high.

Wire fences   These are a necessary evil. Builders seem to have a great liking for them, putting them up to define the boundaries of gardens. If you have any choice in the matter, go for the plastic-covered sort, rather than the ordinary galvanised wire which rusts fairly quickly. Green plastic-covered wire is fairly unobtrusive and lasts much longer. The supports can either be concrete posts, iron pipes or T-irons set in concrete. Corner and end posts must have stays on their opposing sides to take the strain of the wires. You can plant twining annuals such as runner or pole beans or nasturtiums along these fences to make them look more agreeable (at least during the summer).

Walls   These look good but are very expensive compared with fencing or hedges. A 1 m/3 ft wall of concrete, whitewashed stone or brick makes a wonderful background for setting off plants and flowers. If you build a wall make sure the foundations are deep enough to be out of frost danger, usually 20 cm/8 in. below the soil.

If you want fencing of any kind, wood, wire, or a wall of any sort, you may well consider it an investment to have a contractor do the job properly —including the entrance gates and any doors. It will probably look better and last longer if put up by an expert.

A SHELTER FROM THE WIND AND PRYING EYES

Most people like to have a corner of the garden completely private and secluded from neighbours —where they can sunbathe or entertain. Usually this area is close to the house, but in the small gardens of terraced houses creating such an area can be quite a problem.

The simplest solution is to use wattle-hurdles. These are cheap to buy and easy to use. They should be fixed to a light but secure structure of wood or metal tubing. The hurdles will need replacing after some years but this is not very costly.

An even cheaper way of screening yourself is to erect a framework of 2 cm/¾ in. metal piping, and criss-cross this from end to end with lengths of plastic cord. Russian vine or Virginia creeper will soon camouflage the structure. As a rule the wattle hurdles need only be about 180 cm/6 ft high, but they are quite safe up to 360 cm/12 ft provided the structure is bedded in concrete.

This makes a dense green, natural screen and windbreak for the summer. In spring and autumn a piece of canvas or reed matting can be stretched across it.

In the gardens of terraced or semi-detached houses windbreaks and partitions of various kinds

are usually included as part of the building. These often consist of projecting walls or a durable wooden structure. If you want to make your own you will find the necessary details in the relevant illustration.

ROCK GARDENS

If you like rock plants, put a corner of your garden aside for a rockery. Because most of the plants are so minute, even a small rockery will provide room for dozens of them. And there's no need to simulate a vast mountain landscape: a low mound of rocks will do. But take thought: a well-planned rockery is something quite different from a mere heap of stones.

Before you start building a rockery, take a good look at a rock outcrop on a hill or mountain-side, or even at good photographs of such outcrops. You will notice that all the rocks are on their sides, and that they emerge up a gradual gradient to terminate abruptly in a short steep face. That is what you should try to achieve in the garden. The stones should be arranged in irregular groups reminiscent of the rock strata to be seen in mountains. Only one type of stone should be used for each rockery, limestone for example, or tufa. A trough garden, as illustrated above, can also look very charming.

Most rock plants thrive on or between the rocks, and do best on soil rich in lime and humus. Rock tends to retain warmth and moisture. Some rock-plants, however, make quite specific demands as to soil. The blue flowered *Gentiana clusii*, for example, whose natural habitat is mountain pastures, loves a rich loam, together with some turf soil and well-rotted cow dung, when growing in the rockery. Where possible this gentian should be planted on the side of the rockery facing west. This typical rock plant welcomes an occasional sprinkling of water in the early morning as a substitute for mountain dew.

LIVING WATER

Small pools   These can add charm to even the smallest of gardens. There are some delightful plants that thrive in or around the edge of water, and almost any receptacle capable of holding water is a potential pool. An old rain-water butt, or a wooden tub treated with preservative, can be buried in the ground and before long one can have a waterlily growing and flowering in it.

A visit to a scrap metal dealer could be profitable. He might have a tin bath or some similar large strong container that you could buy cheaply. It need not be more than 30–45 cm/1 ft–18 in. deep to hold a few bog-plants or some small waterlilies.

Having purchased your container, the first thing to do with it is to get rid of all the rust. To do this you'll need a liquid rust-killing agent, a wire basket attachment for your power drill, or a really stiff wire brush and a lot of elbow-grease. Once you have got rid of all the rust, paint it inside and out with a rust-proofing agent. When the first coat is dry apply a second and even a third coat. Then sink the container into the ground with about the upper rim left projecting above the soil, and surround it with flagstones. These should be

Rock gardens in sinks or troughs are increasingly popular. Here is a small selection of dwarf shrubs and perennials suitable for this purpose: all very undemanding.

Dwarf shrubs
Cotoneaster dammeri
Dwarf juniper *Juniperus communis compressa*
False cypress *Chamaecyparis obtusa nana gracilis, C. pisifera nana* and so on.
Daphne arbuscula, D. cneorum
Alpines and other perennials
Sandwort *Arenaria tetraquestra*
Cushion pink *Armeria caespitosa*
Artemisia nitida

Whitlow grass *Draba brunifolia*
Tufted harebell *Edraianthus pumilio*
Gentiana acaulis
Cranesbill *Geranium sanguineum*
Dwarf globe daisy *Globularia nana*
Dwarf candytuft *Iberis saxatilis*
Edelweiss *Leontopodium pallibinianum*
Raoulia australis
Rockfoil *Saxifraga aizoon*
Stonecrop *Sedum spathulifolium* 'Capa Blanca'
Houseleek *Sempervivum* varieties
Further information can be found in specialist catalogues

placed over the rim of the container, overlapping it by about 5 cm/2 in. A container 30 cm/1 ft deep requires about 20 cm/8 in. of ordinary garden soil in the bottom, with about 75 cm/3 in. of water above it. The plants should be put in the soil before the water is added. Even a pond no more than 45 cm/18 in. across will grow a dwarf water-lily, a variegated water flag and some reeds. More on the subject of bog and water plants can be found in the section on 'Perennials'.

Another quick way of making a small pool is to bury a concrete cylinder, if possible with a built-in concrete bottom, and again have flagstones over-lapping the edge to camouflage it. These concrete cylinders are used for road drains and can be obtained from builders' merchants.

Plastic sheeting for lining larger pools With heavy gauge plastic sheeting you can build much larger pools, suitable for both fish and water-plants. This sheeting has become very popular because it is so adaptable and easy to handle. It is far more efficient than concrete, and adaptable to a pool of almost any shape.

The first thing you do is dig out the shape of the pool you want. There is no point in making the deepest part of the pool more than 60 cm/2 ft deep: ornamental fish don't go that deep. Leave a shelf all round about 30 cm/1 ft deep: it is on this that you will grow most of the waterlilies and other plants. A shelf about 5 cm/2 in. deep is also useful for marginal plants, but keep it to a small portion of the perimeter. Anything sharp or pointed, like stones or broken tree roots, must be moved, other-wise they will puncture the plastic and the pool will leak. When you have done this, put 5 cm/2 in. of sand over the whole area and lay your plastic sheet-ing on that. If one sheet is not wide enough, use two and join them with a special glue. The two sheets must overlap by at least 15 cm/6 in. Then fill the pool, and fill it slowly, allowing the plastic sheeting to stretch and settle.

Once the pool is full, pull the spare plastic sheeting up over the margins and cover it with earth and then paving slabs to hide it and to hold it firm. The slabs should overlap the water by about 5 cm/2 in.

You are now ready to stock the pool. Put the plants in first and give them a full month to settle down before you put any fish in—otherwise the fish will pull the plants loose, especially the water-lilies. Rather than just put earth in the pond and plant in that, put the plants into proper perforated plastic containers. These are far more satisfactory.

Should you ever want to empty the pool put the hose in it turned full on. Once all the bubbles have blown through the hose turn it off, put your thumb on the tap connection without letting any air in and use the hose as a siphon, drawing the water off to a lower level, preferably a drain.

In winter leave a plastic ball floating on the pool to prevent the surface freezing solid. Never hammer ice to break it: the shock waves travel through the water, concuss the fish and can kill them. If the water freezes really hard, melt the ice by standing a kettle of boiling water on it.

Preshaped fibre glass pools are ideal for use in combination with rockeries, and these are put into

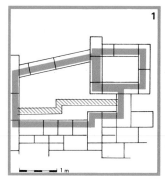
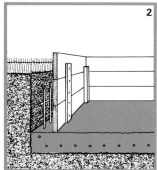
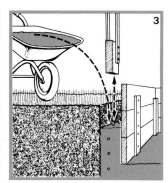

the ground in the same way by excavating a hole and filling it with a layer of sand for the pool to rest on.

A concrete pool If you want a pool that will last for ever, with clean lines and perpendicular or only slightly sloping walls, then concrete is best for the purpose. The various diagrams on these pages illustrate the plan and construction of one of these pools. Concrete is poisonous to fish and it is important to cover the whole surface thoroughly with an impermeable finish before filling the pool and introducing the fish. There are several proprietary products available for this purpose. Four-square pools like these are ideal on patios, especially if they have a deep section for water lilies and fish, with a shallow section for marginal bog-plants.

If you want to make a pool of this sort first make a detailed plan on a scale of 1:10. Then excavate the site for the pool to the planned depth. At the lowest point you should allow for a soakaway point and dig the ground more deeply, then fill the hollow with coarse stones, broken bricks and similar loose material. Tamp the bottom of the pool excavation down and cover it with a layer of rough stone which must also be tamped down.

The next step is putting up the shuttering. It is important to get this right since it determines the final shape of the pool. Follow the sketch-plan here. Mix the concrete in a ratio of 1:5—five shovels of washed gravel to each shovel of cement, and mix them as described earlier.

Before starting to pour in the concrete, fit a 5 cm/2 in. piece of piping above the soakaway at

the bottom of the pool to provide an outlet for the water should you want to drain the pool later. The top of the pipe should be level with the finished concrete floor, so it must be allowed to project 15–18 cm/6–7 in. above the tamped subsoil. Next, pour about 75 mm/3 in. of concrete over the bottom, and tamp this to rid it of any bubbles. Then lay a piece of coarse wire mesh—known as chicken wire in the building trade—over this. Ideally the wire used should be large enough to bend part of the way up the sides of the pool as well to stop any movement between side and bottom. Then top the bottom up till it is level with the top of the drain-away pipe—giving a depth of 15–18 cm/6–7 in. of concrete. At this stage position the wooden shuttering beside the earth walls of the excavation, to act as a mould for the concrete sides. The gap between the shuttering and the soil is built up, the concrete being continually tamped down.

Once all the concrete is in position the whole pool is covered with boards or damp sacking to prevent it drying out too quickly. On hot days it can be kept damp by moistening with a hose. Allow the concrete to dry slowly, then the shuttering can be removed.

While still damp, the inside of the pool should be given a smooth surface with a layer of about 2·5 cm/1 in. of mortar (sand:cement in the ratio 1:1) mixed with a waterproof compound. Round out the corners where walls and floor meet to make future cleaning of the pool easier.

Allow 4 full weeks for the concrete and cement to become really hard, then give the pool a coat of

Building a pool

1 Ground-plan
2 Shuttering—erected on the freshly-concreted floor
  Water lily pools—two depths: 60 cm/2 ft and 30 cm/1 ft
  Bog-plant pools—depth: 30 cm/12 in.
3 Concrete is poured in and tamped down
4 The finished pool ▶

blueish-green waterproof paint. This is particularly recommended for pools with little plant growth—about two-thirds of the pool surface should be free from plants, as overcrowding spoils the overall effect—because this colour is more pleasing to the eye than grey concrete.

If you do not give the pool a coat of impervious paint, then you must wash the concrete clean of any components which might be harmful to plants or fish. This is done by flushing the pool out with water at least three times in a day. Finally it can be filled with clean water and planted up.

Showerbath and bathing pool One of the essentials in any garden is a good water supply. At the time of building, taps should have been positioned along the outer walls of the house. Ideally you then lay pipelines just below ground with a number of outlets at various points all over the garden. Apart from using these to water the garden, you can also use them to water yourselves or the children on really hot days.

A portable shower is inexpensive and easy to install, and can be great fun in the garden on bright, sunny days. There are various models available, usually with their own stand, though you can always improvise one. The water supply is by means of a rubber hose (fig. 1).

Even more refreshing in hot weather is a dip in a large water-tank, 240 cm/8 ft or more in dia-meter. But precautions must be taken to safeguard smaller children: the safest way is to cover deep water tanks with a well-fitting wooden grating (fig. 2).

If you want a real swim in the garden as opposed to a mere splash, you will need a far larger pool and it will cost you far more. Among the lower-priced pools are those made of plastic or reinforced fibre-glass. Pools of this type should be at least 5 m/8 ft in diameter, otherwise you will feel you are swimming in a goldfish bowl. These pools are cheap to maintain.

There are a great number of different types of sunken swimming-pools on the market nowadays. You can assemble the prefabricated ones yourself. The parts are delivered to your door, and these can be assembled at home and built into the garden. Excavation costs—and transport costs for removal of excavated material—must not be overlooked when calculating the overall expense. The minimum size for such a pool if it is to be worthwhile is 7 m/24 ft by 4 m/12 ft with a minimum deep end water depth of 2 m/ 7 ft.

VERY IMPORTANT: If you have young children or grandchildren, or if children come into your garden, fence the pool off to avoid accidents. They happen all too easily, and are on the increase. Falling into an empty pool can be just as lethal as falling into a full one.

2 Of Spades and Lawnmowers

It is often said that it is a bad workman who blames his tools, but when it comes to gardening you have only yourself to blame. There are many jobs you will find it virtually impossible to do without the correct tools. What you need are the right tools, and not too many of them. There are trendy gardeners who rush out to buy every new gadget as soon as it comes on the market, use it once or twice and then, once the novelty has worn off, leave it neglected in some corner. On the other hand, there are gardeners who still struggle on with antediluvian implements like ancient pick-axes, primitive spades and the like. Try to strike a balance between the two extremes. Do not buy more than you need, but be sure that you do have the tools you need for the jobs you are going to do.

Many beginners make the mistake of getting themselves whole piles of bright and shiny garden equipment, much of which they will never use. The money would be better spent improving the soil. A look into the toolshed of an established garden will quickly show you what you really need and what you can do without.

MOTORIZED OR MANUAL?

A quick look round any modern home reveals a variety of electric appliances large and small—vacuum cleaner, washing-machine, electric mixer, dishwasher and so on. Anyone who has any of these machines knows that they only save time and labour if they can be used frequently and if cleaning and maintenance are easy and not needed too often. Just as the size of a house is one of the main determining factors in whether powered appliances are worth buying or not, so too with the garden. It really is only worth buying power tools in gardens of a quarter of an acre or more. Power hedge trimmers may be worthwhile but in small gardens a motor mower does little more than shatter the peace of your neighbours: it doesn't even mow a small lawn as efficiently as a hand mower. Besides, part of the charm of a garden comes from working in it peacefully, away from the noise and rush of everyday working life.

BASIC EQUIPMENT

It is difficult, especially for someone new to gardening, to choose the right tools from the vast and glittering array now offered in garden shops and centres. The following is a guide to those tools which are essential.

Pick and shovel These tools are indispensable in a new garden, and are often needed in the years to come. The blade of the shovel should come to a point, and the shovel should feel well-balanced when held with both hands. It is used not for digging but for shovelling loosened earth, sand and other materials, and also for mixing concrete.

A pick or mattock This is essential for loosening heavy soil and breaking up rocky ground. A mattock differs from a pick in that whereas a pick has each tine approximately the same size, on a mattock one tine is broad and flat. Both can be used for preparing the site of a pool.

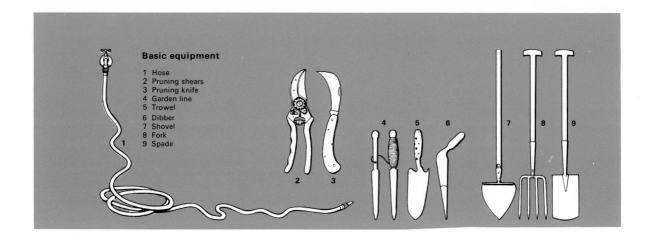

Basic equipment

1 Hose
2 Pruning shears
3 Pruning knife
4 Garden line
5 Trowel
6 Dibber
7 Shovel
8 Fork
9 Spade

The spade This is a classic gardening implement. A spade is to a garden what a plough is to a field. It is the tool that is needed to transform a piece of meadow—or wasteland—into a garden. In later years you will need it for autumn digging of the vegetable patch, for cutting lawn edges, planting trees, bushes and roses, for setting our border plants or replanting shrubs, and many other things. The best type of spade to buy is sturdily built, with a rectangular blade, slightly curved at the bottom. A D-grip is generally less hard on the hands than a T-grip. On heavy clay soils it is worth investing in a more expensive stainless steel blade. This is far easier to work with on such soils than an ordinary metal blade. This is a tool that never gets rusty in the toolshed because it is always being used. While a spade is needed for all rough work and heavy digging, a fork is used for winter work, refining clods of soil turned up by the spade, for summer work on the vegetable garden and so on. It is also useful for turning over the compost heap, or for getting rid of weeds among the fruit bushes, and for harvesting such vegetables as celery, carrots, potatoes and so on.

It is also the only suitable tool for removing deep-rooting and persistent weeds such as couch grass, ground elder, bindweed and so on. A spade would merely cut through the roots, causing them to branch and grow again even more vigorously.

The rake This is used for levelling flower beds or other areas of the garden, especially the vegetable garden. Its purpose is not merely to level the soil, but to bring it to a fine tilth, fine enough for sowing seeds and planting small plants. In the process it can be used for removing stones or larger lumps of earth which can easily be removed from the surface.

A sixteen-tine iron rake is best for general use, but a smaller eight or ten-tine rake is more convenient for keeping the walks between the vegetable beds clean and tidy.

The best tool for levelling larger areas is a wide wooden rake. This is very handy for smoothing the lawn area of a new garden site, and is an essential tool for larger gardens. The long-pronged rake has various uses in a garden. It is meant for raking moss from the lawn, gathering up fallen leaves in autumn, keeping areas round compost heaps clean. Painted metal or cane-pronged models are equally efficient. The latest thing is the nylon sweeper with an aluminium handle.

On larger lawn areas of a quarter acre or more, a wheeled collecting bin with rotary brushes is most useful for collecting fallen leaves. The long-pronged rake would still be needed for raking out moss but the rotary brushes could be used for gathering up the loosened moss afterwards.

Hoes Modern hoes are easy-to-handle tools used for general soil cultivation. You simply walk backwards without having to bend, pulling the implement along the ground between rows of seedlings and plants. The job of cultivating the garden with tools like these during the summer is a real pleasure.

This method of cultivation stimulates plant growth since the soil crust which forms soon after

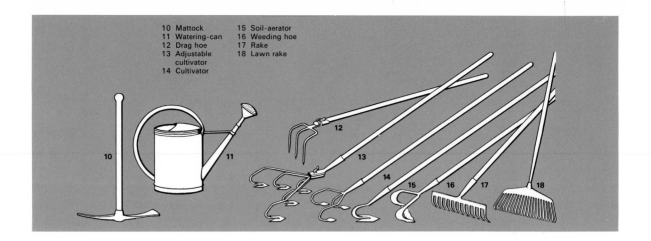

10 Mattock
11 Watering-can
12 Drag hoe
13 Adjustable cultivator
14 Cultivator
15 Soil-aerator
16 Weeding hoe
17 Rake
18 Lawn rake

a fall of rain is quickly broken up, and oxygen allowed to reach the roots of plants, while the residual carbon dioxide can escape from the soil. At the same time, weeds are killed at seedling stage, before they have a chance to get established. Working the soil with a hoe also improves its texture. Other useful, but not indispensable tools include the following.

Adjustable cultivator This tool combines seven individual implements. The shares are interchangeable by means of a wing-screw, and there are seven different heads that can be fitted, each designed for a different cultural operation, but all basically just variants of the hook-rake.

Anyone who is not mechanically minded can find all this changing of heads rather tiresome. In which case they would be well advised to spend a little more money on the following implements. These have the advantage of being always ready for use.

Hooked cultivator This tool has three hooked, fixed blades. Each hooked tine ends in an arrowhead—like blades. This tool is handy for loosening the surface soil-crust on vegetable or flower beds which forms soon after rainfall.

Grubber This looks much the same as the hooked cultivator but is narrower, and its three pointed blades are particularly suitable for use on heavier soils.

Soil-aerator A much-used member of this group of tools, is the aerator which has only one blade. It is used for loosening soil between annuals, border plants and narrow vegetable drills.

If you use these tools frequently and regularly they will be highly successful in keeping weeds down and keeping the soil in good condition. However, if you adopt this method of cultivation you must keep at it. Stop doing it for two or three weeks and the weeds soon reappear. The weeding-hoe has a sharp, wavy, two-edged blade held by two protective side-pieces. You will find it easy to single out weeds from among cultivated plants with this tool.

The handle Not normally considered a tool in itself, there are very few tools that are any use without one. Loose handles are a nuisance, create blisters and can even be positively dangerous. Ideally the length of handle of a hoe, rake or similar tool should be the same as the height of the person using it, to allow them to work comfortably in an upright position.

The hose An indispensable item in the garden today. If used sensibly it should not use up more water than watering with a can would do, and a hose is far more practical and convenient. It is also better for the plants, since it at least attempts to simulate rain. It does not wash soil away from the roots of plants or leave a hard, impacted crust behind, as too easily happens with a watering can. It also saves time and labour, which can be better used on other garden activities or leisure pursuits. The length of the hose you need depends upon

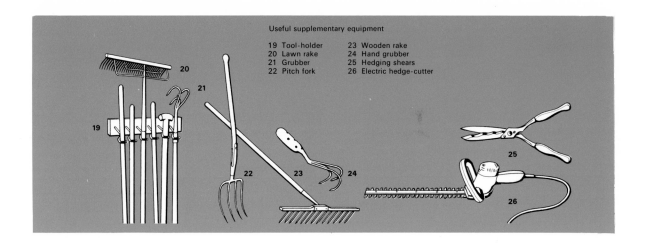

Useful supplementary equipment

19 Tool-holder
20 Lawn rake
21 Grubber
22 Pitch fork
23 Wooden rake
24 Hand grubber
25 Hedging shears
26 Electric hedge-cutter

the size of your garden. It should be long enough to reach into even the furthest corner. The watering can still has a place in the garden today. Its main use is for watering individual plants, and plants growing in tubs or containers. It is most useful to have two cans, a large one for watering the tubs or newly planted shrubs—especially conifers—and a small one, for watering in freshly planted-out seedlings. Generally, plastic cans are best. They last well, don't leak and cannot perish. Set yourself up with a 10 litre/2-gallon can and a $\frac{1}{2}$ litre/1 pint can. The gay colours of plastics and the modern designs of many cans means they can look good left standing beside the water butt in modern gardens, but in cottage gardens they can look rather garish and the traditional galvanised metal ones are more in keeping. Make sure that whatever can you buy is easy to carry when full, and easy to aim when in use.

Small garden implements   Pruning shears are first on the list here, indispensable even in the smallest gardens. You will need them for pruning fruit trees, climbers, roses, shrubs, and for cutting flowers. There are two types available. The anvil-type, where a sharp blade shuts onto a flat surface, and the parrot's beak type where two sharp blades cross. Both are equally efficient. The only important thing is that they should be sharp. A pruning knife which has a solid, curved blade should also be added to the store of small implements. Ask any nurseryman to show you how to use one. It is incredibly difficult to explain how to use them on the written page, and ridiculously

simple to learn when you see someone do it. Like pruning shears, the most important thing about any pruning knife is that it must be really sharp.

You will also need a wooden dibber for planting out seedlings, and a trowel for putting perennials, strawberries or bulbs into the ground. Another useful item is the hand-grubber, especially necessary in rock gardens or for cultivating between clumps of low perennials bordering the pathway.

If you've ever wondered how people manage to plant seeds in a straight row, now is the time to find out. It is done with the help of a line. This consists of two pegs, round one of which a length of waxed twine is kept wound, the loose end attached to the second peg. All you do is push the second peg into the ground, unwind the twine from the first peg, and when you have unreeled enough, push that into the ground. Provided the twine is taut the line will be straight. You can buy these lines, but they are so simple to make it is really better to spend the money on other garden items.

Supplementary equipment   There are implements which, though almost indispensable in some gardens, are not a necessity in every garden. The following are some of these.

The lawn-mower   Since most gardens have lawns, this could well be regarded as basic equipment. In many gardens of a quarter of an acre (0·1 ha) or less the lawn is best mown with a hand mower. A motor mower is a noisy, anti-social machine, that will skid when you brake or accelerate, scuff the turf whenever you turn it, and com-

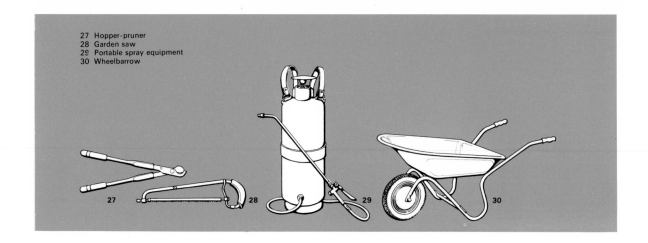

27 Hopper-pruner
28 Garden saw
29 Portable spray equipment
30 Wheelbarrow

27 28 29 30

pact the grass because of its weight. In gardens of this size a motor mower is a status symbol, not a useful tool. If you must have one, keep it in the sitting room to impress the neighbours.

For larger gardens motorised mowers are worthwhile, saving an enormous amount of time. You can choose between motor mowers or electric mowers. The former are noisy and smelly. With the latter you either have a tiresome cable which somehow always seems to be in the way, or a battery which never quite holds its charge long enough to mow the whole lawn. Both, however, are very quiet in operation. The air-cushioned mower, which seems to hover over the lawn surface, does not give a close cut, but is useful in gardens where you have banks to mow: you can also mow right under shrubs with it. However, it is more expensive than conventional powered mowers.

Avoid multi-purpose motorised appliances, which combine a variety of attachments for lawn mowing, rototilling, straight-arm hedge cutting, snow clearing and so on. Though economically tempting, they can be dangerous. You are far better off using separate appliances, each designed to do a particular job.

Further tools for lawn maintenance Short-cut grass and fallen leaves can easily be removed from small areas with a lawn rake. For lawn aeration, you will need a spiker-slitter. Its sharp tines slit the lawn surface into narrow strips, reducing soil compaction, increasing aeration, improving water penetration and drainage, dividing the grass

roots and stimulating growth—and getting rid of moss and creeping weeds into the bargain. Using it, however, is an arduous job but a worthwhile one. You will also need edging shears for trimming the lawn edges.

Sprayers for fruit trees A necessary evil for anyone who grows fruit trees or bushes. The most suitable apparatus for small gardens is a portable plastic container with shoulder-straps. For larger gardens, a solidly-built, high-performance sprayer with a 225 l/5 gal capacity is better. This has a long nozzle flex and is stood on the ground.

Another efficient spraying apparatus is the portable piston-pump with a separate plastic container for the mixture. Although it requires continuous hand-pumping during spraying this is not physically tiring. The plastic containers are interchangeable, so fungicides and insecticides can be kept in separate containers and the residue need not be thrown away every time, nor need the containers be flushed out after use, a time-consuming business.

Wheelbarrow Indispensable when laying out a garden. Once a small garden has been established, you can exist without one, since compost can be collected and carried in plastic buckets.

Hedge-cutters Hedges no more than 10 m/30 ft long can easily be clipped by hand. There are many good makes of shears on the market. The important thing, as with pruning shears is to keep them really sharp. For longer hedges an electric

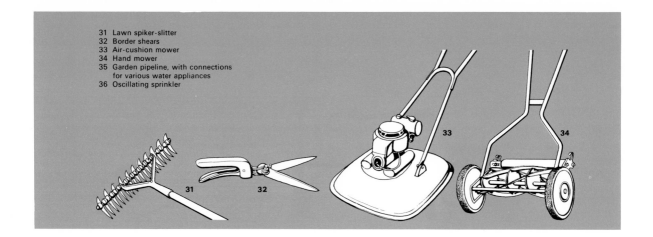

31 Lawn spiker-slitter
32 Border shears
33 Air-cushion mower
34 Hand mower
35 Garden pipeline, with connections
   for various water appliances
36 Oscillating sprinkler

hedge-cutter is essential. You can buy these with teeth on one side only or on both sides of the blade. Always take care to keep the flex well out of the way. Eleven people a year are killed in Britain by cutting through the flexes of their hedge-trimmers —the same number as are killed by lightning. This is a tiny number considering how many powered hedge-trimmers are in use. Nonetheless, treat them with the respect they deserve. If you have no power point available, the alternative is a petrol-driven machine, which is heavier and more expensive.

A tree saw Needed for the maintenance of fruit trees and ornamental shrubs. The best model has a blade which can be tightened when in use.

Loppers These are invaluable for maintaining fruit bushes and ornamental shrubs in larger gardens. They have long handles and good leverage, so that branches up to 5 cm/2 in. thick can easily be cut through. Normal loppers have only a single fulcrum. A model with a double fulcrum means you have to exert less pressure to make a cut. Loppers should be used for cutting any twigs or branches too thick for pruning shears. More pruning-shears are ruined every week by people using them to try to cut twigs too thick for them, than by any other form of misuse or abuse.

A ladder A rigid ladder is an essential if you need to reach tall fruit trees or espaliers. Adjustable ladders made from light metal alloys are best. They are easy to carry and will not rot if left out.

Tool maintenance All tools used for soil cultivation should be thoroughly cleaned with a slightly oily rag after use. The cutting edges of shears, secateurs and so on should be sharpened with a file and the metal wiped with an oily rag before being put away. Unless you are good at sharpening tools, you may find it better to take them back to the shop where you bought them or return them to the manufacturers to have them sharpened. The lawn-mower should be overhauled every winter by an expert.

DE LUXE EQUIPMENT

A sprinkler A garden sprinkler makes a wonderful gift for any garden-lover. Not only does it simplify the task of watering the garden, but at the same time gives a lovely display of mist and spray, especially in the evening with the sun shining through the water.

There are two basic types: those that just spin round for ever, and the oscillating type. The latter are generally more use since they can be adjusted to water a large square, a narrow rectangle, or only to the left or only to the right. Both types are normally run off stand pipes on mains water.

Electric pumps Anyone who has a large rainwater tank near the house can use an electric pump to push this water through the sprinklers. The size and output of these pumps varies from model to model and a filter must be used. Soluble lawn fertilizers can be diluted in the water tank and then sprinkled onto the turf by this means.

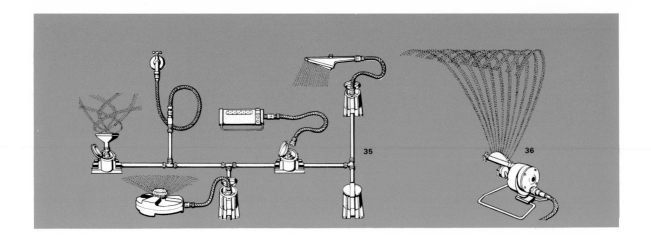

Garden pipelines Though extremely useful these are expensive and are seldom used, except in large gardens. All they are is a system of plastic pipes laid in the ground, with sockets at various points to which sprinklers can be attached. These are most used on lawns where care must be taken that socket-lids are perfectly flush with the ground, otherwise they will damage the mower. They are also useful in large plantings.

The pipeline can be connected either to the domestic water supply or to the rainwater tank—in which case a pump and filter will be needed.

If you want a system of this type you can install it yourself. Just draw a scale plan of the scheme you want then get it checked by a professional garden designer. Although such systems are most easily installed while the garden is being made, they can be added later.

A charming water-display can be created in the garden by operating three of these rotary sprinklers simultaneously along the pipeline at intervals of 5–7 m/16–20 ft.

3 Behind the Scenes – How Plants Live

The average gardener does not need to be a botanist. On the other hand it always helps to know why you do what you do in the garden, not merely how to do it. Besides which, the more you know about the plants in your garden, the more enjoyment you will get from it, and many gardening jobs which most people perform mechanically will take on a new sense and meaning.

THE FUNDAMENTAL UNITS

All plants—whether weeds, weeping willows, peonies, pansies, cabbages or king-cups, are built up of cells so minute they can be seen only under a powerful microscope. The very simplest plants which were also the first to evolve, consist of one cell only: many bacteria and algae are in this group, as are some of the fungi discussed in the chapter on 'Plant Protection'. Throughout evolution the tendency has been for plants to become more complex. From the earliest and most primitive single-celled plants the further plants evolved, and as this happened the different cells within the plants became specialised, different groups of cells performing different functions. Roots, shoots, leaves, stems, flowers, pollen and fruit are all made up of millions of cells. Although the cells in a leaf perform a different function from the cells in a root, the basic structure of the cell remains the same.

Each cell is wrapped in an envelope of cellulose known as the cell-wall or membrane. In the early stages of its life this membrane is quite elastic and flexible, but it gradually hardens and toughens with age. The thick, old cell walls have thin apertures in them through which the exchange of material between cells can continue.

What is actually wrapped up inside the cell-wall or membrane is the basic substance of all living matter—protoplasm. Floating in the protoplasm is the nucleus. In young cells, the protoplasm and nucleus completely fill the space within the cell wall. In older cells the protoplasm shrinks and adheres to the cell wall. In shrinking it forms a cavity, or vacuole, inside the cell, which is filled by a fluid called cell sap.

The nucleus, bedded in cytoplasm, is more or less round. It is between five-millionths and twentyfive-millionths of a millimeter in diameter. This tiny nucleus is made up of several parts. It contains a cohesive fluid which is called the nuclear sap as well as the chromosomes, the units which control the genetic stability of the plant.

The plasma of each individual cell also contains the units of pigmentation. In some fungi, algae and bacteria these are lacking. There are three main pigments units: green (chloropyll), yellow-red (chromoplast) and white (leucoplast). The first of these is of vital interest to the gardener, since it contains the most important of all plant pigments—chlorophyll—the vital substance that enables plants to make use of energy derived from sunlight. The yellow-red pigment gives carrots, tomatoes, rose-hips, and many other blossoms and fruit, their bright colour. It also provides the autumn tints of trees and shrubs. Leucoplast resembles the green pigment in form, but is colourless.

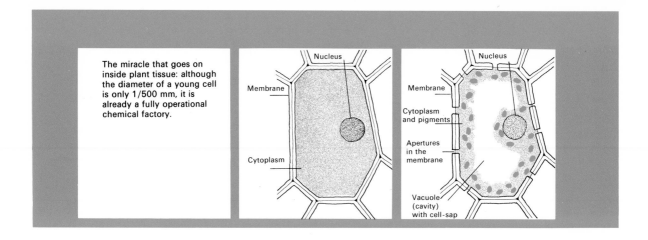

The miracle that goes on inside plant tissue: although the diameter of a young cell is only 1/500 mm, it is already a fully operational chemical factory.

Nucleus
Membrane
Cytoplasm

Nucleus
Membrane
Cytoplasm and pigments
Apertures in the membrane
Vacuole (cavity) with cell-sap

The plasma of many plant cells contains other substances too: there is protein in many seeds, starch in potato tubers and grain kernels; fats and oils in sunflower-seed, poppy-seed and linseed; aromatic substances in pot herbs and medicinal herbs. The cell sap too, which fills the vacuole in older cells contains organic and inorganic salts, various forms of sugar, amino-acids, tannin, and similar substances. Sometimes the cell-sap contains dyes such as anthozyan, which gives cells a blue or red colour. It causes, for example, the red in red cabbage and the purple in copper beeches. It is these dyes, together with the pigments already mentioned, which produce such an astounding variety of colours of leaf, flower and fruit.

Many gardeners out in a gale must have wondered at some time why tall, swaying grasses like pampas grass or lofty windswept trees are not simply broken off by the wind. The reason is that the membranes enclosing older cells in the stems have become toughened and thickened, and this tissue is not only strong but also highly elastic, and can endure the natural exertions of pulling, bending and stretching. However, excessive forces can break the cells or snap branches and stems.

How plants grow A sunflower grows from a seed less than half an inch across into a plant anything from 3–5 m/10–15 ft tall, topped by one or more flowers over 30 cm/1 ft across, all in the space of about 4 months. How on earth does it do it? This is an extreme example, but it does it in just the same way as all other green plants, only faster.

All plant growth results from cells dividing. One cell divides and makes two, two make four, and so on. It is a simple arithmetical progression, not a geometric progression. It is the same whether it is a modest radish or a mighty oak tree.

The rate of growth depends simply on the speed with which the cells divide. The faster they divide the faster the plant grows. The cells in a sunflower divide very much faster than those in an oak tree.

Cell division however, is a complex business. It starts with the division of the nucleus. The original or mother nucleus divides into two daughter nuclei. Each of these will have the same number of chromosomes as the mother cell. The chromosomes are, as it were, coded instructions telling the cell what to do and be. Different plants have different numbers of chromosomes. The number of chromosomes for each species remains constant. A Madonna lily, for instance, has 24 chromosomes; an apple has 34; a Morello cherry 32, and the common horsetail over 200. The same applies to animals. You have 46 chromosomes.

Chromosomes are not, however, the ultimate unit of genetic information. Genes are. Each gene is one unit of genetic information, meaningless in itself. It only becomes meaningful when combined with other genes. The genes are threaded on the chromosomes like a string of beads. It is the order in which they occur on the string that differentiates one plant from another. When the division of the nucleus occurs, the chromosomes split lengthwise and gravitate towards the centre of the cell. Then the halves of the split chromosomes part and pull towards the two

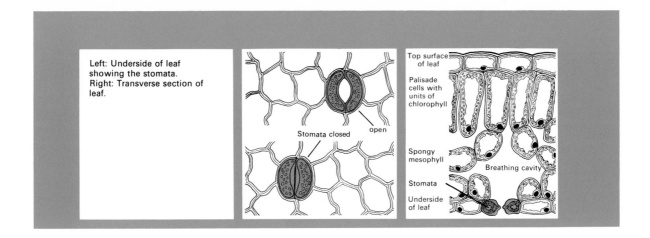

Left: Underside of leaf showing the stomata.
Right: Transverse section of leaf.

Stomata closed / open

Top surface of leaf
Palisade cells with units of chlorophyll
Spongy mesophyll
Breathing cavity
Stomata
Underside of leaf

opposing poles which, meanwhile, have formed inside the cell. There each chromosome forms a cluster of tissue and at the same time a new cell wall is formed. This divides the original cell into two parts, producing two new nuclei. Thus two daughter-cells have been formed out of a single mother cell, and each is identical in every way to the mother cell.

ALL LIFE DEPENDS ON THE GREEN LEAF

Take a pine-needle and a rhubarb-leaf and compare them. They are different in size, shape and colour. They look different, they smell different and they taste different. The leaves of grasses, lilies, horse-chestnuts, maples, hollies, mint and ivy all look, smell and taste different. Yet they are all constructed in a similar way and all serve the same function.

If you put a cross-section of a leaf under a microscope what you would see would be innumerable tiny cells. The upper surface of the leaf is composed of a clear 'skin'. Below this are clusters of long, narrow vertical cells known as palisade cells. These make up about half the depth of the leaf. Below these, and continuing right down to the underside of the leaf the cells are more rounded in shape and irregular in size. They are very loosely arranged, rather like a sponge. These are known as the spongy mesophyll. The spaces between the cells are connected and allow the living leaf to contain air. This enters the leaf through innumerable tiny openings or valves on the underside of

the leaf, known as stomata. These are extremely minute and extremely numerous. The underside of an average-size cabbage leaf has more than ten million stomata.

This structure, simple though it may seem, is the result of millions of years of evolution. In fact, once you fully understand the function it has to perform, you will see that the design is just about perfect. Yet it has taken millions of years to evolve. In primitive plants (mosses, horsetails, algae) the leaves are not so well designed. And perhaps it is just as well that in higher plants the structure functions perfectly, because no life on this planet would be possible without the green leaves of plants. They perform an incredibly clever piece of chemical processing—a process so complex that man has still not been able to synthesise it: they take the energy from sunlight and use it to convert minerals from the soil into complex organic substances. This is the ultimate food source of all animal life. Even carnivores eat animals that ate leaves. The leaves of the plant absorb carbon dioxide (CO_2) from the air during daylight. When water and carbon dioxide molecules come together in sunlight, in the cells containing chlorophyll, they produce sugars and oxygen. The chemical formula for this transmutation is: $6CO_2 + 6H_2O + 675Kal. = C_6H_{12}O_6 + 6O_2$. That means in plain English that six parts of carbon dioxide plus six parts of water (plus sunlight energy) become one part of sugar plus six parts of oxygen. Thus not only are plants the only source of food for all other forms of life. As a mere by-product of that process they also produce

59

the very air we breathe. The system is not however, a one-way one. Man breathes in the oxygen plants give off, and breathes out the carbon dioxide they need to produce more food and oxygen. The plant and animal kingdoms are thus completely dependent on each other.

It may not be quite clear how the carbon dioxide gets into the leaves, since they do not have lungs and cannot breathe it in. It gets in through the stomata or holes on the under sides of the leaves, rather in the way water is soaked up by a piece of blotting paper. It is then absorbed and dissolved in the fluid in the cells, and slowly passes through them to the chlorophyll. The oxygen produced during photosynthesis is slowly released into the atmosphere by a reversal of the process.

That then, is photosynthesis—the fundamental chemical process upon which all life on earth depends. Various other factors determine the rate at which photosynthesis takes place, and whether it takes place at all. The most important of these is sunlight. Photosynthesis can only occur in sunlight. Once the sun sets photosynthesis stops. The second is temperature. As every gardener knows, you need a higher temperature to grow cucumbers and tomatoes than, say spinach. To encourage photosynthesis, as much carbon dioxide as possible must be made available for the plants by giving them plenty of humus, which in the process of decomposition releases this gas.

That, however, is not quite the end of the story of photosynthesis. The leaf has converted water and carbon dioxide into sugar. All this would be rather pointless if it just stayed there. It is stored in the leaf by day in the form of carbohydrates. At night, when photosynthesis stops, it is reconverted into sugar and moves out of the leaf through special conducting tissues known as vascular bundles. These distribute the sugar to all parts of the plant. Much of the sugar is then used by these parts of the plant to build new cells and to grow. Some of it is stored. Substances such as sucrose are stored in the fat roots of sugar beet; starch is stored in the tubers of potatoes.

In addition to photosynthesis there are a number of other processes which plants have to carry out in order to sustain life and grow. Like man and animals, plants breathe. The process is called respiration.

Respiration takes place not only in the leaves but in every cell in the plant, the roots as much as the stem. That is why plants must have air, as well as moisture, in the soil. They can literally drown or suffocate if deprived of oxygen at the roots by water logging or compaction of the soil. The dry weight of green plants is reduced by the process of respiration during darkness, when photosynthesis stops. It is this that causes weight loss in potatoes stored in the dark.

The leaf serves one other vital function—that of transpiration. A plant always tends to take up more water than it can use. This may seem wasteful but there is a good reason for it, which will be mentioned later. The excess, which can be more than ninety-eight per cent, is released into the atmosphere by transpiration. It escapes through the stomata on the underside of the leaves in the form of vapour. The water is taken up by the roots and

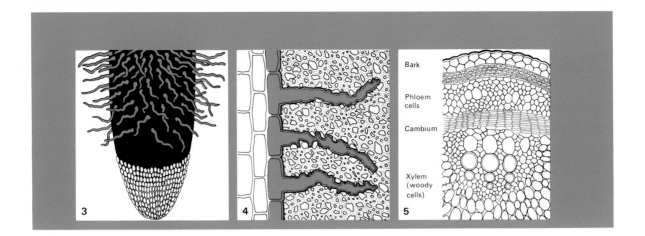

Bark

Phloem cells

Cambium

Xylem (woody cells)

3   4   5

transported by a complicated system of narrow cell tubes to the topmost leaves. The drier the air surrounding the plant, the greater the rate at which evaporation takes place. A tree is capable of transpiring an enormous amount of water in a day. A silver birch, about 4 m/50 ft tall, has approximately 5,000,000 leaves and can give off at least 90 l/20 gal of water a day by transpiration in grey weather—and over 136 l/30 gal a day in hot weather. This is one of the reasons trees dry out the soil round them.

The reason a plant takes up far more water than it can use is this. Dissolved in that water are minute quantities of mineral salts; these are vital to plant growth, and in order to get enough of them the plant has to pump a lot of water through its system, filtering out the mineral salts. It is rather like panning for gold. Since most of the vapour leaves the plant through the stomata, evaporation is greatly restricted when these are closed. Plants normally only close their stomata under extreme conditions, when the demand for water greatly exceeds the supply, and the plant has begun to wilt. In general, the stomata remain open in daylight and closed at night, when photosynthesis stops. Many plants such as cacti protect themselves against excessive transpiration. A glance is often enough to tell an experienced gardener whether a plant requires a lot or a little water for its growth. Large-leaved cucumbers require far more water to grow than, say, onions, with their protective waxy skin. Other plants, such as, for example, mullein, have woolly leaves as a protection from excessive evaporation.

How plants eat By this we mean the roots, which absorb water and nutrients from the soil and send them forth to nourish the rest of the plant.

The roots have two functions. The first is to anchor the plant in the ground. The other is to absorb water and nutrients from the soil and supply these to the rest of the plant. On some plants the two types of roots are quite distinct. There are thin fibrous roots which feed the plant, and thick, coarse roots which anchor it. The difference is not usually that clear, all roots serving both functions.

The organs by which plants carry out the main functions by which they sustain life are situated as far apart on the plant as possible, the leaves at one extreme and the roots at the other extreme.

Roots grow in exactly the same way as any other part of the plant—by cell division. It is the tip of the root that grows, and immediately behind the growing tip is a zone where fine, white hairs spring out on all sides. The older of these tiny hairs are constantly dying and being replaced by new hairs which constantly form immediately behind the growing tip. The life of each hair is very short, so that the active hair zone is always comparatively small. These hairs are so fine that they can penetrate the smallest gaps in the soil. They squeeze themselves between soil particles, and suck up the film of water which clings to them. In order to absorb enough water and nutrients the roots extend over a surprisingly large area, and the active feeding area is at the tip of the roots —at the circumference of the area covered. That

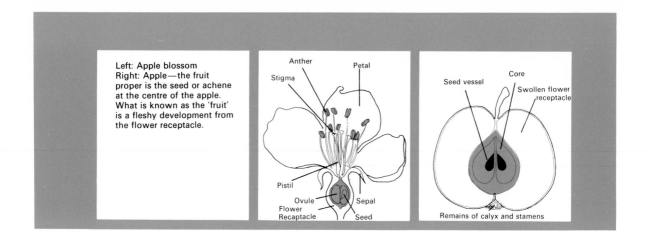

Left: Apple blossom
Right: Apple—the fruit proper is the seed or achene at the centre of the apple. What is known as the 'fruit' is a fleshy development from the flower receptacle.

Anther
Petal
Stigma
Pistil
Ovule
Flower
Recaptacle
Sepal
Seed

Seed vessel
Core
Swollen flower receptacle
Remains of calyx and stamens

is why it is a waste of time to water or manure a plant with a far-reaching root system, such as a fruit tree, close to the trunk only. The place to put the manure and do the watering is far away from the trunk at the furthest reach of the branches; that is where the active roots will be.

Stems and trunks   These have two functions. The first is to provide the plant with a support system sufficiently strong to hold it up off the ground and prevent it breaking in wind or rain. The second is to connect all the different parts of the plant together. All stems contain two types of cell tubes. One is composed of long cells with woody walls, making up a tissue known as xylem. These are the tubes through which water and a weak solution of mineral salts is transported from the roots to the remotest leaves. The other is composed of long, soft-walled cells called phloem. This carries sugars and other foods manufactured by the leaves during the process of photosynthesis to all other parts of the plant.

In dicotyledonous plants (plants whose seedlings have two seed-leaves, including most trees and shrubs and many flowering plants) there is another layer of cells between the xylem and the phloem. These are the only active cells in stems or trunk, and are called the cambium. These cells divide rapidly. As they mature, those on the inner side of the ring change to woody cells (xylem), and it is this which makes the branches grow thicker. The cambium is particularly important for gardeners when grafting.

This dual system of cell tubes runs through the whole plant from the root tips to the finest veins of the leaves. Water absorbed by the roots is moved through these cell-tubes to all parts of a plant by capillary action.

Although water reaches every part of the plant, most of what is absorbed passes all the way along the system to the leaves where it is transpired through the stomata into the atmosphere.

Blossom time   Man has become so arrogant in his supposed mastery of nature that he probably presumes, if he stops to think about it, that the only reason the plants in his garden produce such a wealth of flowers in such a variety of sizes, colours, shapes, forms and scents is for his delight alone. It is sobering to realise that the first flowers appeared on the face of the earth about 35,000,000 years ago—long before evolution got round to the first mammals, let alone to man. Man merely uses flowers for his own ends: they have a function of their own: simply and solely to reproduce themselves and preserve the species. Insects are lured into flowers by colour or scent usually in search of nectar. As they push their proboscis deep into a flower their legs get covered in pollen, some of which rubs off onto the reproductive organs of the next flower they enter. Flowers are thus a kind of mating display, though mating itself can usually only be carried out by means of a third party—the insect. Among the decorative plants, only grasses, conifers, ferns and the plants which produce catkins can do without this seductive 'make-up'. They are pollinated by the wind.

The whole process of pollination, fertilization

and seed formation is complicated and fascinating.

Both the male pollen grain and the female ovule are created in the normal way by cell division. There is only one thing different here: each has only half the normal number of chromosomes. For a new plant to be formed the two have got to get together to produce the full set of chromosomes.

A bee or other insect brushes past the stigma of a flower as it enters. If the stigma is, as it were, in season, it will be sticky, and male pollen will stick to it. If both are ripe and from the same species of plant, the sticky substance on the tip of the stigma will make the pollen grain germinate. It will then grow a long tube down through the tube in the middle of the style of the ovary. A male sperm from the pollen grain then swims down this tube and unites with the female nucleus of the ovule. The new cell formed by this union, the embryo, then has the full compliment of chromosomes for that particular type of plant.

After this, another male nucleus forms inside the long tube, and moves down into the ovary where it fertilizes another nucleus (secondary embryo-sack nucleus). This nucleus has double the normal amount of chromosomes. A cell nucleus with three times the normal number of chromosomes is thus created. From this second fertilization is formed the protective and nutritive tissue which encases the growing embryo.

Fruit and seed Once this double fertilization has taken place, and the embryo has been formed inside the seed case, cells begin to divide extremely rapidly. Within a surprisingly short period the cells have multiplied to become, in effect, a plant in miniature, curled up, like a foetus inside the seed case. There is a radicle—a minute, primitive root, which will push into the soil and turn into a real root. There are the seed-leaves or cotyledons which will sustain the seedlings until the root is sufficiently established for the plant to put on true leaves. And there is the endosperm, which is to a seed what the white is to the yolk of an egg. Once these things have formed, together with a hard outer casing, the process stops. The seed becomes dormant. Only after it has been planted in the earth, where it has the necessary conditions of darkness, moisture, air and warmth, can the young seed germinate and begin to grow.

The seed stage is a rest period for plants. It bridges seasons, droughts, and so on. To carry seeds through this period they contain oil, starch and protein which is why so many seeds are good to eat. During the germination process these substances are changed into a form readily acceptable to the seedling.

The devices by which seeds are dispersed are many and ingenious. The seeds of dandelions drift gracefully on the wind, borne up on fragile parachutes. Those of maples spin to the ground on membranous wings. Burrs stick to the fleece of animals, and fall where the animal finally rubs them off. Some are eaten by birds and carried in their digestive tract sometimes hundreds of miles before being ejected. Some seeds are scattered by an explosion of the seed case: brooms do this and on a still, hot summer day you can hear them exploding with a pop like a pop-gun. The lupin

also scatters its seed by exploding, blasting seeds up to 15 m/50 ft away.

The period during which seeds remain usable—that is, retain the ability to germinate—can vary enormously. Some seeds, like those of parsley or carrots remain usable for only a few weeks, while the seed of some alpine plants and water lilies can remain usable for 150 years—more than twice the span of a human lifetime. Rumour has it that seed of the sacred lotus of Egypt remains usable for a thousand years. However, no one has actually proved that yet.

APPLYING THE BOTANY

Now you know the basic biology of plant life, its worth seeing how you can actually apply this knowledge in a practical way in the garden. Take cucumbers, for example. Suppose you manure them, then a couple of days later they look 'scorched'. Can you work out why?

What went wrong was this. Inside each plant cell there is a liquid solution called cell sap. This contains a variety of dissolved mineral salts and other substances, mainly organic. The cell walls are partly pervious, and this enables a process called osmosis to take place. The principle is that the solution inside the cell is stronger than the solution outside it. The stronger solution draws the weaker solution to it through the cell-wall. In a normal situation the solution inside the cell is stronger than the solution outside it. The cell therefore absorbs the solution outside. However, if the solution outside the cell is the stronger of the two, the process will be reversed and the solution inside the cell drawn out. That is what happened when you manured those cucumbers. The manure was too strong. The plasma in the cells was drawn off, the cell walls collapsed, and the plant started to wilt. The only cure is to weaken the manure by applying an enormous amount of water—but that will only work if the collapse has not gone too far. And you may drown the plant trying to wash the nutrients out of the manure. Roots need air as well as moisture in the soil.

Another point many gardeners wonder about is whether the leaves of celery and tomatoes should be removed. For some reason, many people think this results in bigger sticks of celery, or tomatoes that ripen earlier. Having read the vital role of the green leaf in building up the plant, it should be apparent that the plants cannot grow without leaves. The purpose of manuring plants and safe-guarding them from pests and diseases is after all to help them to develop strong, healthy leaves, which will in turn enable them to grow into large, healthy fruit and vegetables. No market-gardener would go to the trouble and expense of doing that if he thought he could grow good big sticks of celery and large, well-coloured tomatoes without leaves.

On the other hand one does quite often see the leaves of strawberries being removed after harvest. This is only done when the leaves have been affected by leaf spot disease and have therefore ceased to function properly. If the diseased foliage is removed immediately after harvest and the area manured, the soil loosened and watered sufficiently

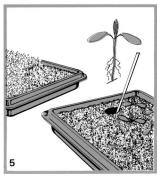

Sowing and pricking out
1 Cover bottom of seed-box with broken crocks, then fill up with seed compost.
2 Firm down the fine soil and make a firm, level surface.
3 Sow seed and gently cover with fine sandy soil.
4 Press seed in and sprinkle with water.
5 As soon as true leaves appear, prick out seedlings. Nip off root-tips a little (to encourage more compact root growth).

in dry weather, in a few weeks the plants will produce a vigorous display of fresh green leaves. This healthy foliage can assimilate very intensively, and build up the plants very rapidly. The decisive factor here is that the old foliage should be cleared away immediately after harvest, since the new blossoms are already forming between the end of August and the beginning of September. By that stage the newly-formed leaves must already be fully operational. Experiments have shown that yields are not lowered by this treatment. It should not, however, be applied to healthy strawberry beds.

The leaves of cuttings usually wilt after being placed in the ground, and one of the problems facing anyone propagating plants from cuttings is to prevent this. The wilting occurs because the leaves continue to transpire—give off water. However, having no roots, they are inadequately equipped to draw up water to keep the leaves supplied. To reduce transpiration, cuttings of shrubs are usually partly stripped of their leaves, those remaining being cut short, before being put into a propagating case or under plastic sheeting. These cuttings must be kept in warm, moist, close conditions, until roots form to minimize transpiration from the leaves. The propagation frame must of course be shaded against the sun. Once roots begin to form, less water is needed and more air can be allowed in.

A similar procedure must be followed when pricking out seedlings in a propagating case or under plastic sheeting. They too need a close atmosphere, so the lights are kept shut and the seedlings are watered frequently. The seedlings have of course, already grown roots, but these tend to get damaged in the process of pricking out, so that the leaves temporarily lack a sufficient water supply.

Apart from accidental damage during pricking out, the long white roots of the seedlings should be nipped off between forefinger and thumbnail to encourage the fine feeding rootlets to branch out in a compact little ball. By the time the seedlings are ready for planting out they no longer need such close conditions. They can be lifted from the frame carefully so that their fine root fibres are not damaged. By this time their root system is sufficiently well developed for them to take up water and nutrients readily from the soil and continue to grow without first 'sulking' for several days.

Jiffy pots are a marvellous invention for plants whose roots will not tolerate any root disturbance. The pots are made of compressed peat, and the seedlings can be planted in the ground in their pots. The roots simply grow through the peat into the surrounding soil.

While on the subject of roots it is worth looking at a botanically interesting member of the vegetable family—the black radish. The eatable part is not the actual root but a development of the seed-stem (*hypocotyl*) which connects the root with the seed-leaves. This curious fact can be put to practical use. If radish seed is sown thickly and the seed-box kept in a warm, dark place until the seed-stalk has formed, the seed-stem can be deliberately forced to make leggy growth. Wait until the seed-stalk is at least 65 mm/2½ in. long before planting

Propagation in multi-pots

Jiffypot

out. The result will be exceptionally long radishes.

Applying the botany you now know you should be able to work out why it is that the roots of turnips, tomatoes and carrots, and the fruits of apples and cherries sometimes suddenly split open. During long spells of dry weather a woody material known as lignin forms in the cell-walls of the plants, causing them to harden and lose their original elasticity. If the dry spell is followed by heavy rain there will be a sudden build-up of water pressure inside the plant, and the roots or fruits will burst open. Regular watering during dry spells can help to prevent this from happening.

However, with kohl rabi and turnips, splitting may be caused by an insect pest. Some cabbage varieties split open for quite different reasons. The highly-cultivated form of the cabbage makes it difficult for the plant to flower. That compact, tightly-curled head is unnatural. Every now and then a flower stalk tries to thrust its way through and in the attempt splits the cabbage-head. This is particularly likely to happen with early crops of white cabbage. These early varieties should therefore be gathered as soon as they are ready.

The bolting of lettuce is caused by something different again. The length of daylight is the main factor. In most plants the moment at which flowering is initiated is goverened by the length of the day. Short-day plants will only flower when the days are short: long-day plants only when days are long. There are also neutral plants, where flowering is governed by other factors than day-length. When a lettuce bolts it is simply starting to flower. Cabbage lettuce fall into two groups: one belonging to the long-day group, the other to the neutral. All the early varieties are long-day plants. They will bolt as soon as the days grow long enough for them to start to flower. Therefore early varieties should only be planted during short days—in spring and again in late summer. For summer cultivation, neutral sorts such as 'All the Year Round' or 'Feltham King' should be planted.

Another well-known long-day plant is spinach. Since spinach is grown for its edible leaves, not for its flowers, it should be sown in spring or autumn.

For spring cultivation the dividing line between short- and long-day lies towards the end of May; for autumn cultivation, towards the end of July/ beginning of August. This should be kept in mind when planting spinach and early lettuce. Hot, dry conditions promote flowering. Translated into gardening practice, this means that spinach must be given plenty of water in spring.

The pea, a long-day plant, is interesting in this context. Unlike the other plants mentioned so far, it is grown for its fruits and so must flower. It would be wrong to conclude from that that it should be planted in the long days period. If that were done they would develop blossom and fruit very quickly. Foliage, however, would be sparse and the yield low since there would be insufficient leaves to build up enough nutrients. Instead, peas should be planted early in the spring. During the short-day period they will build up a rich growth of foliage, providing a large area for photosynthesis, thus providing adequate materials for the plants to produce a rich crop of flowers and fruit during the long days.

4 Colour Your Garden

WHY EVERY GARDEN NEEDS ANNUALS

Annuals, as the name suggests, are plants that complete their life cycle in one season. They therefore have to be replanted annually. Planting annuals out every year may seem rather a bore, the unnecessary repetition of a needless chore, when one could so easily put the whole garden down to shrubs and perennials, planting them once and once only and then leaving them for ever. However, annuals have one great thing in their favour. They can out-flower any other type of plant. They have to. To ensure the continuance of the species they have to produce enormous quantities of seeds and to do that they have to produce equally enormous quantities of flowers. These flowers, because they have to attract pollinating insects, are usually the most brilliant colours—reds, blues, pinks, whites, oranges and yellows. Plant for plant, annuals produce more sheer flower-power than any other type of plant.

SOWING IN THE OPEN

Many annuals can be sown in the open ground where they are to flower. This should be done during April and May. The seeds should be broadcast evenly and sparsely, the soil lightly raked over, and then given a light sprinkling of water. Once the seedlings are up, most varieties should be thinned, leaving about 30 cm/12 in. between each plant.

The following annuals are all specially colourful: many are also suitable for cutting for vases or small table decorations.

Godetia 45–60 cm/18–24 in. The silky blossoms come in a whole range of pastel shades—pink, red and white. Since godetias are easily transplanted they can be sown out of doors in a seed-bed and the seedlings moved to their flowering position in May. Good for cutting. Tender in the north of the U.S.A.

Californian poppy *Eschscholtzia californica* Up to 75 cm/30 in. These bloom from early summer well into October. The brilliant creams, golds and reds of the poppylike flowers blend splendidly with the cooler pastel shades on the petals. Suitable for filling empty spaces between shrubs and perennials. Once sown in a garden the Californian poppy seeds itself freely, even begins coming up on gravel paths or close to a sunny wall.

Cape daisy *Dimorphotheca aurantiaca* 30 cm/1 ft. Has daisy-shaped flowers in a beautiful mixture of orange, salmon pink, white and golden yellow. Because of their susceptibility to frost they should not be planted out of doors until the middle of May onwards. Ideal in empty spaces on the rock garden against a sunny wall. Good for cutting.

Annual cornflower *Centaurea cyanus* 1 m/3 ft. These resemble the wild cornflower in the colour and shape of the flower. Single and double varieties. Splendid as cut flowers. The sweet smelling variety sometimes seen is *Centurea moschata* with pink, purple, yellow or white flowers.

Portulaca *Portulaca grandiflora*, 10–15 cm/4–6

in. One of the most brilliantly coloured of all annuals, this is a little succulent from South Africa. Single or double daisy-like flowers in every colour except blue. A striking annual, needing light sandy soil and a sunny situation. When the sun goes in, the flowers close. Ideal for a rock garden or for edging. Seeds itself annually in places where it is happy. Thin seedlings to 10 cm/ 4 in. apart.

Marigold *Calendula officinalis,* to about 60 cm/ 2 ft. Flowers daisy-like from pale yellow to orange and shades of apricot. A long-blooming annual that flowers brilliantly right up to the first frost. Good for cutting. The petals are tasty in salads. Self-feeding, so they renew themselves each year though the size and colour of the flowers deteriorates year by year.

Candytuft *Iberis amara; Iberis umbellata,* to about 30 cm/12 in. The first variety is white, and blooms from May till August. *Iberis umbellata,* on the other hand, is mauve and purple and flowers from June till August. Both varieties are suitable for borders and edging. Self-seeding, they look delightful in the narrow gaps between paving stones.

Cosmos or Cosmea *Cosmos bipinnatus,* 1–2 m/ 3–6 ft. Daisy-like flowers in lilac, scarlet, violet and pure white. Green fern-like foliage, giving a delicate, feathery appearance. They will bloom earlier if planted in a nursery bed in April, and later transplanted, than if sown where they are to

flower. Dead head the taller varieties, since this will encourage them to keep on flowering. Do not dead head the dwarf varieties. Does best in poor soils. In rich soils you get all leaf and little flower. Flowers cut still in bud will keep up to two weeks.

Calliopsis *Coreopsis tinctoria,* 38–100 cm/15–36 in. Daisy-like flowers, gold with a purple centre. Best mixed with other annuals or used as a filler between perennials. These are excellent for cut flowers.

Marguerite *Chrysanthemum carinatum,* to about 60 cm/2 ft. Daisy-like flowers with bright red, yellow, and brown bands on a white background. Other combinations include mahogany, bronze and yellow. Often considered one of the most beautiful annuals. Should be sown in as wide a range of colour combinations as possible. Plant in good soil: the richer it is, the more flowers you'll get. And the more flowers you cut for decoration, the longer the plants will keep producing new flowers.

Sunflower *Helianthus annuus,* up to 4 m/15 ft. Colours range from yellow to bright red. There are both giant and dwarf forms. Can be sown where they are to flower, though seed should not be sown out of doors before the beginning of May, or raised in small pots and planted out in the middle of May. Plant at least 60 cm/2 ft apart. Save the seed and put it out for wild birds in winter. With luck the plants will seed themselves. The dwarf varieties make good cut flowers.

Delightful collection of herbaceous plants all of which enjoy a dry, sunny position. In the background yellow achillea, in foreground violet-blue salvia, red lychnis and scabious. Also grasses and small shrubs.
From left to right: tiger lily, ornamental grass *Stipa barbata* and *Allium albopilosum*.

Alyssum *Lobularia maritima*, 7–30 cm/3–12 in. according to variety. Starry white, pink or mauve flowers produced in enormous quantities. Useful dwarf annual for edging paths and borders. Can also be sown thickly to form a white, pink or mauve carpet in a flower bed, with taller flowers among them. The white variety, 'Carpet of Snow', which grows 10 cm/4 in. tall looks most attractive between red or deep pink polyanthus. The polyanthus need to be planted further apart than usual, so that the carpeting of alyssum can get enough sun. Alyssum is also self-sowing, thus producing a quickly spreading carpet.

ANNUALS FOR TRAINING AGAINST FENCES AND TRELLISES

There are several annuals that are climbers. These are both useful and decorative when sown where they are to grow at the foot of a fence or trellis. Many are fast-growing and will provide a dense green screen by early summer.

Sweet peas *Lathyrus odoratus*, climbing up to 2 m/8 ft. These are among the loveliest of annual climbers, producing large trusses of pea-like flowers in every imaginable colour over a very long season. Sow the seeds in rows in April, and when the seedlings are 5–7 cm/2–3 in. high, thin them out, leaving about 23 cm/9 in. between each plant. If seeds are sown in two or three batches four weeks apart you will have plants in flower from July right into the autumn. The more blooms you cut, the more flowers the plants will put on.

In dry weather water and feed well. Figure only on May–June flowering in northern U.S.A.

Scarlet runner beans *Phaseolus coccineus*, up to 3 m/12 ft. Though usually grown for their beans these plants were originally cultivated for their flowers. Both flowers and beans are decorative. Seeds should be sown outside but not before the beginning of May. Alternatively they can be sown in pots in frames from mid-April onwards, and planted out from mid-May. 'Prizewinner' has brick red flowers. 'White Giant', white flowers. America's favourites are 'Kentucky Wonder' with large beans and 'Purple Pod', which, as its name suggests, has stunning purple pods (which alas, go green when cooked). You can create a most interesting effect by growing different varieties together. They are suitable for high fences, and make a very good windbreak when trained up canes or trellises, since they stand up well to rough weather. The beans must be gathered while still young, not allowed to get stringy.

Nasturtium *Tropaeolum majus*, up to 3 m/12 ft. Delightful plants with round, grey leaves and large trumpet-shaped flowers, bright red, orange or yellow with long spurs. They need some training to grow up wooden or wire fences or over sheds. Sow in the first week of May, placing the seeds about 10 cm/4 in. apart.

Morning glory/Convolvulus *Ipomea purpurea* and others. Height depends on the variety and ranges between 2–3 m/6–12 ft. Flowers huge,

trumpet-shaped, in remarkably clear colours—blue, red, white and striped flowers. The silky flowers of *Ipomea coerulea* 'Grandiflora' and *I. tricolor* 'Heavenly Blue' are of a rare and exquisite blue. Seed can be sown where the plants are to grow *in situ* from the beginning of May onwards, about 10 cm/4 in. apart. You will usually get better results however, by sowing seed under glass in pots and planting out towards the end of May, in a warm place protected from the wind. The flowers open at about four or five o'clock in the morning, and close again between ten and twelve o'clock. Only on dull days do they remain open longer—if they face west until the late afternoon. This should be taken into account when choosing a spot to plant them. New flowers open each day throughout summer. Prepare the ground well before planting and dig in plenty of compost. Do not use manure otherwise the plants will revert to their wild state. The plants need a lot of water to flower well.

Ornamental Gourds *Cucurbita pepo* CVS. These climb to a height of 5 m/18 ft or more. These gourds are grown for their fruits, which come in a wide variety of shapes, sizes and colours. The leaves are like those of cucumbers, to which gourds are closely related. Once established, gourds can cover large areas: walls, balconies, trellises and so on. Large plants are very heavy and because of this you should only grow them on trellis-work you know to be really secure. You can either sow seed outside in early May, or in pots under glass in April, as for morning glory. The strange and beautiful fruits should be gathered before the first frost. If dried and varnished they will keep for many months, and make striking winter deocrations in bowls or shallow baskets. They need a sheletered spot in the garden, and the soil should have plenty of compost dug in. No artificial fertilizer should be added.

ANNUALS FOR WINTER FLOWERS

These are not heroic little annuals that push their flowers up through snow and frost—alas, there are no such annuals—but summer-blooming plants whose flowers last almost for ever once dried—everlasting flowers. These, together with ornamental grasses, can be used to make pretty bouquets and arrangements for the winter. You can either fill different flower beds with different varieties, or plant several together as fillers between shrubs. If you only want them for drying for winter you may find it better to plant them in an out-of-the-way corner.

Everlasting *Helichrysum bracteatum.* 60–100 cm/2–3 ft. Available with white, yellow, orange, crimson, rose, mauve or brown flowers. These are very hardy plants and bloom early. If you sow them in nursery beds in April, transplant them in mid-May. Alternatively sow them thinly *in situ* at the end of April where they are to flower, and thin to 5 cm/2 in. apart. If you want to dry them, cut the flowers just before the buds open. Remove the leaves and hang the flowers, still in bud, head downwards, in an airy, shaded place.

Far left: annual ornamental grasses.
Left: Everlasting flowers and helipterum. The latter is particularly attractive with its delicate pink petals and yellow centre.

Right: ornamental gourds.

Helipterum *Helipterum manglesii,* 30 cm/1 ft. These everlasting flowers come in shades of red and pink. *Helipterum roseum* produces extra large flowers in shades of pink, crimson and yellow. Sow seed as for everlastings in a warm, sunny place. Transplant to 15–20 cm/6–8 in. apart. Dry as for everlastings.

Squirrel-tail grass *Hordeum jubatum,* 45–60 cm/18–24 in. An attractive annual ornamental grass that should be sown where it is to grow. Sow seed at the end of April or the beginning of May, in a sunny spot. If you want to dry the grass cut it before it is ripe. This will usually produce a second crop of heads in late summer.

HALF-HARDY AND GREENHOUSE ANNUALS

All the annuals mentioned so far are what are called hardy annuals. That means they are hardy enough to spend the whole of their life-cycle out of doors. (A plant is called hardy if it can withstand frost.) The annuals dealt with in this chapter are half-hardy—that is they are only hardy enough to spend half of their lives out of doors—the adult half. The seeds and seedlings would never succeed out of doors, so the seeds have to be sown under glass and the seedlings kept under glass until they are robust enough to survive in the open garden. The term 'under glass' is a rather vague one; it means in the house, greenhouse or a frame.

The seeds of half-hardy annuals should be sown in seed-trays or boxes and either placed on a window sill, on a bench in the greenhouse or in a garden frame. If they are put in a frame the glass of the frame should be covered with sacking or coconut matting at night if frost is forecast. Seed should be sown in late March or early April, so that the seedlings can be planted out into a nursery bed by late April or early May.

It is important that the soil in both the seed box and the nursery bed should be properly prepared. For seed boxes buy some seed compost from your local garden centre. The soil in the nursery bed should be improved by digging in washed sand and peat, and care should be taken that no rotting or half-decayed vegetable matter remains in the soil. The surface should be firmed with a levelling board and fine soil sprinkled over it. The seedlings should then be put in individual holes made with a thin dibber, in rows. Each row should be clearly labelled, each label showing the name of the plant and the date seed was sown.

Take care never to allow the seed boxes to dry out, either before germination or after the seedlings have come up. Above all, do not let seedlings become leggy. If germinating the seeds in the house, keep the seedlings as near a bright window as possible. On warm days open the window so that the seedlings remain as short and sturdy as possible. And plant them in the nursery bed just as soon as the weather permits.

The time to plant the seedlings out is once their second pair of leaves have developed fully. The first leaves to appear are seed leaves: the next pair are true leaves. It is once these true leaves develop that the seedlings should be pricked out. The true

73

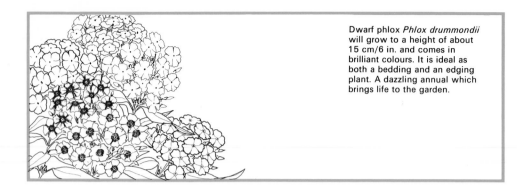

Dwarf phlox *Phlox drummondii* will grow to a height of about 15 cm/6 in. and comes in brilliant colours. It is ideal as both a bedding and an edging plant. A dazzling annual which brings life to the garden.

leaves are completely different in shape from the seed leaves. Prick out the seedlings about 5 cm/2 in. apart. At the same time look out for slugs and snails. Zinnias, dahlias and marigolds are especially in danger from these, so slug pellets should be liberally scattered over the seed bed as soon as these are planted out. If you are lucky enough to own a warm greenhouse or heated frame, you can grow the annuals on for longer, until they are almost in flower, before planting them out. It is only when you don't have these facilities that you need to hurry the seedlings on. The following half-hardy annuals are suitable for average sized gardens, and will provide a brilliantly colourful display.

Ageratum *Ageratum houstonianum*, depending on type—from 15–60 cm/6–24 in. Colour, blue. The dwarf variety is the one to use as an edging plant. It is very compact and has a spread equal to its height. The taller varieties are suitable for cutting and are useful between other dwarf annuals, or as fillers between shrubs. The azure blue and lavender blue of ageratum are most effective when planted among yellow, white or pink annuals. They maintain an excellent display throughout the summer right till the first frost. Sow seed about the end of March, or buy young plants about the middle of May.

Aster *Callistephus chinensis,* depending on the variety, 20–60 cm/8–24 in. These are among the most popular annuals. There are ostentatious double ones and simple, single-flowered ones.

Many people prefer the single ones partly because they are particularly good for cutting and look very effective with their simple yellow centre surrounded by a ruff of red or blue petals, but also because they tend to be less liable to wilt, a disease which often affects asters, and for which there is no known treatment. The double asters, which rather resemble blousey chrysanthemums, come in a far wider range of colours.

The dwarf varieties, which form compact little bushes with a mass of double blooms, are ideal for bedding and edging. They can also be used for filling in any gaps between plants during the summer, since they can easily be moved, even when in flower. It is even worth keeping a reserve bed filled with a few asters, just for this purpose. The reserve bed is usually best out of the way near the compost heap. Asters should be sown at the beginning of April and planted out from the beginning of May onwards. Asters need lots of sun, good soil, plenty of water in dry weather, and an occasional dressing of liquid manure—treatment appreciated by most half-hardy annuals.

Begonia *Begonia semperflorens*, 10–20 cm/4–8 in. This is a reliable popular bedding plant which—like ageratum—will provide a delightful carpet of reds and pinks for months. White semperflorens begonias seem less popular but you can buy them and they look effective mixed with the reds and pinks. Begonias grow equally well in sun or half-shade. Buy the plants from a nursery in May. Seed is as fine as dust and it takes some practice to germinate it successfully.

Cone flowers *Rudbeckia* bloom all summer long and provide an unlimited supply of flowers for cutting.

Mignon dahlia *Dahlia variabilis*, about 30 cm/1 ft. These simple, free-blooming, compact little annual dahlias make a splendid show, and should perhaps be more popular than they are. Seed can be sown in frames at the end of March, and seedlings planted outside at the end of May, or young plants can be bought from a nursery about the same time. The growing tips of young plants should be pinched out in the nursery bed, to make the plants grow as bushy and compact as possible.

Busy Lizzie *Impatiens sultani*, 30–60 cm/12–24 in. The busy lizzie is well-known as a free-blooming pot plant but it is not often realised how useful it is as a bedding plant out of doors, particularly in shaded positions where it will bloom continuously until killed by frost. There are forms with variegated or bronze leaves and flowers of red, orange, white or magenta. It must be well watered and given an occasional liquid feed. Sow seed at the very latest at the beginning of April. Pinch out growing tips to make a compact, bushy plant. Difficult to raise satisfactorily from seed: easy to buy from a garden centre.

Lobelia *Lobelia erinus*, 15–30 cm/6–12 in. The blue of these flowers is much deeper than that of ageratum. As well as the popular form with cornflower blue flowers, there are also red and white varieties. These make ideal carpeting plants, and are useful for filling empty spaces during the summer. Sow seed at the very latest, by the beginning of April. Plant in clumps for maximum effect. Usually bought from nurseries.

Snapdragon/Antirrhinum *Antirrhinum majus*, 60–100 cm/2–3 ft. These are among the easiest and most popular bedding plants. The larger sorts make a grand display when massed, while the smaller sorts make excellent edging plants. The modern F_1 hybrids are especially splendid. If dead-heads are not cut off, you may find young seedlings will appear the following year. These will occasionally survive a mild winter, and when they do they make particularly sturdy clumps though the flowers are usually smaller. Sow seed at the beginning of March, and plant out in mid-May, 15–30 cm/6–12 in. apart, or buy plants from a garden centre.

Annual pinks There are two of these, *Dianthus caryophyllus*, which grows to about 45 cm/18 in. and *D. chinensis*, which grows to about 30 cm/1 ft. Both look like the familiar perennial pinks and come in almost every colour except blue. The taller, *D. caryophyllus* with its heavily frilled petals, is best for cutting. Seed should be sown in February. The smaller *D. chinensis* is ideal for borders and edging. A pretty effect is created if these are mixed with the double Japanese pinks *Dianthus chinensis hedewiggii plenus*. Seed should be sown at the beginning of March and planted out at the beginning of May.

Phlox *Phlox drummondii*, 15–30 cm/6–12 in. These produce large trusses of flat-headed, wide open blooms in a delightful range of colours—mainly pinks and mauves. They create a riot of colour, and make stunning edging plants. Sow

75

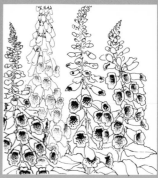

From left to right—the sweet William is one of the most popular of the biennials and looks lovely when mixed with blue campanulas. The foxglove and poppy are also popular flowers from this group.

seed at the latest at the beginning of April and plant seedlings out about the middle of May.

Sanvitalia *Sanvitalia procumbens*, 15 cm/6 in. Sanvitalia makes a charming free-flowering carpeting or edging plant. The flowers are daisy-like, bright yellow with a jet-black central cone. They look rather like miniature zinnias, and need a warm sunny position. Sow in April and plant out in May.

Black-eyed Susan *Rudbeckia hirta*, 60–100 cm/ 2–3 ft. Colours range through gold, orange and yellow with bronze and mahogany shadings. The annual rudbeckia is very like the perennial rudbeckia with daisy-like flowers. Outstandingly good as cut flowers, for filling the flower beds, and between shrubs. The variety 'Goldsturm' is particularly beautiful with orange-gold petals and a black centre. Once established, rudbeckia seeds itself, new plants appearing every year without assistance. Sow seed in April and plant out in May, about 30 cm/1 ft apart.

African marigold *Tagetes erecta*, 70–100 cm/ $2\frac{1}{2}$–3 ft depending on variety. Variously known as African or French marigolds, these plants in fact came originally from Mexico. Flowers chrysanthemum-like in brilliant shades of yellow and orange. The F$_1$ hybrids with their giant, globe-shaped blossoms 10–13 cm/4–5 in. across are very striking. The taller varieties are good for cutting, and superb when used in massed plantings. There is also a double dwarf variety, *Tagetes erecta*

'Nana plena', which grows to about 25 cm/10 in. The single dwarf African marigold blooms—*T. patula* 'Nana' which also grows to about 25 cm/ 10 in. is a delightful plant, compact and bushy, and ideal for both bedding and edging. There are mahogany-shaded varieties as well as the yellows and oranges. African marigolds can easily be transplanted while in bloom. Propagation is easy: sow the seeds in the middle of April and plant out the seedlings in mid-May.

Verbena *Verbena hybrida*, 20–60 cm/8–24 in. Verbena is a splendid annual with many uses. It comes in all colours, multi-colours and some forms have a white eye. It can be used equally well for bedding, edging and cut flowers and, if moved in clumps, will continue flowering without interruption. Despite the rich variety of colours verbena never looks too showy. Sow seed from the end of March till mid-April and plant out seedlings from the middle of May till early June. Pinch out the growing tips of seedlings to encourage bushy plants.

Zinnia *Zinnia elegans*, height; 75–150 cm/$2\frac{1}{2}$–5 ft. These are among the gayest of all half-hardy annuals, and come in almost every colour under the sun. Their sturdy, stiffly upright habit of growth shows them off to advantage when planted next to more delicate annuals and produces an eye-catching show—a wonderful contrast. The catalogues of any good seed firm will tell you all about the latest varieties.

Among the best varieties are 'Envy' growing to

Many annuals (tagetes, antirrhinum, and so on) and also biennials (pansies and double daisies) are offered in the seed catalogues as F₁ Hybrids. These are hybrids raised afresh every year by controlled cross-pollination, as they themselves do not produce true-to-type seed. Such an F₁ Hybrid, is the dark pink *Bellis* 'Hen and Chickens'. These compact plants produce dozens of flowers throughout the spring and early summer.

30 cm/12 in.—an excellent bedding plant and particularly popular with flower arrangers, and 'Tom Thumb', a new break and a true dwarf growing only to 15 cm/6 in. The compact, double flowers are especially good for edging, for small beds and in the rockery garden.

Finally it should be pointed out that many of the flowers often used in window-boxes and tubs are also suitable for use in borders. Planted in sunny spots perlargoniums (the sort known as geraniums), petunias, and the brilliant yellow calceolana, can produce a lovely show of colour. Many do well in shaded parts of the garden.

SOME RELIABLE BIENNIALS

Biennials are particularly useful, since they often flower early in the year before the annuals get going. Biennials are like annuals in that they only flower once then die. They differ from annuals in that they take two years to do this instead of one. The first year they simply grow, building up their strength. In their second year they flower, produce seed, then die. Most are almost as floriferous as annuals. All those named below are best sown in a small seed bed in the garden between the middle of June and the middle of July, where possible in pots filled with fine earth, which can be placed under a polythene cloche. If a propagating frame is available, then the seeds can be sown there. They should be kept in a damp, shady position until they germinate. Then they should be gradually hardened off—exposed to the air, in half-shadow. Finally the plastic or glass can be com-

pletely removed, so that the young seedling can grow as healthily and sturdily as possible. As soon as the plants are big enough to move they should be pricked off into a reserve bed about 6 cm/2½ in. apart. By autumn they will be ready to be moved to their flowering positions. They will bloom in spring or early summer, then die.

Sweet William *Dianthus barbatus*, 30–45 cm/ 12–18 in. Flowers between June and August. If you look at the flower heads closely you will see that each individual head is very like that of a pink, which is also a dianthus species. The flowers come in pinks, reds, purples, white and bi-colours. They need plenty of sun, and a well-drained soil.

Foxglove *Digitalis purpurea*, height; 100–160 cm/3–5 ft. A tall, stately and dignified plant, producing its slender spires and flowers between June and July and growing equally well in sun or shade. Colours—pink, reds and white—in various shades and combinations of colours, usually heavily spotted in the throat. Sow the seed in an outdoor seed-bed in spring and move the seedlings to their flowering positons in August. Thinning is unnecessary. Plant 20 cm/8 in. apart, preferably in bold clumps. The plants contain a strong heart stimulant, which can be poisonous, a fact which should be pointed out to children. Once you have foxgloves in the garden, they will continue to seed and flower year after year.

Double daisies *Bellis perennis*, 15 cm/6 in. The double varieties have large flowers, up to 5 cm/

Campanulas, with their blue and white flowers add a homely touch to the garden. These are 'cottage garden' flowers, sweet williams, hollyhock and viola.

From left to right: the bulbs and corms of crocuses, snowdrops, scillas and other can be scattered about. Plant them where they fall. Use a trowel or a spade to lift up the turf, and place the bulbs in the ground. ▶

2 in. across, so double they are almost ball-shaped, flowering from March to June in pinks, reds and white. The seeds are very fine and are best mixed with sand and sown in rows from June onwards. Pricking out is not necessary. As soon as the seedlings are strong enough, plant them out 15 cm/6 in. apart. Though they will seed themselves, most of the resulting plants will have single blooms. Any plants which are particularly fine can be increased by dividing them in spring.

Wallflower *Cheiranthus cheiri*, 60 cm/2 ft. Dwarf varieties to 30 cm/12 in. Flowers from April till June, flowers yellow, red, brown or purple, sometimes streaked or flecked. Sow the seed from May to June. Prick out the seedlings and transplant in the summer 25 cm/10 in. apart. They do best in poor soils, in really well drained positions, and enjoy all the sun they can get. Sometimes they will survive mild winters, but if they do so they tend to become leggy, so it really is better to start them from seed each year.

Iceland poppy *Papaver nudicaule* 30–45 cm/ 12–18 in. Delicate-looking dainty poppies that make a stunning splash of colour—orange, red and white—flowering from June till September. Plant out in August, 25–35 cm/10–15 in. apart. Once planted they will seed themselves freely.

Mullein or Aaron's rod *Verbascum olympicum* and others, 1–2 m/3–6 ft. The invariably yellow flowers are produced between June and August in tall, narrow spires from a large basal rosette of silvery leaves. It likes dry soil and a great deal of sun and is not worth growing unless these conditions can be supplied. Easily grown in suitable positions by simply scattering the seed where the plants are wanted.

Hollyhocks *Althaea rosea*, 2–3 m/6–10 ft. Popular old-fashioned cottage garden plants, flowering between July and September, flowers pink, red, yellow or white. Sow seed of mixed colours in spring and plant out where they are to flower in late summer. They should be spaced at least 45 cm/ 18 in. apart to allow the foliage room to spread. They do best in ground that has been heavily manured. They are prone to a disease called rust. At the first sign of this, spray the plants with a fungicide and repeat the treatment every two or three weeks. This should be effective. If it isn't, dig the plants up and burn them and do not try to grow them again in the same soil for at least five years.

Canterbury bell *Campanula medium*, 60–100 cm/2–3 ft. Flowers between June and July. Colours: blues, pinks and white. An old-fashioned flower, which lasts well when cut, and it is ideal for filling gaps between shrubs. When the plants have come up, they should be pricked out and transplanted to their permanent beds in the autumn 30–45 cm/12–18 in. apart.

Sweet rocket *Hesperis matronalis*. 110–150 cm/ 4–5 ft. Flowers from May till July. Purple. Another old-fashioned cottage garden favourite,

like so many of the biennials. It is a shame that this plant is not more popular, since it is very easy to grow, and blooms for two or three months, quite oblivious to sun or rain. It looks particularly fine mixed with yellow flowers, against a white wall or dark green conifer. Sometimes the plants will need staking. Sweet rocket is particularly valued for its fragrance, which fills the warm May evening air. The plants seed themselves.

Pansy *Viola x wittrockiana* hybrids, 20–30 cm/ 8–12 in. Blooms in autumn and again in spring to early summer. Most colours, nearly all with striking eyes of contrasting colours. A very wide range of pansies is available, as can be seen from any good seed catalogue. The Hiemalis pansy which is particularly hardy, blooms in the autumn, with a second flush of flowers again in spring as soon as the snow melts. The giant pansies are the showiest of all. The young plants should be planted out in late autumn about 15 cm/6 in. apart. They can be easily moved even when in full bloom.

Forget-me-not *Myosotis alpestris*, 12–25 cm/ 5–10 in. Blooms from May to June. Colours: traditionally sky-blue, but there are also pink and white forms. Sow seed and plant out as for pansies. Forget-me-nots thrive particularly well in damp soil. They make a colourful display when combined with tall, stately, yellow or pink tulips, or with cream coloured narcissi.

The annual and biennials have purposely been dealt with in great detail, since during the spring and summer months these give the most lasting colour to the garden. Shrubs, on the other hand may only blossom for a few weeks or even a few days, besides which they are permanent, whereas if you don't like annuals or biennials you can simply try something different next season.

BULBS, CORMS AND THEIR LIKE

Spring-flowering varieties On a sunny day few sights are more delightful than the bright colours of tulips, daffodils and hyacinths, together with primulas, forget-me-nots, pansies and wallflowers—all blending their yellows, blues, mauves and whites in perfect harmony. The sight has been praised by poets and pop-singers for generations. Among the early blooming bulbous plants the following are the most popular: snowdrops, anemones, winter aconites, crocuses, chionodoxa, the species tulips such as *Tulipa batalinii, T. eichleri* and *T. kaufmanniana* hyacinths, irises, grape hyacinths, narcissi, fritillaries, scillas and many varieties of the larger cultivated tulips, all blooming up to the end of May.

What to plant where The smaller subjects— snowdrops, winter aconites, crocuses, scillas—look best planted in informal groups beneath shrubs or in an herbaceous border. They look dreadful planted in regimental rows. If you want to create a natural effect, take a handful and toss them into the air, planting them where they fall. If you leave them alone once planted, they will spread of their own accord, forming ever widening colonies, and producing more and more flowers year by year.

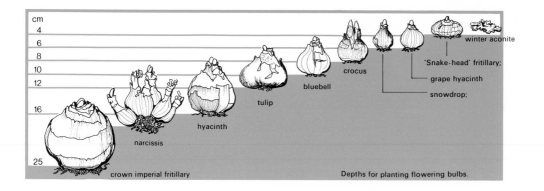

cm
4
6
8
10
12
16
25

winter aconite
'Snake-head' fritillary;
grape hyacinth
snowdrop;
crocus
bluebell
tulip
hyacinth
narcissis
crown imperial fritillary
Depths for planting flowering bulbs.

In winter the shrubs under which these bulbs have been planted are bare, allowing enough rain to fall on them and remain in the soil to start them into growth. When they flower, the shrubs are still bare, allowing sufficient light to fall on the flowers and leaves. Later, when less light reaches the plants, the leaves begin to fade. In summer, when the shrubs are in full leaf they pump the soil under them dry, giving the bulbs a good baking, which is what most bulbs need.

A small helpful tip: there are points in the garden where the snow tends to lie for a long time, and others where it melts at the first sight of the sun. Look out for these latter spots wherever they are for that is where the early crocuses, snowdrops and winter aconites will flower earliest. Cream narcissi and yellow daffodils look especially good against a dark green background of conifers. They could be planted under the grass, (see diagram) if a suitable spot in the lawn can be found.

Species or botanical tulips are ideal for naturalising. They should be planted in a protected spot— possibly near the house—if they are to bloom early. The scarlet *Tulipa eichleri* looks splendid standing above a carpet of yellow-green thyme; or the delicate *Tulipa linifolia*, mixed with the pale yellow *T. batalinii* against a background of steel blue fescue grass. This last species grows only 10 cm/4 in. tall.

Tulipa praestans 'Fusilier' grows about 40 cm/ 16 in. tall and the brilliant scarlet blooms are carried up to four on a stem. Planted in a carpet of white arabis and among little clusters of scillas, this sight is really arresting.

Tulipa sylvestris, another botanical tulip, grows about 30 cm/1 ft high and has golden yellow flowers, which look particularly effective pushing up through a carpet of pale aubretia. There are many combinations of tulips and carpeting plants that can be experimented with to make magnificent spring displays.

In complete contrast to the unpretentious botanical tulips are the stiff regal hyacinths. To do well these need a very deeply dug and richly manured bed. Because of their rather stiff, portly habit and rather artificial appearance, they look decidedly odd if you try to naturalise them. They are perhaps the only bulb that looks really good planted in formal rows in a formal bed.

Exhibition tulips on the other hand, which also need a well fed and well prepared bed, are often best grouped in the herbaceous border. There they will bloom for weeks. The first tulips to bloom are the only single simples, followed by the Mendel, Triumph, Rembrandt, Breeder and Darwin varieties.

Two varieties bloom in May and are different in shape from most other tulips. These are the elegant lily-flowering tulips, and the exotic parrot tulips. These look so unusual that they should be planted separately from other varieties. Their stems are not quite straight, which also adds to their unusual appearance.

Tulips look best planted in close clusters of five to fifteen of each colour. They look even better in beds with pansies or forget-me-nots.

If you want an informal garden, but one which does not involve too much work, here is a sugges-

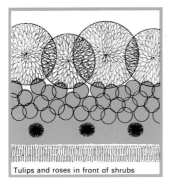
Tulips and roses in front of shrubs

In spring

In summer

tion. Plant some shrubs at the back of a wide bed, leaving at least 1 m/3 ft in front, to allow the shrubs to spread. In front of the shrubs, near the edge of the lawn plant a row of roses—all of the same variety, and behind those plant several rows of early flowering tulips or daffodils.

When these bulbs are in flower, the roses will hardly have started into growth so you will see the tulips and daffodils through them against the background of shrubs. Once the tulips are over and the foliage is beginning to fade, the roses will be in full leaf hiding the fading tulips leaves. From then onwards, throughout the summer and the autumn, the roses will bloom one after another.

Another way of using spring bulbs is to plant crocuses or other bulbous plants round the base of a fruit tree or an impressive ornamental shrub. These look charming pushing up through the grass. The only disadvantage of growing bulbs in this way is that you must not cut the grass where they grow till the leaves have died down. The bulbs need to complete their cycle of growth, and the leaves are needed to build up supplies of food-stuffs in the bulbs to produce the following year's flowers. Nor should the lawn be trodden on in these places. Clusters of scillas can also be planted in the same spot. These come into flower just as the crocuses are beginning to fade, and prolong the springtime scene.

Planting and care If you want to plant bulbs in the lawn, this is the simplest way to do it. First raise a patch of turf by cutting it on three sides with a spade and folding back. Dig and loosen the

soil beneath, then plant crocuses, scillas or daffodil bulbs in the ordinary way, replace the turf and lightly tread down.

In cultivated ground you can plant tulips, narcissi and other bulbs with the aid of a trowel or a useful tool called a 'bulb-planter'. The soil should be well dug beforehand. Avoid planting bulbs in waterlogged soils. They will simply rot. In heavy soil make the hole for planting rather deeper, and seat the bulb on a handful of coarse sand. There is a correct depth for planting each type of bulb and this is shown in the diagram on page 92.

Bulbs occasionally get attacked by fungus diseases. They are also a favourite part of the diet of moles and mice. There are preparations available to protect them against both evils. Since the chemicals gardeners are allowed to use are always changing, ask at your garden centre. They will tell you what is currently permissible and effective.

Cheap bulbs are not usually the best Don't be deceived by catalogues that offer a large selection of bulbs at a low price. These are usually undersized bulbs that won't flower for a year or two, or else will produce small flowers. Tulip bulbs need to be 11 cm/$4\frac{1}{4}$ in. in circumference if they are to give a good quality bloom. There are exceptions: the bulbs of early tulips and Rembrandt tulips are somewhat smaller. Even smaller are those of the botanical tulips.

After-care In March of the year after planting, apply bonemeal at the rate of one or two handfuls

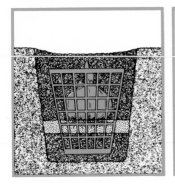

To protect lily bulbs from field mice they can be planted in wire containers, available from garden centres and garden shops. A handful of sand should be placed under the lillies as they need good drainage. In soils which have a tendency to accumulate water, gravel should be placed beneath the container.

to each m² or square yard, sprinkling it between tulips, hyacinths and daffodils. When the flowers wither cut the heads off. Letting them produce seed takes strength from the bulb and means smaller or no flowers the following year. The foliage, on the other hand, should be left to wither and die since the base of the leaves stores food-stuffs for the coming year.

After a few years the bulbs should be lifted at the end of June and divided. The largest bulbs should be planted again in October, but the smaller ones are not worth keeping. Buy a few new bulbs each year to increase the range of shapes and colour.

Bulbs in containers If you want to have bulbs in flower in pots or bowls in the house in spring you need to start them off in early October. First put a 2·5 cm/1 in. layer of charcoal chips at the bottom of the bowl, then fill it with bulb fibre—which you can buy at any garden centre. Plant the bulbs 5–7 cm/2–3 in. apart, water them freely and keep them in a cool dark place until the first shoots begin to appear. Then gradually increase the amount of light the shoots get, as well as the amount of warmth, until the bulbs are ready to be placed on a warm, sunny window-sill to flower. Tulips, daffodils, hyacinths and crocuses can all be forced in this way.

Where to find out more about bulbs Catalogues are the prime source of information, giving details of numerous varieties, together with all the relevant cultural information about each. They usually have good colour photographs which make it easier to see what you are going to get. Visits to botanic gardens or any of the great gardens open to the public are also useful, since in these gardens you can see the bulbs as they really grow. A trip to the bulb fields of Lincolnshire or Holland is even more worthwhile, since there you will see almost every imaginable bulb growing and growing well.

LILIES

Lilies are among the most exotic-looking of all the flowers which can be grown in the garden. So gorgeous are they, that most people think they are too difficult to grow. This simply is not so. The great majority, like the Madonna lily, the tiger lily and the beautiful hybrid lilies raised over the last few years, mainly in America, are about as easy to grow as any other border plant.

The hybrids in particular make good garden plants. They come in an enormous range of colours and colour-combinations, whites, pinks, reds, oranges, yellows and creams, often spotted or streaked, frequently strongly and deliciously scented, the flowers trumpet-shaped, upturned, outward facing, or with recurved petals.

Cultivation Lilies should be planted in October or November—the earlier the better. The only exception is the Madonna lily, which should only be planted in late August.

Lilies like a fairly light and well drained soil. If your soil is heavy you can make it lighter by digging in plenty of peat and sharp sand, and by raising it 7–15 cm/3–6 in. above the surrounding

Dahlias come in many shapes and sizes, and in both brilliant and muted colours. The pompom dahlias (left) with their small flowers are very pretty, as are the Mignon dahlias (right). In the centre is a particularly attractive variety—the orchid-flowered dahlia.

soil. When planting lilies, always put a handful of sharp sand under each bulb. Where there is any danger of mice eating the bulbs, plant them inside wire or plastic containers.

The depth at which you plant lilies is critical. Too deep and the bulbs will rot, too shallow and the flower stems will fall over. As a general rule, the bulb should be planted at 3 times its own depth. Thus, if the bulb is 5 cm/2 in. tall, it should be planted 15 cm/6 in. deep—that is with 15 cm/6 in. of soil over the top of it.

An exception to this rule is the Madonna lily. This should only have about 5 cm/2 in. of earth over it.

Lilies belong to that awkward category of plants that like their heads in the sun and their feet in shade. The easiest way to provide these conditions is to plant the lilies among low perennials or grasses.

Lilies like a light, rich soil. However, on no account feed them with manure or artificial fertilizers. What they like is a good thick mulch of 7–10 cm/3–4 in. of well rotted leaf mould every year—and that is all.

Unlike tulips and many other bulbous plants—which can easily be lifted when dormant—lilies must be left in position. In time they will form large clumps. Only when the flowers begin to deteriorate should they be lifted and moved to another part of the garden.

Lilies are prone to several diseases. As a precaution, apply a systemic insecticide. Snails and slugs are also nuisances, so slug repellents should be sprinkled around the plants.

DAHLIAS, GLADIOLI AND OTHER BULBOUS PLANTS

Dahlia Dahlias, with their large showy flowers are one of the glories of the summer. Natives of Mexico, they were cultivated as sacred plants by the Aztecs centuries before Europeans discovered them. They are neither bulbs nor corms. They grow from a fleshy rootstock called a tuber. According to variety they will grow from 30 cm– 3 m/1–8 ft. They flower from July up to the first autumn frosts. They need a rich soil and lots of sun. The flowers come in a great variety of shapes, from small, simple daisy-like flowers to huge double globes, and in every colour except pure blue. The tubers should be started into growth by being placed in a deep box full of peat stood in the sun in early April. At night they must be protected from frost. Then plant them out about the middle of May. Allow at least 60 cm/2 ft each way for large varieties, and about 25–30 cm/ 10–12 in. for smaller varieties. And the tiny Mignon dahlias, which have been mentioned before among the annuals, can be placed even closer together. Plants can be increased by cutting the tubers with a sharp knife just as the buds begin to swell. Each piece must have at least one growing bud. Portions without buds will never grow. The top of the tuber should be covered with at least 5 cm/2 in. of earth. Protect young growth against snails and slugs with repellants.

Once the plants are growing well, give them a liquid feed every 2 to 4 weeks. The larger varieties should be staked firmly, otherwise they will be

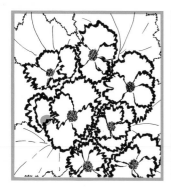

An attractive begonia with a red picotee edge on a white ground *Begonia crispa* 'Marginata'. Like the other varieties, it blooms unceasingly from May to late autumn. Even in complete shade, it is astonishing how abundantly it blooms.

The tiger flower *Tigridia pavonia* is most exotic. Butterfly gladioli have nothing rigid about them. They are ideal both for flower arrangements and the flower bed. ▶

knocked to the ground in bad weather, and the tubers damaged. Dead-heads should be continuously removed. In the autumn the tubers should be left for as long as possible in the ground. When the foliage is blackened by frosts, the stalks should be cut down to ground level and the tubers carefully lifted with a fork, avoiding damaging them in any way. The water should be drained from the hollow stem, and then the tubers stored in dry peat for the winter in a dry, drafty, frost-proof place. Each plant should have a label tied to the dead stem stump. Most dahlias take up an enormous amount of space so are best not mixed with other flowers, but grown in borders or clearings of their own. The exception is the Mignon dahlia, which is just right for the smaller garden. Simple in shape and only 30 cm/12 in. or so high, they go very well with herbaceous plants. Since there are so many varieties your best way of finding the ones that appeal most to you is to refer to a good gardening catalogue, or visit flower shows.

Gladioli These elegant plants with their tall spires of huge flowers springing from a sheath of sword-shaped leaves, are just as popular as dahlias, and just about as spectacular. Again, the flowers come in almost every colour except true blue. The corms should be planted from March to May about 10–15 cm/4–6 in. deep, in rows or clumps 15–20 cm/6–8 in. apart. The taller varieties grow to as much as 150 cm/5 ft, the dwarfs to about 60 cm/2 ft. By planting a sequence of early, middle and late varieties, you can have gladioli in flower from July until the first frost.

Gladioli are liable to attack by aphis and by the minute sucking thrip. Symptoms of thrips are silver or brown streaking or patching on the leaves, which gradually spreads over them completely. Bleached and dry spots may also appear on the tips and edges of the flowers. This can completely spoil the flowers. The red and pink varieties are particularly liable to attack. If a plant is attacked and damaged, the flowers and leaves should be removed and burnt. Otherwise the insect will move down into the corm in the autumn and spend the winter there. So, when you lift the corm for winter put it in a box containing E605 dust and give it a thorough shaking. To prevent mildew attacking the corms during storage, they should be treated with Dithane or Orthocid Dust. Store gladioli corms in just the same way as you store dahlia tubers. When the foliage has died down dig the corms up, and allow them to dry out. Remove the dead foliage and store the corms in a frost-proof place for the winter.

Gladioli are usually planted in their own beds, and are considered ideal for cut flowers. Because of their stiff and splendid appearance they do not look good mixed with other summer flowers. One exception is the butterfly variety. These are smaller than the large-flowered varieties and look very dainty, thus opening up new possibilities for mixed borders.

Montbretia These are similar to gladioli, but smaller, daintier in flower. They are cultivated in the same way as gladioli. In frost-free areas the corms can be left in the ground in the autumn,

but should be covered up during severe winter weather.

The beautifully shaped flowers in yellows and reds are very weather resistant. The plants come into flower in the end of July and continue until October. The corms should be planted in a sunny spot in a rich, well-fed soil, about 10 cm/4 in. deep in April.

Tiger flowers *Tigridia pavonia*. These exotic plants have huge flowers like brilliant butterflies up to 15 cm/6 in. across. There are 3 large petals and a central bowl to the flower: the bowl is usually heavily spotted. The wild form has a brilliant scarlet flower, but there are also pinks, yellows and a pure white variety. The corms should be planted in April 10 cm/4 in. deep in rich soil. The brilliant blooms appear in June, on plants about 45 cm/18 in. high. Although each flower lasts only one day, flowers follow each other in succession. In the later summer the corms should be lifted and dried. They are best stored in dry peat during the winter, at a temperature of between 10–15° C/50–60° F.

Tuberous-rooted begonias are not only useful in window boxes facing north or east, but also in the garden. They flourish in shaded or semi-shaded positions—which are areas useless for annuals, except busy Lizzies and provide a brilliant splash of colour. They grow to about 30 cm/1 ft and bloom ceaselessly from June until the frosts. The colours range from white to yellow and orange, and from pink to dark red. The corms should be started in March, in shallow fruit boxes

or in flower pots. These should be filled with peaty soil and the corms pressed into the mixture. The plants can be put out into the open ground from the middle of May onwards. If you don't want the trouble of raising plants from corms, you can buy the plants already in flower from a nursery in May. Throughout the summer, begonias should be given a liquid feed every few weeks. After the first frost the plants should be cut back, the corms lifted and stored, as with gladioli and dahlias. Begonias like a well-fed, peat-enriched, damp soil. Best known are the large double-flowered sorts. Less common, but no more expensive is *B. crispa* 'Marginata Lutea' with an unusual yellow flower with a delicate ruched red edge. *B. crispa* 'Marginata Alba' has white flowers with a red picotee edge.

THE VARIED WORLD OF PERENNIALS

Perennials are probably the most diverse of all groups of plants; they come, quite literally, in every imaginable size, shape and colour. They vary from the dwarf plants 10 cm/½ in. high that creep and crawl along the ground, to plants with leaves 1–2 m/6–8 ft across and from plants that grow in stony deserts to plants that grow with their feet in water. They are grown not only for the variety of the flowers, but also for that of their foliage, which apart from varying almost endlessly in shape, can be almost every colour besides green.

So what exactly is a perennial? Perennials are plants which last for many years—that is the simplest definition, since it distinguishes them from annuals and biennials. Normally the word is used to describe plants with permanent roots but whose top growth springs up early each year and dies down in winter—a typical herbaceous border plant. A few perennials, however, do not loose their leaves in winter. This being the case many gardeners make the mistake of thinking that perennials can be planted, then left alone to look after themselves. This is quite wrong. Most perennials need a lot of attention, unlike shrubs. The flower stems should be staked, dead heads removed, the ground hoed and kept free of weeds and manured, and every 3 to 5 years most will need to be lifted, divided and replanted.

The great advantage of perennials is that they last for many years, and new plants do not have to be bought each year. They have one disadvantage compared with annuals—they do not bloom for nearly so long.

THE MOST IMPORTANT BORDER PLANTS

Perennials play a major role in the smaller garden, providing the bulk of the background colour; mainly in the summer and autumn. In spring, the bulbs, forget-me-nots and other temporary plants can be used to give colour. These plants are larger than most annuals and need quite a lot of attention. The ground must always be kept free from weeds. In April and again in June, bonemeal should be scattered over the ground. Taller plants like the delphiniums should be carefully staked to avoid them getting damaged during bad weather.

Biennials mix well with perennials in the herbaceous border; forget-me-nots, wallflowers, violas, campanulas and sweet Williams are ideal as are some of the single roses. Also, where you have a choice, go for plants that have a long season of interest. Spaces should be left between these and filled with dwarf varieties. Prominent plants that produce a succession of flowers throughout the year include peonies, delphiniums, summer phlox, heliopsis, rudbeckia, helenium and Michaelmas daisies. You could then fill the gaps between these taller plants with some of the following: crown imperial fritillary, globe flowers, bleeding hearts, doronicum (leopard's bane), lupins, carnations, erigeron, poppies, lychnis, lysimachia, coreopsis, helenium, gypsophila, Shasta daisies, achillea, Madonna lilies, *Lilium regale* and other lilies, golden rod, camellias, salvias, asters and chrysanthemums.

This is only a small selection from the enormous range of perennials available. In some cases there are as many as 30 or 40, sometimes even 100, different varieties. So many are there, that making a selection for a small garden can be quite a problem. To make things easier for you the most important of these perennials are listed below. You can find hundreds more in catalogues. Plants are listed here according to time of blooming. If you follow it you can have a good show of flowers from spring until late autumn.

Yellow doronicum *Doronicum austriacum, D. cordatum* blooms from April till early summer. Height, according to variety, 25–75 cm/10–30 in.

These are among the first perennials to flower in the year. The yellow flowers keep for quite some time, both in the garden and as cut flowers. They are very easy to grow and make a striking effect when planted among blue forget-me-nots and red tulips.

Bleeding heart *Dicentra spectabilis* blooms from May to June. Height, 1 m/3 ft. This plant is familiar to most people. The delicate pink of the little heart-shaped flowers creates an enchanting picture when combined with the blue forget-me-nots. If you grow it in the herbaceous border, do not plant more than one or two since they finish flowering early in the summer.

Peony *Paeonia lactiflora* and others. Flowers in May and June. Height 60–100 cm/2–3 ft. Flowers white, pinks, and reds. There are 3,000 or more named varieties, single or double. The single are most beautiful, the doubles most popular. Peonies are probably the most ancient plants grown in our gardens. Many botanists believe that they, together with their first cousins the buttercups, were among the earliest of flowering plants to evolve, perhaps as much as 25 or 30,000,000 years ago. They have also been cultivated for longer than any other decorative plant; the Chinese are reputed to have cultivated them nearly 5,000 years ago. The plants in our gardens today are nearly all hybrids between several of the Asiatic species. The European and Russian species, though beautiful, are seldom grown. The 3 North American species are rather tender.

The important thing about growing peonies successfully is to plant them properly and then leave them well alone. First prepare a hole 45 cm/ 18 in. deep and put 15 cm/6 in. of well rotted manure at the bottom of this. Then fill the soil back to its original level and plant the peony in this soil, its growth buds just peeping through the soil. Shallow planting is important: the usual reason peonies fail to flower is that they have been planted too deeply. Once planted they need a year or two to settle down to flowering freely. Leave them for 15 years before lifting, dividing and replanting.

Peonies, like bleeding hearts and other early flowering plants, should be placed towards the back of the border, so that after they have finished flowering they will be hidden by the later blooming summer and autumn perennials.

Lupins *Lupinus polyphyllus* hybrids. Flowers in June. 70–100 cm/2½–3 ft. These plants with their dainty fan-shaped leaves and showy spikes of bi-coloured pea-shaped flowers, after a decline in popularity, are once again much in demand. Colours range from pure white, through yellow, orange, pink, red and blue to a deep blue-black. Some varieties are not suited to chalky soils, and the plants do not last very long there. Except for the delicate yellow variety, lupins are generally very hardy. When the flowers have finished the head should be cut off, since seed-formation weakens the plants and shortens the plants' lives. They should be planted at the back of the bed. To gain the maximum colour effect, plant a group of several lupins together.

Bearded iris *Iris germanica* varieties, bloom between May and June. 70–100 cm/2½–3 ft. Lovely plants with sword-shaped leaves and flamboyant flowers. Many hybrids have been developed over the years, and there are now more than a thousand named varieties in every colour and colour combination except black. Plant them in a sunny well-drained spot. Keep them well watered while in growth, but allow them to dry out after flowering. The rhizome should be planted flat, so that the topside just shows above the surface of the soil.

Oriental poppy *Papaver orientale*, blooms from June to July. 100–130 cm/3–4 ft. These plants have gigantic, poppy-type flowers over 23 cm/9 in. across, red, orange or pink with black blotches at the foot of each petal and a marvellous golden centre. They are very showy and easy to grow. Plant them towards the back of the bed, so that when flowering is over they will be hidden behind other flowers, as they then look rather ugly. They make great mounds of silvery foliage and established plants can have a leaf-spread of over 1 m/3 ft. *Papaver orientale flore pleno* is a dwarf variety growing to about 23 cm/9 in. high with double orange flowers, ideal for small gardens.

Erigeron hybrids bloom from June to July and August to September. Height 45–60 cm/18–24 in. This flower is not as well known as the other perennials, which is a shame, as it is one of the most attractive. The more flowers you cut in June and July, the more you'll get in the second flush.

The flowers keep for up to two weeks in water; they should be cut when fully open, since the buds do not open in water. The colours are blue, pink and white. Erigerons look good planted with helenium, heliopsis, rudbeckia and gypsophila; and also with roses and grasses.

Delphinium hybrids bloom from June to July and September to October. Height 1–3 m/3–9 ft. Truly regal plants, whose stately spikes of flowers tower majestically above the dainty feathered leaves. The flowers are among the finest bluest of all, and come in every shade of blue from off-white to almost black. Recent breeding, mainly in North America, has produced some strains with bright red or yellow flowers. These are just beginning to appear in seed catalogues.

To see this gorgeous flower to advantage and appreciate its varying shades of blue it should be planted in bold groups and each plant must be allowed plenty of room to grow. It should remain in the same spot for several years and must be fed frequently with liquid fertilizer and during dry periods watered liberally. The flower spikes must be carefully staked so that gales and rain do not damage them. As soon as the first flowering is over, cut the plants down to just above the ground, to encourage a second blooming in the autumn.

Lychnis *Lychnis chalcedonica*, blooms in June and July. Height up to 1 m/3 ft. The flowers are a dazzling scarlet, and contrast beautifully with delphiniums, the dark blue of monkshood or white marguerites. Any soil. Very easy.

In spacious gardens, larger perennials can be planted at irregular intervals against a plain background. In small gardens, plants are best sited because of lack of space, in a herbaceous border. Care should be taken that the greater part of the available area should be filled with small and medium sized plants. If these are mixed with a few taller, sturdy varieties, a lively, irregular picture is achieved.

Perennials mix very well with small shrubs and roses. Some small areas could be left for annuals that harmonize well with perennials. There are several annuals that would be eminently suitable for this purpose.

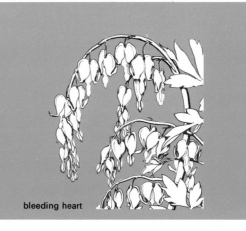

bleeding heart

Loosestrife *Lysimachia punctata,* blooms from June to August. Height, 76 cm/30 in. This is a cultivated species of a quite common wild flower, and is suitable not only for a 'naturalised' spot in the garden, but also for the herbaceous border, where its golden-yellow flowers are so numerous that the foliage can hardly be seen. Because of its brilliant yellow colour it looks well when placed near delphiniums, monkshood or red roses. It has a tendency to spread, so that at times it needs to be checked, and plants removed.

Tickseed *Coreopsis verticillata,* blooms from June to October. Height, 45 cm/18 in. A good border plant because of its brilliance of colour and constant blooming from June into October. It has clear, bright yellow flowers and needle-like leaves. Every three years plants should be divided and replanted.

Helenium hybrids bloom from June to October, according to variety. Height, 76–180 cm/30–72 in. One of the most useful of the perennials, helenium comes in many varieties in shades of yellow and bronze. The earlier varieties are smaller than the later ones. Bees swarm round these flowers, which are ideal for cutting; and when mixed with delphiniums, phloxes, rudbeckia and Michaelmas daisies, they make a really stunning colour combination. They are ideal plants for the herbaceous border.

Monkshood *Aconitum* varieties, bloom from July to September, depending on variety. Height 45–150 cm/18–60 in. Like peonies, phloxes and Madonna lilies, Monkshood is one of the mainstays of the cottage garden. Plants should be left as long as possible in one position. For best results manure the soil well. The general effect of Monkshood is similar to that of delphiniums but less showy. They go well with white Marguerites, phloxes and yellow plants.

WARNING: Monkshood is exceedingly poisonous, so handle it with care.

Achillea flowers from July till September. Height, 45–150 cm/18–60 in., depending on variety. Will grow in all sorts of soil and are most useful because of this. However, to get the best results plant them in a well-fed soil, which is not too dry. The most commonly seen variety is *A. filipendulina,* looks good planted with blue Monkshood and red lychnis. There is also a dark red achillea, *A. millefolium,* which is smaller, reaching only 45 cm/18 in. It, too, is very attractive.

Catmint *Nepeta x faassenii,* flowers June till September. Height, 20–30 cm/8–12 in. This small, bushy plant blooms unceasingly throughout the summer. With its lavender flowers, and silver-green leaves it has many uses in the herbaceous border and in other parts of the garden. It should be placed near yellow flowered plants and roses.

Shasta daisy *Chrysanthemum maximum* flowers from July till September. Height, 60–90 cm/2–3 ft. There are several varieties of which the large single-

flowered ones are especially useful in the herbaceous border. They should be planted sparingly, since their dazzling whiteness outshines other plants. Divide and replant every 2 to 4 ﹍rs.

Phlox *Phlox paniculata*, flowers from July till September, (depending on variety). Height 90–120 cm/3–4 ft. One of the most useful border plants, phlox are available in shades of reds. They need a rich soil that does not dry out in summer since they are shallow rooting. There is a little trick you can use to increase the flowering period. When the first flower buds are forming, pinch out about one-third of the leaf shoots, new flowering shoots will then develop from the leaf joints and flower later in the season. Phlox combine well with monkshood and white Shasta daisies.

Heliopsis, flowers from July till September. Height, 70–150 cm/30–60 in. These produce brilliant yellow flowers throughout summer. A very hardy plant it can stay in the same spot for many years. Does well on dry soils, but if allowed to get too dry, the leaves will begin to wilt. Give it a good dressing of fertilizer during the summer. Its bright yellow goes well with delphiniums or monkshood, phloxes, white daisies, mauve erigeron, orange helenium, or Michaelmas daisies. It flowers so prolifically one hardly notices when flowers have been picked.

Golden rod *Solidago* hybrids, flowers from July till September. Height, 60–70 cm/24–30 in. Many of the new varieties with their plumes of brilliant yellow remind one of the mimosa of Mediterranean countries: very popular with bees. If it spreads too much and begins to crowd out surrounding plants, divide the roots and replant them. Goes well with bronze helenium and blue and mauve Michaelmas daisies. Keeps for a long time in water.

Coneflower *Rudbeckia* blooms from July to October. Height 60–180 cm/2–6 ft, depending on variety. All the rudbeckias have long-lasting yellow flowers. Excellent, easy plants in the herbaceous border, and good for cutting. They do well even in shaded positions.

Michaelmas daisies flower from September into October. Two species are known by the same name. The first is the shaggy *Aster novae-angliae,* growing 90–120 cm/3–4 ft. Because they grow large they should be planted individually, but if you have room it is well worth planting several individual plants, each some distance from each other. They are among the most reliable plants in the garden, and there are some very brilliantly coloured varieties. They are ideal for shaded positions, but unfortunately the flowers close on dull days and in the evening. The second species is *Aster novi-belgii* which blooms at the same time and grows to 90–180 cm/3–6 ft. Like the above-mentioned species they need a well-fed, rich soil to grow well and should be well-watered on sunny autumn days, otherwise they will dry out. The larger varieties need to be staked so that they will not be damaged by heavy rain. They are unfortunately, rather susceptible to mildew if grown in dry positions.

The *Aster dumosus x novi-belgii* hybrids are dwarf plants at only 30 cm/12 in. high. These should be planted in clumps, in a sunny position, so that their brilliant colours can be fully displayed.

Chrysanthemum *Chrysanthemum* species, hybrids and varieties, bloom from September till November, depending on variety. Height, 60–150 cm/2–5 ft. The most richly coloured of all autumn flowers, available in every colour except blue and in numerous forms with single or double flowers. One of their great advantages is that they can be transplanted when already in bud, or even in full bloom. They are excellent for cut flowers, since they are very long lasting. The single varieties, with their yellow centres and bright petals, resembling daisies are particularly fragrant. The small pom-pom varieties are becoming more popular, particularly for cutting.

In September and October, when the first frosts threaten, the flowers should be protected by placing plastic bags, sheets or muslin sheets over the blooms. If an Indian summer follows, then they will continue blooming well into the autumn.

With the exception of one or two hardy single-flowered varieties, chrysanthemums should be cut to ground level after the first frosts and stored in a frost-free place over winter.

PERENNIALS FOR SHADED POSITIONS

As you may have noticed, most of the perennials mentioned so far need to be grown in a sunny position. However, since most gardens have beds or borders in shade or half-shade (i.e. shade for half the day) it is worth seeing what you can grow there. From the perennials mentioned above the following are suitable: delphiniums, the tall Michaelmas daisies, the yellow doronicum, lysimachia and the blue monkshood. These last three display their true beauty under such conditions. There is in fact, a whole range of perennials which do particularly well in shade or half-shade. Amongst these are the Christmas rose, which begins to bloom around early January; the violet primula, primroses, polyanthus, the blue and yellow linum, the yellow dronicum, the blue forget-me-not and the inexhaustible *Bergenia cordifolia*, with its heart-shaped, leathery leaves and flowers in pink, red or white. The old-fashioned Columbine, growing to about 70 cm/2½ ft, blooms in May and June and enjoys half-shade. The modern long-spurred hybrids, in all the colours of the rainbow are even better than the older varieties. Flowering about the same time, perhaps a little earlier, is bleeding heart, which looks particularly lovely when planted together with forget-me-nots and cream-coloured narcissi. A brightly coloured flower for shade is the geum, which, depending on variety, blooms from May to August, enlivening the border with fiery orange, bright yellow or crimson flowers.

The foxglove, which is a true shade-lover, comes into flower in June or July. It is best to plant a large group, when they will flower well and abundantly. They reach up to 60 cm/2 ft tall, and look their best when towering out of a bed of

low carpeting plants. Another brilliant display at this time even in complete shade, if the ground is rich and damp enough comes from the astilbes. They will not grow under shallow rooted bushes, since they will not find enough moisture in such a position, and results would be poor. Depending on the variety these graceful, fragrant plants bloom from the end of June till September. The colours are white, pink, red and mauve, and the height varies between 50–100 cm/18–36 in. Astilbes should be planted in groups if possible. They are so distinctive in height and colour that they could be left on their own without any other flowers around them. However, ferns make suitable companions as do silver foliaged plants and ornamental grasses. The most effective background for their pastel shades would be dark evergreen shrubs. Astilbes can be planted in a bed on their own. If at one end of the bed Japanese anemones or a late-blooming silvery cimicifuga are planted, with tulips between the astilbes, then there will be a succession of colour in the bed for many weeks. Astilbes are attractive not only when in flower, but also when the young red shoots first appear. The foliage is pretty in its own right.

In July the blue monkshood *Aconitum fischeri* starts to flower, lasting right through until September. It's another good plant for light shade. Very useful too, is the July-flowering *Cimicifuga racemosa*, whose white flowers reach 80 cm/36 in. high and which blooms at the same time as the astilbe. Then follows *Cimicifuga cordifolia* and its varieties in September. The latter is only 70 cm/30 in. tall, has sycamore-like leaves, and

elegant, stiff candle-shaped flowers. It blooms in August and September. These mix well with Japanese anemones, ferns and carpeting plants.

For July to September colour hostas are the best of all shade-bearing plants. They are grown primarily for their attractive foliage. The leaves can be green, yellow, steel blue or striped, splashed or edged yellow or white. Most varieties produce attractive spikes of violet or white flowers. They are the perfect plant to add colour to a bare, dark spot.

A particularly important group of shade-bearing perennials are the Japanese anemones. These flower from August to October, single, or double, in white, pink, or dark red, with brilliant golden-yellow stamens. Height ranges from 30 cm/12 in. to 60 cm/2 ft. The foliage of Japanese anemones never dies down, and the plant prefers a moist soil. They should not, once planted, be disturbed, and take several years to settle down to flowering freely. Once established they spread in all directions, so each plant should be allowed plenty of room.

GROUND-COVER PLANTS

These serve two functions, one decorative and the other labour-saving. A great many plants look best when grown as individual specimens thrusting up out of a carpet of low-growing plants. The other is that they suppress all weeds. To do this effectively, however, the ground must be completely cleared of all weeds first—especially the deep-rooting and persistent weeds such as ground-elder, bindweed or couchgrass. In shaded places, plants such as astilbe, Japanese anemones and ferns really come into their own only when grown in this way.

Ground-cover plants cannot however, be used in a herbaceous border in a sunny position, or between roses, where the ground must be kept clear. They are, on the other hand, ideal for 'natural' spots; for instance those in half shade, where a carpet of colour is useful, and from which individual rose bushes, grasses, or other taller plants can push up.

Ground-cover plants for dry, sunny places
Thyme, in its green or yellow form, is ideal here, as are the stonecrops *Sedum* spp.; the silver-grey speedwell *Veronica incana*, with its blue flowers, and the silver-grey dwarf artemesia *A. schmidtiana* 'Nana'. Dwarf phlox and aubretias are also ideal in full sun.

Ground-cover plants in half-shade   Creeping bugle, with its violet-blue flowers, *Cotula squalida*, with fresh green fern-like foliage, and golden-yellow flowering creeping Jenny *Lysimachia nummularia*, are suitable for such positions. When it comes to covering larger areas under trees and shrubs the rose of Sharon *Hypericum calycinum* is almost unbeatable, with its huge golden flowers, as is knot-weed *Polygonum affine*, with its pink-red flowers, and the inexhaustible stachys *Stachys olympica*, the flowers of which should be removed as soon as they appear, since they give an untidy appearance to the closely woven silvery carpet.

Ground-cover plants for full shade   For fully shaded spots the evergreen *Asarum europaeum, canadense* or *caudafum*; the popular lily-of-the-valley, the luxuriant but unpretentious woodruff, the small-leaved ivies, the evergreen Japanese spurge *Pachysandra terminalis*, or its silver variegated form; the many spreading periwinkles and the equally dense *Waldsteinia ternata* with its almost perpetual crop of bright golden-yellow strawberry-like flowers. And finally an all-purpose ground-cover plant that does just as well in sun or shade, remains green all winter, and always looks pleasant, *Cotoneaster dammeri*. This is a shrub that grows only about 16 cm/6 in. high but spreads in all directions, rooting as it goes.

DWARF PLANTS FOR EDGING PATHS

These plants hide harsh ugly edges, and at the same time provide a splendid splash of colour in the spring. They are just as good for the rock garden, as for thickly carpeting the ground with brilliant colour in May. Plant them about 30 cm/12 in. apart. During the first couple of years there are of course, gaps, but this is a necessary evil for achieving the final effect.

Plants most used for this purpose are: the dazzling yellow alyssum; white arabis and quickly spreading aubretia. Candytuft *Iberis* is also white, and the dwarf iris *Iris barbata* 'Nana' comes in all colours—pale blue as well as gold, red, mauve and purple. Dwarf phlox is an essential edging plant, coming in white, slate blue and deep pink shades.

All these ground-cover plants bloom in April

95

Left: The best months for planting water-lilies are May and June. After planting, the soil should be covered with washed gravel.

Right: To set the container at the right depth in the water, place it on stones.

and May, and are 7–15 cm/3–6 in. high. When they are used as edging plants, gay annuals should be planted close behind them, otherwise the path would look rather dull during the summer. There are other edging plants which bloom in early summer—cerastium, armeria, and dwarf pinks. One other thing: these dwarf plants do not form regularly shaped clumps, since some grow faster than others, so the edge will not be absolutely straight which is just what one wants. When arabis or phlox get straggly and out of hand, the untidy stems can be pulled out by hand.

PLANTS FOR WATER OR WATER'S EDGE

The *prima donna* of all water plants is the water lily. There are many different varieties beside the common white one *Nymphaea alba*, which requires about 100 cm/3 ft of water to gtow well. There is also the blush pink *N. marliacea* rosea, and the red *N. laydeckeri* 'Purpurata' which will grow in about 45 cm/18 in. of water. The deep red *N. froebelii* will also thrive at that depth as will the white *N. odorata* 'Superba'.

If you only have a pool with a water level of 10–15 cm/4–6 in., then the dwarf white *N. tetragona*, *N. pygmaea* 'Alba', and the canary-yellow, fringed, dwarf *N. x helvola* are best. Wherever water depths are mentioned in relation to water lilies the depth is that from the water surface to the top of the plant container.

Water lilies should be planted in April or May, either directly in earth, which is placed at the bottom of the pool in specially designed plastic plant containers, or in a willow basket. Round containers should be at least 30 cm/12 in. in diameter; square ones should be 30–40 cm/12–15 in. across. The containers should be at least 30 cm/12 in. deep. Garden soil can be used to fill the containers. Well rotted compost should be added or an organic fertilizer such as bonemeal. When the water lilies have been planted, the surface of the soil should be covered with washed gravel. It is best if the container is first placed on some stones, so that the water is only 10–15 cm/4–6 in. above the new leaves. As the leaves grow larger and taller, the container can gradually be lowered until it is eventually at the required depth. If you possibly can, fill the pool with rain-water rather than tap-water. The problem with tap-water is that it contains a lot of chemicals; algae quickly develops, living on these chemicals and ruining the appearance of the pool. If goldfish are put into the pool they will keep it free from insects. Both plants and fish will do best if the pool is in a sunny position.

As spectacular in their way as water lilies are the arum lilies *Zantedeschia aethiopica*. These can be planted in ponds in exactly the same way as water lilies, but not so deeply. They must be deep enough for roots not to get frozen in winter. Normally only 10 cm/4 in. of ice forms on a pond, but in severe winters it can be as much as 15 cm/6 in. There are several other pond plants worth growing, mainly for their interesting foliage. These only require about 7 cm/3 in. of water over the roots. Amongst these are water plantain *Alisma plantago*; mare's tail *Hippuris vulgaris*, arrowhead

In this round pool arrow-head, mare's tail, and lesser reed mace or cat tails have been planted. Round the edge of the pool creeping Jenny shows off its pretty green foliage.

Sagittaria sagittifolia and the rush *Scirpus lacustris*, whose stem rather resembles a leek. *Scirbus tabernaemontani zebrinus*, which has bands of green and white running round its stem, looks rather zebra-like and most unusual. The reed mace or cat tail *Typha* is also rather attractive. For smaller areas *T. angustifolia*, with its narrow leaves about 90 cm/3 ft high and *T. minima* 60 cm/2 ft high, are better suited.

If you want to enjoy the fish in the pond, don't over plant it. Only a third of the pond should be occupied by plants. The rest should be open water. This also shows the plants off to best advantage.

In small ponds, plant each plant in a pot of its own, in the pond, with as many bricks beneath it as are needed to bring it to the correct depth in the water. Apart from making it easy to settle each plant at the correct depth, there is the following advantage: reeds, water plantains and arrowhead spread very rapidly, and if they reach a stage where they look like overcrowding the water lilies, some of them can be removed at once.

Not only the pond itself, but also its margins, should be planted with suitable perennials, so that the whole area forms a composite picture of colour and life. Ideal plants for the dry ground immediately surrounding the pond are the narrow leaved perennials such as red-hot pokers or torch lilies *Kniphofia*, beardless irises *Iris sibirica* and day lilies *Hemerocallis*. A handsome plant at every season is the hardy *Sinarundinaria murielae*, which looks very like a bamboo.

Plants with large, lush leaves are ideal if the ground round the pond is wet. Some of the best of these are the ligularias *Ligularia przewalskii*. Snails and slugs are very fond of their leaves, so scatter some slug pellets round them, Creeping Jenny *Lysimachia nummularia*, knotweed *Polygonum affine*, and different varieties of stonecrop *Sedum* also look attractive around the pond. A particularly unusual plant, easily as tall as a man, is the willow-leaved sunflower *Helianthus salicifolius*. At the slightest breath of wind the leaves rustle and dip into the water and the plant looks just as good without the flowers as with them. The flowers are small, yellow and do not appear until late autumn.

If you want something rather different round the pond, Japanese water irises *Iris kaempferi* are ideal. Their shape and fine colouring are strangely attractive. They should be planted so that the roots are always covered with about 15 mm/$\frac{1}{2}$ in. of water. When the flowers bloom each of the flowers of this far-eastern beauty lasts only a few days, but for those few days it is one of the glories of the gardening year.

GRASSES

Several annual grasses have been mentioned when dealing with annuals. All grasses mentioned here are perennials. To most people the mention of grasses conjures up images of endless moorlands, meadowlands, marshes or heaths clothed with nothing but grass, and indeed, the grasses are probably in evolutionary terms, the most successful group of plants to appear so far, with species and genera capable of colonising almost every

corner of the world. One of the reasons for their success is that they have abandoned the insect pollination method of most of the plants we grow in our gardens, for old-fashioned wind pollination.

As for grasses in the garden, at the mere mention of them most gardeners immediately conjure up a vision of continuously pulling up couch grass. Ornamental grasses are something quite different.

Graceful, simple fragrant grasses, with the wind rustling softly through them, can combine beautifully with coloured flowers—blue, yellow and red —especially with the tall, more natural perennials. The best grasses for planting in the herbaceous border are *Miscanthus sinensis,* millet grass *Pennisetum compressum,* tall marsh grass and clumps of *Avena sempervirens.*

Grasses must occasionally be dug up, since they do tend to spread. If you want to restrict their spread, plant them in concrete rings or in a box with the bottom knocked out. In sunny positions miscanthus could be planted in the soil. These tall, stately grasses, with reed-like, drooping leaves, make their greatest effect when growing in a clump. The giant species, *Miscanthus japonicus* grows to a good 2·50 m/9 ft *M. sinensis* 'Gracillimus', with its narrow hanging leaves, grows to only 180 cm/6 ft and is suitable for smaller gardens. Interesting but rather stiff is the zebra grass *Miscanthus sinensis* 'Strictus', with yellowish diagonal stripes on the leaves: height 135 cm/4½ ft. *M. sinensis* 'Silver Feather' is also very useful. It grows to about 180 cm/6 ft high, with narrow drooping leaves and silvery, feather-shaped flowers in the autumn.

Tall marsh grass, *Spartina muchauxiana* 'Aureomarginata' growing to a height of 135 cm/4½ ft has elegantly drooping leaves with a vertical gold stripe.

Pennisetum compressum grows about 45 cm/18 in. high and looks fine in sturdy lush green clumps. The flowering-heads develop in autumn, and look very attractive in a vase. *Avena sempervirens* grows to about 45 cm/18 in. but the flowers reach 135 cm/4½ ft in the summer.

The various species of feathery grasses *Stipa barbata, S. cappillata* and *S. pennata* grow about 60–75 cm/24–30 in. The long, feathery 'whiskers' wave gently in the slightest breeze. The 'star' of the tall ornamental grasses is the pampas grass *Cortaderia selloana*—an overpowering beauty, taller than a man, with great feathery flower plumes. It makes a great effect when on its own, or in small groups against a background of shrubs— on a terrace or next to the pond. It should grow in the lawn or in the middle of a carpet of dwarf plants. The plant needs a lot of water while growing and in the autumn should be given a generous feed of liquid manure, in spring the previous season's leaves should be removed. The simplest way to do this—drastic though it sounds—is to set fire to them, but make sure you do this before the first new growth appears. There are a few more low clump-forming grasses that enjoy full sun. These can be planted in small groups or over a wider area —both will be effective. The fescue grasses *Festuca punctoria* and *F. glauca* belong to this group growing only 20 cm/8 in. high with spikey blue leaves. Just as attractive is *Festuca scoparia,* which forms lush green clumps. Mountain sedge *Carex montana* also looks pretty in the smaller garden, when planted with ferns and dwarf conifers. This sedge grows to a height of 20 cm/8 in. and has green, hanging, tufted heads which become golden or dark brown in the autumn. These also thrive in half-shaded positions.

In shaded positions   Giant sedge, *Carex pendula* 90 cm/3 ft high, does well in shade. The same applies to a wavy *Deschampsia caespitosa*, which may grow to 30 cm/1 ft in height. The yellow-brown flowers appear in summer and reach about 75 cm/30 in. As soon as the flowers have finished blooming they should be cut off, as they are no longer at all decorative. The tufts of leaves are left until spring. This grass is also suitable for sunny positions. The greater woodrush *Luzula sylvatica* grows about 25 cm/10 in. high and can be planted under shallow-rooting trees as a ground-cover plant. Even round the trunk of such trees as the birch, the leafy tussocks give a splendid effect. They are also suitable for very shaded spots. All the grasses named above should be planted in spring—there would be few survivors if they were planted in the autumn. The taller varieties should be treated as individual plants, and should therefore be planted separately. The leaves, and even the flowers, if present, remain intact throughout the winter in the majority of species. These look very charming when covered with frost or snow. In spring they should be cut down to the ground. Many of the dwarf varieties such as the fescue grasses, whose leaves are blue or green, do not need

to be cut back. They just need to be carefully tidied up, i.e. the dry and yellowed leaves pulled out by hand.

PROPAGATION, PLANTING AND CARE OF PERENNIALS

Most perennials are very easy to propagate. All you do is dig them up in winter when they are dormant, and divide them, literally tearing or wriggling the clump of roots into two, three or however many satisfactory clumps you can get from the original clump. With most small perennials, stonecrops, grasses, ferns and many ground cover plants, you can do this with your hands. For perennials with tough or woody stems and roots, use a knife or spade to cut the clump into several parts, on each of which there must be a new shoot. Or you can do this by pushing two garden forks back to back into the middle of the clump allowing them to lever it apart. Amongst perennials needing spade, knife or fork to divide them are day lilies, achillea, Shasta daisies, delphiniums, heleniums, heliopsis, rudbeckia, astilbe, Siberian irises, phlox and begonia. The plants should be divided every few years whether you need extra plants or not, otherwise their roots overcrowd the ground and the flowers begin to deteriorate. Use any spare pieces to swap with gardening friends and neighbours for new plants. Some perennials such as primulas, poppies, lupins, dianthus and colombines are propagated from seed, just like annuals.

Perennials are in general best planted from the

99

Many perennials can simply be divided by tearing them apart with the hands. Others, however, have very strong root growth, and therefore you need a spade to divide the plant into fist-sized parts.

Many perennials can simply be divided by tearing them apart with the hands. Others, however, have very strong root growth, and therefore you need a spade to divide the plant into fist-sized parts.

beginning of September till the end of November and throughout the winter if mild weather prevails. Planting can also be done in early spring and, with a few exceptions, should not be left later than the end of March. Today many plants come in pots, and these can be planted throughout the year. For marsh and water plants the correct times for planting are April–June, after the water has had time to warm up a bit. All grasses, and the torch lily, chrysanthemums, Shasta daisies, Michaelmas daisies and lupins should be planted in spring, except when planted from containers. Lilies should be planted in late summer or early autumn, or in the spring. Only the Madonna lily should be planted in August–September.

The herbaceous border should be no wider than 180 cm/6 ft otherwise it will be too difficult to look after. At the back of the bed should be planted a few tall, long-lasting plants: only one or two per square yard or m². These will form the backcloth to the border, and should be planted individually or at the most in groups of three. Then come the medium-sized plants and in front the dwarf varieties. The medium-sized plants can number three to five to a square yard or m², the small ones ten to fifteen to a square yard or m².

Before planting—even before the plants are bought—a plan should be prepared to a scale of 1:10. When doing this, spaces should be left in the bed for groups of polyanthus and floribunda roses, and smaller spaces for annuals. Only by doing this can you achieve a really effective show of colour. Under no circumstances should the herbaceous border be filled only with tall and medium sized

plants; taken as a whole it would look most unsatisfactory and muddled. On the other hand the border would look most attractive if the taller perennials, planted within small groups or individually, rise up out of a colourful carpet of smaller plants. Before planting, soil preparation is absolutely crucial. It should be well dug and fed with peat or compost. At the same time couch grass and other persistent weeds should be removed—the roots should be dug up, or these nusiances will recur. Planting should be done on a dull day because the roots are extremely sensitive and can dry out rapidly on sunny or windy days. On a still cloudy day lay the plants out on the soil in small groups where you want them and then plant them. If the plants have been ordered from a nursery and arrive at an inconvenient time, these can be heeled in temporarily, very close together, in a shaded position in the garden. This small temporary bed should be prepared with damp peat. The plants can remain there for a week or more without coming to any harm. So that you don't compact the soil you have so carefully prepared, put a plank down on the earth, and stand on this while planting. Planting should be done from the back of the bed towards the front. Long fibrous roots should be cut back, with a sharp knife, to about 10 cm/4 in. before planting. Begonias and irises should be planted horizontally and shallowly. Finally all the plants should be watered thoroughly, using a watering can without the rose.

As soon as the ground has superficially dried out after rain, it should be loosened with a hoe. In any prolonged dry period, the ground must be fre-

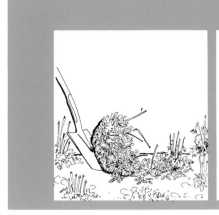
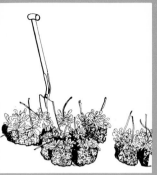

Perennials need dividing when a new bed is being planted, or when the flowers begin to deteriorate. The best time for division is just after the plants have finished blooming. With perennials with 'stem' roots, division is hardly possible, e.g. lupin, poppy, alyssum, and so on. Such varieties are increased by seeding, cuttings or layering. Usually when perennials are finished, the beds are replenished by buying from a nursery.

quently watered. In autumn or in spring the border should be covered with approximately a layer 5 cm/2 in. deep of an organic fertilizer such as well-rotted compost. In March a handful of a chloride-free fertilizer can be added, but this must not be sprinkled on the leaves, only on the soil. A well-proven fertilizer for the herbaceous border is a mixture of peat with nutrient salts and other organic materials. A layer about 5 cm/2 in. thick should be spread over the bed and then lightly hoed in. Just as useful is a fertilizer containing bonemeal which should be used according to the instructions on the packet. Marsh and pond plants do not need to be manured if a bonemeal preparation has already been added to the soil.

It is very important to realise that these fertilizers should only be used for highly cultivated perennials or border plants. Under no circumstances should they be used for wild plants or dwarf carpeting plants, which would rapidly become straggly and lose their attractive shapes and colours: they should be given compost. Many alpine plants and various pot herbs such as speedwell, dwarf artemesia, thyme and so on, are even allergic to artificial fertilizers. They like to live as quietly as possible.

It is also important to cut off the dead-heads of all perennials. By so doing the plant can conserve its energies for new blooms, instead of forming unwanted seeds. You can either pick off the dead-heads or cut them off with scissors or pruning shears. Delphiniums, erigerons, lupins and others should be cut down almost to the ground. By so doing there will be a second flush of flowers in late summer, although it may be a poorer one than

the first. In late autumn cut the dead growth back to close to the ground. The ground round the plants should then be forked over, taking care not to damage the roots, and all weeds removed.

After five years at the latest, the main part of a perennial should be transplanted. This is done by lifting the plant, dividing it and replanting in a bed that has been prepared with either peat or compost. There are of course plants which benefit from remaining for as long as possible in one place. These include bleeding heart, fritillaries, crown imperial, heliposis, day lilies, varieties of lilies, begonia, Christmas roses and some varieties of rudbeckia—*R. laciniata, R. nitida*. Many of the naturalised perennials which prefer to remain where they were originally planted for as long as possible have not been mentioned here; only the Christmas rose, which is often found in the herbaceous border, should be left well alone.

Several perennials need some form of protection in the winter—mainly those which have shoots or leaves above the ground during the winter. The most important among these are the rock garden plants, which, without the ideal protection of a covering of snow, may be in some danger. These are easily covered with evergreen twigs. Newly planted perennials and late-planted bulbs benefit from a light covering of twigs or foliage.

NO ROSE WITHOUT A THORN

Roses in the garden A garden without roses is almost inconceivable. There were supposed to

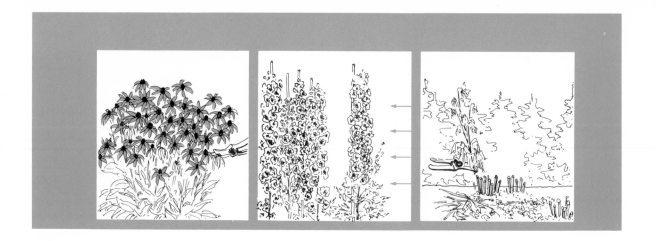

have been over five thousand varieties at the end of the last century: there must be three or four times as many today. Roses are big business now and specialist firms spend their lives trying to raise new varieties that will be winners.

There are more ways of using roses than most people ever dream of. They do not need to be grown in splendid isolation in beds all on their own —which is how they are usually grown. They can be used round the house porch instead of other climbing plants or on trellises on the summer house. A bed of twenty to thirty floribunda roses, placed near a patio presents a very charming picture; or two or three rows can be placed beside a path to good effect. Rose bushes can be planted near garden seats or to conceal a compost heap. Floribundas can also be used in herbaceous borders, or mixed with ornamental grasses, and hybrid tea roses could even be included in the vegetable garden although they do not mix well with other flowers in an ornamental garden. These long-stemmed roses look beautiful in a vase. A rose enthusiast can transform a small garden or part of a garden into an imaginative scene of fragrance and colour.

In such rose gardens the large-flowered hybrid teas go very well, especially when planted in small square or rectangular beds, and edged with a dwarf box hedge kept carefully clipped, or with germander *Teucrium chamaedrys*. The fragrant white gypsophila mixes very well in such a rose garden. An attractive feature can be created when roses are planted in a large bed, at larger than usual intervals, with clumps of the white annual alyssum between.

Buying, planting and general care If roses are to be planted in the autumn, an order must be placed with the nursery by the beginning of October at the very latest. By spring many varieties will already be sold out, and you will have to make do with alternatives. The best time for planting is between late October and March, in mild weather when the soil is still workable. In hard winters it is better to wait until March to plant, when the earth should have dried out sufficiently. Roses can be planted in containers at any time of the year.

If roses are ordered from a nursery a long way away, unpack them as soon as they arrive. Immerse the roots in water for several hours and plant in position immediately. If this is not convenient, place them in damp leaf-mould in a temporary position. Before planting, the stronger roots should be shortened, and any damaged ones cut off. The ground should be well dug and a phosphate fertilizer spread around. The top soil should be dressed with compost—two or three bucketsful to a square yard or m², or five in heavier soils. During the first year of planting the roses will need no other fertilizers, but a year later well-rotted farm-yard manure, or a mulch of compost should be liberally spread round the bushes or trees. Hybrid tea and floribunda roses and other varieties should be planted just deep enough for the place where the rose was grafted, which is seen as a bulge on the root, to be about 2 cm/1 in. beneath the soil surface. If the rose is planted too deep, it will not grow away well. If the graft shows above the surface, it may be ruptured by frost. When planting a rose,

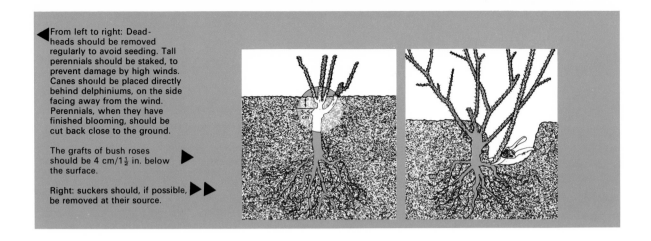

From left to right: Dead-heads should be removed regularly to avoid seeding. Tall perennials should be staked, to prevent damage by high winds. Canes should be placed directly behind delphiniums, on the side facing away from the wind. Perennials, when they have finished blooming, should be cut back close to the ground.

The grafts of bush roses should be 4 cm/1½ in. below the surface.

Right: suckers should, if possible, be removed at their source.

dig a hole with a spade, place the rose in it, and fill the hole with earth—the roots should not be bent back while doing this. Then water the rose well. If planted in the autumn, they should not be pruned, unless the plants are especially tall, when they should be shortened by a third. If rose trees are planted in the spring, they may possibly have dried out on the way from the nursery. They should therefore be immersed for half or even a full day in water, before planting. When planted they should be well pruned and covered with sufficient earth or damp leaf-mould so that only a few of the shoots remain visible. Only when the plants are well rooted, and begin to grow new shoots, should this extra covering of earth be removed, on a dull day. The roses should be kept well watered, particularly during a dry period.

As for planting distances, you can plant 9 shrub roses every square yard or m²—a distance of 30–35 cm/12–15 in. between each bush is enough but the more vigorous need about 45 cm/18 in. between them. Standard roses should be placed 90–180 cm/3–6 ft apart. If used to form a hedge, then they should be no more than 45 cm/18 in. apart. In a small garden a single rose bush can be used to give emphasis to a particular spot. If three rose bushes are planted in a triangle, with 45 cm/18 in. to 60 cm/2 ft between them, the effect is particularly attractive. Plant roses which are to climb up walls, about 270 cm/3 yards apart; however, if they are to be planted along a fence, to form a thick flowering wall, 180 cm/2 yards is sufficient between each rose.

In the spring—towards the end of March or at the beginning of April—roses which were planted in the autumn should be pruned. Floribundas, hybrid teas and standard roses should all be pruned down to three to five 'eyes' from the base of the shoot. 'Eyes' are the new leaf buds, which will later give flowering stems, and which grow at the junction of the leaf with the stem. In general this means that at least half or even two-thirds or three-quarters of the length of the shoots is removed. Prune roses planted in the previous autumn or the present spring particularly severely. It will be obvious from the 'eyes' where the shoots should be cut back to—especially on vigorous lower shoots. Shoots of newly planted climbing roses must be reduced by at least half their length.

Work for the spring Roses not pruned in late autumn or early winter should be pruned in March/April. First, all weak, dead or possibly frost-damaged parts must be completely removed from rose bushes and standard roses. The remaining shoots should be cut back to three or five eyes, but with the more vigorous growing varieties a few more leaf buds could be left. Basically, the weaker varieties should be more rigorously pruned and the sturdier ones more lightly. If, in unusually cold winters, the roses have been badly affected by frost they should be cut back to healthy eyes, even if these are near the base of the plant. Where the floribunda or hybrid polyantha roses are planted more informally, they will not need such heavy pruning as those confined to flower beds or borders. For these it is enough to remove any dead wood or weak shoots and cut back about a quarter or a third of their growth. If after several years the stems are bare and no longer bloom, these need to be 'rejuvenated': i.e., all the old, dead wood must be removed and other branches rigorously cut back.

The old-fashioned shrub and species roses should only be thinned out; i.e., the dead and weak shoots, or those growing too thickly should be removed. The natural shape must be kept: the more unconstrained and freely they are allowed to grow, the more attractive will the bushes appear. Only those varieties that grow very long shoots need be reduced in size—by about half. Otherwise they would bow under the weight of dozens of blooms at the end of these long shoots, and the flowers would end up in the mud after a heavy rainfall.

Climbing roses should not be pruned too severely. Only the three-year old and older shoots should be cut back to ground level, especially if young shoots have been developing near the base. The healthy young shoots, which are so often regarded as suckers, are most valuable to the climbing rose, and should under no circumstances be removed: they will carry next year's flowers. Climbing roses should not be rigorously pruned, but merely thinned out. An old climbing rose with bare basal stems can be renovated either by removing all the old wood down to the young shoots or—a much more radical measure—cutting the whole rose back close to the ground. With either method, the result is healthy new growth.

Fertilizers are very important In March, compost or leaf-mould should be placed between the roses, and worked into the ground. At the same time a proprietary rose fertilizer could be sprinkled over the ground. In addition, an organic mineral fertilizer containing potassium nitrate, sulphate of ammonia, potassium sulphate and calcium superphosphate should be added. The gardener can make up this mixture for himself or buy it under a number of proprietary names: it incorporates all the necessary nutrients. Bonemeal or hoof-and-horn fertilizers are also excellent for roses.

In April, when the buds are forming, give a feed with a nitrate-free liquid fertilizer. Towards the middle of June the manuring should be repeated—once again either a natural or artificial fertilizer can be used. At the beginning of July give the plants another dressing of liquid manure. It has a rapid effect, and encourages the second flowering in late summer.

A fertilizer containing nitrate should not be used late in the season. It merely encourages the plants to throw up long, soft, sappy new shoots, which have no chance of flowering before the frosts. Before the winter sets in, give the plants a dressing of potash or phosphate fertilizer. This helps the roses to build up firm shoots which are particularly hardy and frost resistant.

In summer, work the soil shallowly, so that the roots do not get damaged. A mulch of lawn mowings about 10 cm/4 in. thick can be spread around the rosebushes which both feeds them and keeps weeds down. Leaf-mould can also be used in the same way. Further, the ground does not then need to be

worked since the earth beneath the mulch remains moist.

If, during a long dry period, the roses have to be watered, the leaves should not be allowed to get wet, so it is best to use a hose to water the ground between the plants. Leaves which are damp for some time are particularly susceptible to mildew and rust.

There is a section later in the book which deals with the diseases and pests which affect roses and the remedies for these.

If roses are cut for the vase they should be cut with the stems as long as possible. This encourages the rose to produce healthy new shoots. Also, when removing the dead-heads, cut the shoots back two or three leaf joints. You can usually see exactly where the cut should be made, since the new shoot has already begun to grow below the dead flower.

If you have in your garden hybrid tea roses that are wanted not merely for garden decoration but also for cutting, you will have to ensure that, when cutting the blooms, two or three leaves still remain on the stem. It is also very important that these plants are well pruned in the spring, down to two or three eyes on a strong shoot.

The dead blooms of species roses need not be removed, since the hips are very attractive and add colour to the garden. But with all other roses and climbing roses the work of dead-heading must not be neglected or the second flowering will be very small and weak.

Choosing roses To help the garden enthusiast,
a selection of roses that are proven favourites and possess many good qualities is given below. Since the quality of roses varies from one district to another, look around you and see which roses do well in your district. You can learn a lot from attending exhibitions, flower shows, visiting botanical gardens, rose gardens and other places where roses are displayed in the neighbourhood. Make notes not only of the names of roses that appeal to you, but also of their height, colour and so on.

Incidentally, in case you are not already familiar with roses, they are grouped into various categories, and it is worth knowing the main characteristics of each group. Polyantha roses (e.g. the well-known 'Paul Crampel') have large clusters of flowers but their individual flowers are small. Hybrid polyantha roses also have flowers in clusters, but have larger individual flowers. Flori-bundas have even larger individual flowers. They are similar to the hybrid tea blooms, but grow in large clusters.

These three types can quite happily be planted in large beds and borders, since they give a magnificent display of colour. The hybrid tea roses are particularly suitable for cutting. They have fewer, but much larger blooms.

Each year the catalogues offer new varieties, which—according to the advertising blurbs—excel all other varieties in beauty, abundance of bloom and fragrance. Take it all with a pinch of salt and if you want to try out a new variety, buy only one or two plants. The new rose may not be all you expect of it.

Rose bushes and standard roses before and after pruning. Weak shoots should be removed, and the rest cut back to three to five 'eyes'.

POPULAR VARIETIES

Shrub roses

'Munich Carnival' red	Height 150 cm/5 ft. The full blooms of this new variety come in giant clusters. The fiery blood red colour, does not fade even in rain. Very resistant to most diseases. Blooms throughout the whole summer up to the end of October.
'Director' red	Height 180 cm/6 ft. The semi-double, glowing blood red blooms appear right into late autumn. Vigorous growth.
'Bischofastadt Paderborn' red	Height 120 cm/4 ft. This is a new rose, which has simple cup-shaped flowers of flaming orange. Ideal for use as a hedge.
'Stadt Rosenheim' salmon pink/orange	Height 120 cm/4 ft. The salmon coloured blooms which are similar to the hybrid tea are intensely brilliant. Glossy, healthy, light green foliage.
'Elmshorn' pink	Height 120–180 cm/4–6 ft. The delicate blooms are deep pink with a salmon sheen, and form large clusters. They are good for cutting (for small arrangements).
'Sparriehoop' pink	Height 120–180 cm/4–6 ft. The single cup shaped flowers are mother of pearl pink and form large clusters. Blooms until late autumn.
'Snow White' pure white	Height 90 cm/3 ft. The pure white flowers resemble those of the hybrid tea, but bloom in large clusters, which continue blooming until the frosts. Very suitable for hedges.

Climbing Roses

'Parkdirektor Riggers' red	A very vigorous variety. Velvety blood-red semi-double blooms in clusters, produced in abundance, very long lasting.
'Gruss an Heidelberg' red	Blooms freely into late autumn. An intense fiery-red colour, with dark green foliage. Very fragrant.
'Sympathy' red	Certainly it is one of the most beautiful of all the red, repeat-flowering climbers with large blooms, similar to those of the hybrid tea varieties, in a velvety dark red. Sweet smelling.
'New Dawn' pale pink	Well known, useful variety in a delicate pink, fragrant, free-flowering throughout the summer until the autumn. Vigorous growth and foliage; very hardy, and very good for cutting.

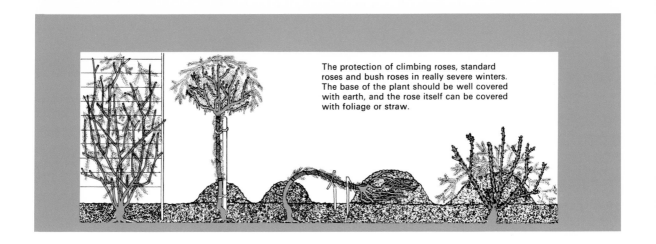

The protection of climbing roses, standard roses and bush roses in really severe winters. The base of the plant should be well covered with earth, and the rose itself can be covered with foliage or straw.

Polyantha hybrid and Floribunda roses

'Lilli Marleen' deep red	Height 60 cm/2 ft. Possibly the most beautiful of all the deep velvety red roses, flowers in great profusion, right into the autumn. Very healthy lush green foliage.
'Marlena' red	Height 45 cm/18 in. A dwarf, long lasting 'Lilli Marlene'. The bushy plant is covered with brilliant dark red double blooms. Ideal for a rose bed filled with smaller varieties, and especially suitable for smaller gardens. The flowers remain unharmed by the rain and bloom continually until the frosts.
'Europeana' red	Height 60 cm/2 ft. The brilliant blood-red flowers have a strong fragrance and are very abundant. A vigorous foliage.
'Saraband' red	Height 60 cm/2 ft. The red of this single, geranium-coloured rose is unusually brilliant. Vigorous growth, and long blooming.
'Northern Light' red	Height 45 cm/18 in. Dazzling scarlet—especially brilliant.
'Irish Wonder' red	Height 60 cm/2 ft. Velvety orange-red flowers. The colour remains consant, hardly any fading. It is a prolific flowerer, and quite brilliant.
'Meteor' red	Height 45 cm/18 in. Vermilion flowers, rather similar to 'Irish Wonder' but somewhat lighter.
'Evelyn Fison' ('Tropicana') red	Height 60–80 cm/2–2½ ft. The full, hybrid-tea type blooms, which are a brilliant orange/red, have a very powerful perfume.
'Viennese Waltz' red	Height 60–80 cm/2–2½ ft. A large flowering floribunda with noble, velvety brilliantly fire-red blooms. These keep for a long time, so are very suitable for cutting.
'Queen Elizabeth' bright pink	Height 80 cm/2½ ft. Blooms with great profusion into November. Each individual bloom is of small hybrid tea type, and is very well formed. The colour is a pure clear pink. An excellent variety and a strong grower.
'All Gold' golden yellow	Height 45 cm/18 in. The flowers are a pure golden yellow; unaffected by bad weather. Very free growing and flowering.
'Pink Parfait' salmon pink	Height 45 cm/18 in. Splendid blooms in salmon pink, with the bright golden yellow stamens gleaming from the centre. The blooms soon fade, and so must be picked off. Has a lovely perfume.

1 Hybrid polyantha 2 Floribunda 3 Hybrid tea

Hybrid Tea Roses
(A small selection of the most popular and highly recommended varieties)

'Earnest H. Horse' red
This is a new variety with velvety red blooms. The growth is strong and upright.

'Red Star' red
The buds are rather elongated, but produce well formed, full, long lasting bright red blooms, which are excellent for cutting.

'Alec's Red' red
Deep vermilion red flowers perfectly shaped, large and full.

'Wendy Cussons' pink
A wonderful rose with perfectly formed pure pink flowers. Excellent for cutting.

'Picadilly' red and yellow
An unusual variety in shades of salmon-yellow-red. One could almost believe that there was a candle glowing behind each bloom. An ideal cut flower with a lovely perfume.

'Superstar' orange
A fantastic variety, whose colour is difficult to describe exactly—pure light vermilion. It is very vigorous in growth, fragrant and blooms into autumn.

'Fragrant Cloud' orange and red
A very long stemmed rose with red/orange/yellow flowers. An excellent rose for cutting.

'Gloria Dei' golden yellow
This has enormous, long lasting blooms. The petals are a golden yellow in bud, and as they open change bright yellow tinted slightly with red. It is extremely vigorous, healthy and hardy.

'Grandpa Dickson'
A splendid rose for cutting with golden yellow flowers, a distinctive perfume and healthy foliage.

'Peace'
The exquisitely shaped creamy-yellow blooms are full petalled. They are ideal for cutting and have a heavy perfume.

'John F. Kennedy' white
The large splendid brilliant pure white blooms are very fragrant and also very attractive.

1 *Viburnum farreri (=fragrans)*

2 Snowberry

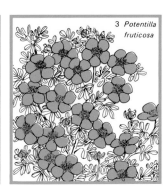

3 *Potentilla fruticosa*

ORNAMENTAL SHRUBS HAVE MANY USES

Ornamental shrubs can be used for forming a barrier around the garden, or near the patio. There are so many delightful shrubs that it would be impossible to describe them all in this book. There are many good books on shrubs and numerous nursery catalogues which give you all the information you need, and usually have colour illustrations. You can learn even more by visiting a garden centre, nursery or one of the great gardens open to the public.

Besides, local nurserymen are the best people to advise you as to what does best in your area.

To get the best from shrubs, plan their positions carefully. To see them at their best give them plenty of room to develop. Plant them at least 150 cm/5 ft apart. Try to avoid planting them in regular rows, which would present a rather boring picture: stagger them instead.

Below is a brief selection of some of the most useful ornamental shrubs in order of their season of flowering.

By March both the witch hazel *Hammamelis mollis* and the cornelian cherry *Cornus mas* are already in flower. Both grow to a height of about 4·50 m/15 ft, so must be planted farther apart than usual. A first-rate flowering shrub, literally covered with golden-yellow flowers is the popular forsythia, blooming a little after the cornelian cherry. *Viburnum farreri,* often sold under its old name, *V. fragrans,* has a lovely perfume, and displays its pink and white flowers throughout winter. Among the larger ornamental shrubs that flower in April/May are the different varieties of Japanese cherry. After these comes the June berry *Amelanchier laevis,* often sold as *A. canadensis,* an attractive shrub, pleasant not only for its white flowers in spring, but also for its summer berries and brilliant autumn colours.

Various forms of cotoneaster *Cotoneaster dielsianus, C. frigidus* and others, are of interest on account of their elegant shape and foliage. The flowers are rather insignificant, but the berries are spectacular in autumn. Excellent flowering shrubs with white and pink flowers, are the various types of deutzia. Taller and stronger shrubs that come into their own in spring are laburnums and lilacs. The latter come in many varieties, three of the best are: 'Souvenir de Louis' Spath (dark red, single); 'Michael Buchner' (pale mauve, double) and 'Madame Lemoine' (pure white, double). Bridal wreath *Spiraea arguta* and other spiraeas, including *Spiraea* 'van Houttei', look just like freshly fallen snow as they bloom in May/June. The fragrant beauty bush *Kolkwitzia amabilis* is an ornamental shrub that looks attractive throughout the year, particularly in June, when it is covered with pink blossom; while the Jew's mallow *Kerria japonica* brings some yellow to the garden. Then there are the different sorts of viburnum, some of which are fragrant: most have white flowers. The popular mock orange *Philadelphus* species much loved for its fragrant white flowers, follows the viburnums. *P. microphyllus, P.* x *purpurea maculatus,* so delicate in their effect among the other shrubs, are also in bloom at this time. Another

Ornamental shrubs before and after being thinned out.

Hedge planting. After the ground has been prepared, a small trench is dug, and the bushes planted as straight as possible. Deciduous bushes should be cut back, if they are without berries. If they have berries, then the tips should be shortened to a uniform height.

splendid flowering shrub which can be thoroughly recommended is the white *Spiraea nipponica*, which is almost as beautiful as its earlier-blooming varieties.

The different varieties of weigela in mauve, pink and red flower from July until the autumn.

Shrub roses could also be planted with these ornamental shrubs, but it would be best if they were planted either separately or in small groups, in front of the green wall of shrubs.

Standing alone in another part of the garden, a buddleia makes a very pretty picture and the flowers are very attractive to butterflies.

If you like plants with coloured leaves in the garden, the white-leaved dogwood *Cornus alba* 'Albo-marginata Elegans' is superlative—one of the finest of all variegated shrubs. It is a very robust plant, which looks attractive throughout the whole year.

Shrubs with red leaves include the purple hazel *Corylus maxima* 'Purpurea', the dark-red leaved *Berberi thumbergii* 'Atropurpurea' with almost black-red foliage. This reaches about 5·50 m/18 ft with a corresponding spread; this must be taken into account when planting it. A pretty yellow leaved bush, up to 4·50 m/15 ft, is a little maple, *Acer negundo* 'Aureo-variegatum'.

Two vigorous ornamental shrubs, which are suitable as specimens are: *Buddleia alternifolia* with graceful, bright violet, hanging spikes of flowers and *Buddleia davidii*, already mentioned. The spring tamarisk *Tamarix parviflora*, with its delicate pink flowers and feathery foliage, is attractive in April/May. A shrub with a weeping

habit and abundant white flowers is the previously mentioned *Spiraea nipponica*, also the well-known *Spiraea arguta*. The spiraea family display their real beauty in open situations. The very decorative *Cotoneaster dielsianus* has lovely overhanging foliage, but its flowers are inconspicuous.

PLANTING A HEDGE

It must be remembered before planting a hedge that it will need clipping twice a year, once in June and again in the winter. Conifer hedges need be cut once only, in July, when new growth has ceased. Hedges should be kept wider at their bases than at the top—see diagrams—otherwise the lower parts soon become bare.

Conifer hedges should only be planted where the natural conditions are favourable to their growth and there is adequate moisture. The result will then be a thick hedge, which will provide seclusion even in winter. Under no circumstances should a conifer hedge be planted next to a wooden fence, since the lower parts would soon become bare. A wire fence, through which the branches can grow, is quite suitable.

If the hedges can be trimmed at the correct times of year—and an electric cutter makes this much easier—you may prefer to surround your garden with a hedge rather than with free-growing ornamental shrubs. Hedges have the advantage that they take up little ground space and provide a very dense screen. Before planting, a strip at least 45 cm/18 in. wide and two spits deep must be dug and thoroughly prepared as for the perennial and

rose borders. Persistent weeds must be removed before planting. On average, you will need 4 to 5 plants for every yard or metre, (in the case of thuyas, two and a half plants per yard or metre). If the deciduous or coniferous trees are very small —only two or three years old—then up to ten can be planted per metre or yard and thinned out later as they grow. After the ground has been prepared, a trench of about 20 cm/8 in. wide and approximately the same depth should be dug. Put plants in it in a straight line at the correct distance apart, fill back with soil, tread it down till really firm and finally, water thoroughly.

Two- to three-year-old plants should be well cut back, while the taller hedging plants should be trimmed to an even height and tidied up at the sides, so that they will present an orderly picture and produce healthy shoots. Deciduous hedges should be planted in the autumn and spring, conifer hedges in August/September.

Hedges between 75 and 90 cm/2½ and 3 ft high
For low, well cut hedges the common privet *Ligustrum vulgare* is very suitable, or even better, *Ligustrum ovalifolium*. *Ribes sanguineum* and the popular berberis *Berberis thunbergii* 'Atropurpurea' with deep red leaves, are also good. Hornbeam, too, can be used, if kept rigorously to height.

Hedges between 90 and 180 cm/3 and 6 ft high
This is the height most used for enclosing gardens. Since the main purpose of the hedge is to prevent the garden from being overlooked 180 cm/6 ft is generally high enough.

Privet or red-leaved berberis can be used for this purpose though the deciduous hornbeam is both neater and more attractive. Hornbeams form good thick hedges. The brown dead foliage remains for the most of the winter. The same is true of beech, another popular hedging plant. If you want an unusual hedge, try the Cornelian cherry *Cornus mas*, especially the variegated form, *Cornus mas* 'Variegata'.

In city gardens, when an evergreen hedge is needed, *Thuja plicata* (planted young) is very suitable. If something special is wanted, then the perfect hedging plant is *Thuja plicata* 'Semperaurescens' with its bronze twigs.

For the garden of a bungalow or a villa of Mediterranean character, *Thuja occidentalis* 'Fastigiate' can look magnificent. This variety keeps its lovely green colour even in winter, and without the need of any cutting on the sides, forms a slim, close hedge. Height is kept in check by trimming the tips. Common yew, *Taxus baccata* is traditionally the finest of all hedging plants. Relatively slow growing—about 45 cm/18 in. a year—it makes a very neat, dense hedge.

 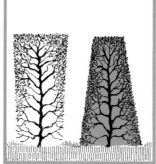

To ensure the hedge looks neat after trimming, a line should be laid at the right height before cutting. Hedges should be thicker at the base than at the top. Grown this way they remain thick at the base.

For low, free growing hedges the following are suitable:

English name	Height in m/ft	Colour of flowers	Time of flowering	Botanical name
Deutzia	1/4	white	May/June	*Deutzia gracilis*
Hypericum (St. John's wort)	1/4	golden yellow	June–October	*Hypericum patulum* 'Hidcote Gold'
Mock orange	1·5/5	white	June/July	*Philadelphus* x *lemoinei* hybrids
Shrubby cinquefoil	1/3	golden yellow	June–October	*Potentilla fruticosa* 'Farreri'
Spiraea	60 cm/2	dark red	July/August	*Spiraea* x *bumalda* 'Anthony Waterer'
Spiraea	1/3	dark pink	June/July	*Spiraea bumalda froebeli*

For taller, free growing hedges the following are suitable:

Cotoneaster	1·80/6	red berries	in autumn	*Cotoneaster dielsia nus* and *C. divarica tus*
Forsythia	1·80/6	golden yellow	April/May	*Forsythia intermedia* 'Lynwood Gold'
Forsythia	1·80/6	pale yellow	April/May	*Forsythia intermedia* 'Spring Glory'
Scottish wild rose	2/8	dark red	June	*Rosa rubiginosa*
Japanese wild rose	1·80/6	pink–bright red	May–October	*Rosa rugosa*
Spiraea	1·80/6	white	May	*Spiraea arguta*
Spiraea	1·80/6	white	May/June	*Spiraea vanhouttei*
Snowberry	1/4	white	in autumn	*Symphoricarpus rivularis* 'White Hedge'.
Rouen lilac	2/8	mauve	May	*Syringa* x *chinensis*

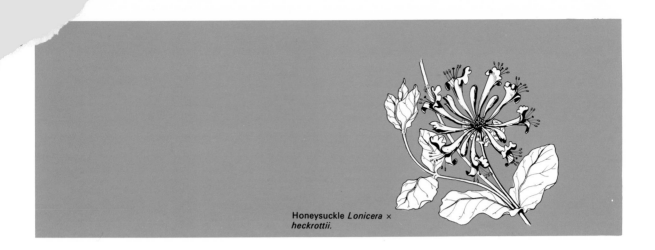

Honeysuckle *Lonicera* × *heckrottii*.

CREEPERS AND CLIMBERS

Planted round a porch, a climbing plant creates a link between house and garden. A porchway entwined with leaves and flowers makes an attractive feature: the same applies to pergolas and trellises, when climbers wind their tendrils round posts and through lattice work. Even the starkness of a garden shed can be relieved by a single climber. Climbing roses have already been mentioned; some other climbing plants given below:

Dutchman's pipe *Aristolochia macrophylla* (= *durior*). This is a vigorous, hardy plant, with large, luxuriant, heart-shaped leaves. In a small garden, care must be taken that the heavy leaves do not look out of place.

Clematis varieties The small-flowered varieties look quite enchanting: *Clematis montana rubens*, pink, which blooms in May; *Clematis viticella*, with violet purple flowers, which bloom in July/August; *Clematis tangutica* with yellow flowers, blooming from June to September. The last-named has also attractive seed-heads resembling small silver wigs! The plants can climb to a height of 810 cm/9 ft and are therefore ideal for covering fences. Best known are the large-flowered hybrids, which come in different shades of blue and even in pink and white. All clematis needs shade on their roots. They should be planted rather deeper than usual, the soil well prepared with compost or peat. Place a large stone over the roots to shade them.

Ivy *Hedera helix*. This well-known small-leaved climber will, without much encouragement, quickly cover a house right up to the roof. Ideal for shaded and half-shaded positions.

Honeysuckle *Lonicera*. A delightful variety is *Lonicera heckrottii*, which blooms from June to the autumn, and has elegantly formed lip-shaped flowers. The colours are crimson-pink, opening to a golden-yellow inside. Grows to about 3·5 m/12 ft. Before blooming, loniceras are often attacked by greenfly. As long as the flowers remain unopened, spray the plants with a systemic insecticide, which should deal with the problem. If the greenfly is noticed only after the flowers have opened, then a weaker solution of insecticide should be used. Another attractive honeysuckle is *L.* x *tellmanniana*, which blooms in May and June, with golden yellow flowers, which look particularly good against a dark background. There is also a useful variety, *L. henryi* which grows to 3·5 m/12 ft and whose leaves remain green throughout the winter.

Virginia creeper *Parthenocissus quinquefolia* (also listed as *Ampelopsis g.* and *Vitis g.*). This climber is so well known that not much need be said about it. The most popular of all varieties is the large-leaved *Parthenocissus quinquefolia* (*P. tricuspidata veitchii*). It grows well on a north-facing wall. Grows to 6 m/20 ft or more. The beautiful red autumn leaves make a delightful picture.

Russian or rule-a-minute vine *Polygonum baldschuanicum*. This vigorous climbing plant will

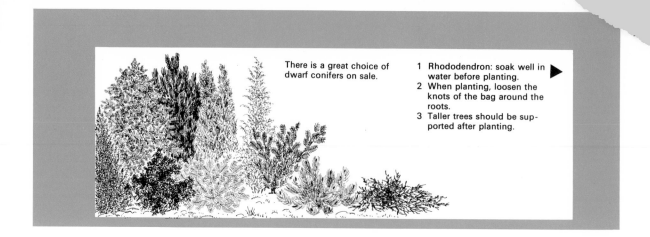

There is a great choice of dwarf conifers on sale.

1 Rhododendron: soak well in water before planting.
2 When planting, loosen the knots of the bag around the roots.
3 Taller trees should be supported after planting.

quickly cover a large area. It can grow 3·5 m/12 ft in a single season. Its fragrant white flowers are decorative from summer to autumn. Definitely not suitable for small gardens since it will quickly overwhelm everything near it.

Wistera   A most impressive climber, which looks particularly good against white house walls. The long blue sprays of flowers appear in May. Wistera loves warmth and should be planted on a south or west wall. The fragrant lilac-like flowers give great pleasure in early summer.

Conifers and evergreens   Conifers turn a 'six-month garden' into a 'twelve-month garden'. They look attractive throughout the year and are particularly valuable in winter, when perennials are dormant and deciduous trees have lost their leaves. They are perhaps at their most beautiful when snow or hoar frost sparkles on their needle-shaped leaves. Once planted, conifers do not require a great deal of care and attention.

Small spruces look particularly attractive, but most of them do not remain small for long. In an average sized garden they would soon become overpowering, since they may reach a height of up to 27 m/90 ft, with a spread of 6 m/20 ft or more. The same applies to the pines, firs and larches. There are, however, among all these popular trees miniature varieties which grow less vigorously.

The Siberian spruce *Picea omorika* a tall tree, always remaining slender, has attractive hanging branches; and is often used in gardens. The eastern variety *Picea orientalis* 'Aureospica', which grows

to only 270 cm/24 ft in height, is a golden-yellow in colour, while growing. *Picea breweriana* should be planted on its own. The long, thin side branches hang downwards in a frost—they look like Christmas trees covered in tinsel. This tree grows to a height of 9 m/30 ft and, like the Siberian spruce, can be planted in the average sized garden. Among the massive growing firs, which can only be used in parks and very large gardens, there is one variety which is suitable for the smaller garden: the Korean fir *Abies koreana,* which reaches only 180–360 cm/6–12 ft, and produces masses of violet-purple cones even on young plants. In some gardens, the blue spruce stands as a special showpiece and focus of interest. The best-known form with deep silvery-blue needles, is *Picea pungens glauca* 'Koster' which will grow to between 9–18 m/30–60 ft. So one should plant it with care.

The larch also makes an attractive addition to the garden. Recommended is a weeping variety *Larix kaempferi* 'Pendula' which grows to a height of only 4–5 m/15–18 ft. It should be planted on its own to display its lovely hanging branches to advantage.

The common Scots pine *Pinus sylvestris* is really a forest tree. It does however have a place in the garden. Rhododendrons could be planted under it, so receiving the shade they require, while not interfering with the roots of the pine. The dwarf mountain pines *Pinus mugo*, especially the little bun-shaped forms 'Mops' and 'Gnome' are useful since they do not take up too much room, and reach a height of only 60 cm/12 ft after 10 years. An

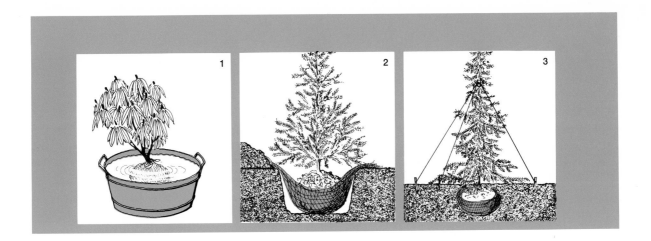

impressive slow-growing pine, with silver-blue needles is *Pinus sylvestris* 'Beurovensis' which is quite suitable for a small or average sized garden, since it reaches a height of 180 cm/6 ft.

Besides those mentioned above there are many more conifers, which do not grow too tall, including the evergreen dwarf varieties, most of which only grow to between 15 cm/6 in. and 60 cm/2 ft. These can be used to great advantage even in the smallest garden. They include dwarf varieties of spruce, juniper and the pine. Any nursery that sells trees keeps a good selection of dwarf trees in varying shades of green, yellow and blue.

Returning to broad-leaved shrubs, there are quite a few that keep their leaves throughout the winter. The best-known are the rhododendrons, which need some shade and an acid soil. A decorative evergreen variety of cotoneaster, with pendulous twigs, is *Cotoneaster salicifolia* 'Floccosa'. Other evergreen shrubs include: holly (*Ilex*), honeysuckle (*Lonicera*), Oregon grape *Mahonia aquifolium*, *Pyracantha coccinea* and the large-leaved *Viburnum rhytidophyllum*.

Conifers and evergreen trees are best planted in spring before growth begins. The plants are usually sold with their roots packed in sacks. If the roots have dried out on their way to you they should be placed for several hours in a bucket of water. Rhododendrons in particular should be soaked for a whole day.

The hole where the tree or shrub is to be planted must be sufficiently large for the soil to be mixed with damp peat. The plant is then placed in the hole, and the space between the tied up roots and the sides of the hole filled with soil. The sacking is cut from round the top of the root, but left in the ground round the plant, which is then well watered and the earth covered with damp peat.

Taller conifers should be anchored securely to the ground by three wires. So that the wires do not cut into the trunk, a piece of bicycle tyre, sacking or similar material should be placed around it. During dry periods, the newly planted trees must be well watered each week. As soon as the taller conifers have established themselves—after about a year—the wires can be removed. Otherwise the wire, despite its lining, can cut into the thickening trunk, possibly causing it to break during a storm.

The green lawn A patio opening directly on to the lawn can be delightful. It should be connected with the sitting area or there should be a seat from which to enjoy a view of the garden. One specimen tree planted two-thirds of the way down the lawn will draw the eye to it, emphasising the smoothness and tenderness of the lawn. Whatever you do, do not dot the lawn with several fruit trees; that would merely spoil the grand effect of the lawn and make both lawn and garden look smaller. Flower-beds and borders belong at the edge of the lawn, if only because that makes it easier to care for the lawn.

Inaccessible corners should not be included in a lawn, they would otherwise have to be cut with shears. If the lawn is walked on a great deal in one particular part, put stepping-stones down. These are placed a pace apart (about 60 cm/2 ft between each stone) and laid on a 5 cm/2 in. bed of sand.

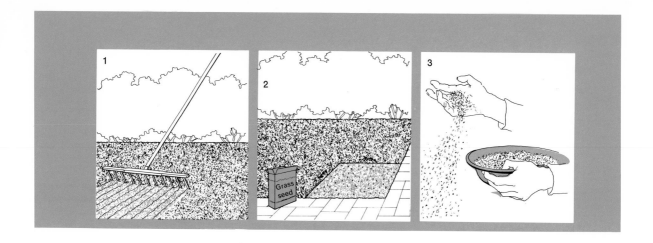

The area which is to be made into a lawn need only be dug one spit deep, then raked over to level the ground. The lawn does not, however, have to be absolutely dead level with the patio. A gently rolling or undulating surface produces a pleasant, natural effect and makes the garden appear larger. The soil should then be improved with a surface dressing of peat-based fertilizer. Grasses are shallow-rooting so this does not need to be dug in.

The ground should be allowed to rest for about three weeks before seeding—though one is tempted to seed straight away in order to see a green lawn as soon as possible. During this time thousands of weeds will spring up, and should be sprayed with a soil-neutralising weedkiller to get rid of them right from the start. The next day sowing can begin, since these preparations become ineffective directly they touch the soil, working only on green leaves.

The lawn seed mixture is very important. There are more than 4,000 different grasses and a lawn should consist of several different varieties. A good one will contain equal proportions of tuft-forming and spreading grasses. The spreading type will grow around the tufts of grass, thus forming a close-knit turf. But what type of lawn do you want? A luxurious lawn, like a carpet of green velvet, looks delightful but is far too precious to be spoiled by children playing. Besides, it needs a great deal of regular care to keep it in such beautiful condition, for which few gardeners would have the time.

The ideal solution is a lawn that can be used: one that isn't treated like a sacred cow; one on which children can play without ruining its appearance. Only during the first few months after sowing should the lawn be spared and not trodden on, but after the first mowing it can be used normally. A third solution would be a real country meadow-type lawn, in which wild meadow flowers are allowed to bloom. This has its appeal, since not only is it attractively natural looking, but also, weekly mowing is unnecessary. Such a lawn needs only to be cut with a scythe, twice a year. Unfortunately this kind of lawn is hardly practicable in the average garden, since it needs a large surface area and is only suitable for people without children: a lawn of flowers can only be trodden on for a short time—just after being cut.

When buying lawn seed go to a good garden centre: they will know what mixture of grasses is best for the type of lawn you want. Don't try to economise when buying lawn seed. It is in fact cheaper to buy the more expensive seeds of which you will need less per square yard or square metre than you would with cheaper seed. Before sowing, the seed should be placed in a sack or plastic container and shaken, so that the different seeds are evenly distributed throughout the mixture. Then scatter the seed evenly over the whole area and rake it. The best times to sow are April/May or August.

In warm damp weather seeds begin to germinate within a week. Since seeds during germination have a tendency to dry out the whole area should be kept moist until the grass appears. The first mowing is very important. As soon as the grass reaches about 7·5 cm/3 in. high it can be cut. The cutting

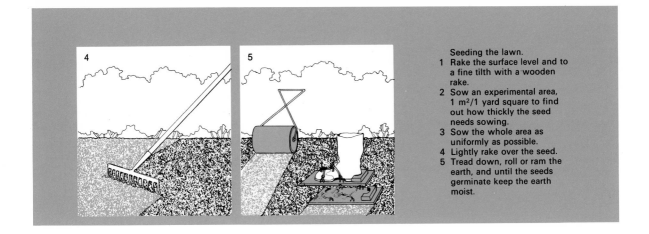

Seeding the lawn.
1 Rake the surface level and to a fine tilth with a wooden rake.
2 Sow an experimental area, 1 m²/1 yard square to find out how thickly the seed needs sowing.
3 Sow the whole area as uniformly as possible.
4 Lightly rake over the seed.
5 Tread down, roll or ram the earth, and until the seeds germinate keep the earth moist.

blades of the mower must be very sharp so that the young grass is not torn out. The mower should be set as high as possible, so that only the tips of the grass are cut: it should under no circumstances be cut short, since the green blades are essential for producing the materials necessary for the healthy growth.

Mowing plays an important role in lawn care: it should be done regularly—but the cut should not be too close. In spring and early summer, when the growth is particularly vigorous, the lawn should be mown once or twice a week; about once a week in summer; and less frequently in autumn.

The correct cutting height depends on the lawn; a decorative lawn at 2–3 cm/1 in.; a more practical one at 4 cm/1½ in. If the lawn is allowed to get too long, when it is finally cut it will look an unhealthy yellow colour, and can become scorched. This can easily happen when you go away on holiday for a couple of weeks. On your return you should set the blades as high as possible, and mow the grass on a dull day.

Thick, healthy grass on the surface indicates good root growth. When the roots penetrate below the earth as deeply as the grass stands above the surface, then the correctly cut lawn is not so sensitive to the long dry periods that occasionally occur during the summer as a close cut lawn would be.

It is very important that the blades of the lawn mower are kept sharp. Hand mowers should be re-sharpened at least once a year. Otherwise the grass will be torn, not cut. Before mowing, all stones,

metal pieces and so on that could damage the mower must be removed.

A good lawn cannot be achieved without dressings of fertilizers. A sparse lawn can be greatly improved by the correct fertilizer. If you think about it, regular lawn cutting means that a great deal of the living green mass is removed, so it becomes obvious why lawns need feeding. If all the cutting from one blade of grass during one year were laid end to end, they would be over 90 cm/3 ft long.

Grass likes a neutral or slightly acid soil. If the soil is too acid the lawn tends to become matted and mossy; if the ground is too alkaline, weeds and coarse grasses will grow.

Nitrogen is the most important ingredient in any lawn dressing, since it produces a good green colour and healthy growth. But other foods and elements play their part in the health and hardiness of a lawn. In March, spread a good fertilizer over the grass. During the growing period—between April and September—every three or four weeks after cutting give the lawn a dressing of nitrogen fertilizer. It is important to spread the fertilizer as evenly as possible; otherwise 'burnt' patches could alternate with pale ones where too much fertilizer, or not enough, had been added.

There are many excellent and proven lawn fertilizers on the market. These should be applied two or three times a year according to instructions. These products do tend to be rather expensive, but are much easier to use, and even distribution of fertilizer is assured.

A lawn needs watering in dry weather; and twice

A well cared for lawn can be achieved by the application of a top-dressing in spring. Use a long-toothed rake or fork to pierce the ground at intervals. Peat, sand and an organic fertilizer, mixed in equal parts and then spread over the lawn, using a nylon mesh bag to scatter it uniformly. Or, instead of this top dressing, a proprietary lawn fertilizer can be used. In this way the lawn is both aerated and fed.

Right: To mow a lawn correctly, follow this sort of pattern.

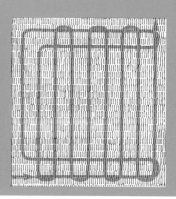

as much water is needed under trees as on the open lawn. It is also very important that the lawn is aerated. With a lawn rake or spiker, moss and tufts can be removed. The sharp knife-like prongs scratch the surface of the lawn and encourage new growth. It is an arduous task, but results are rewarding. The job can also be done with a barbed roller.

Lawn weeds can be destroyed with special weed killers that leave the lawn unharmed. But it is important that the instructions on the label are carefully followed. There are many suitable preparations on the market that will do the job adequately. Some are even effective on newly sown lawns without causing any harm to the young grass.

5 Fruit Trees in the Garden

Fruit trees and bushes probably give more pleasure and satisfaction than any other area of gardening: in springtime, there is the splendour of fruit trees in blossom; then there is the satisfaction not only at the rewarding fruits you have grown yourself but also at the money saved. There is no comparison between the taste of a juicy pear picked from the tree and even the best that the supermarket can offer.

A single apple or pear tree creates an interesting focal point in a garden, while a hedge of fruit can make an attractive boundary between neighbouring gardens.

FRUITS FOR SMALL AREA

Apples grown on dwarfing root-stocks can be planted even in small gardens. Warm, dry and south-facing situations are not suitable, and the plants would find it hard to thrive there. For the same reason it is not advisable to place an apple espalier on a south wall.

In small gardens pears, too, can be grown on dwarfing stock; and also in the form of fruiting bushes; they can also be grown as half or full standard trees, especially if one wants the tree to be a conspicuous point in the garden. Half and full standard trees are grafted on pear seedling stock and therefore grow more vigorously. Pears tend to grow upwards rather than outwards.

Plums of many kinds are common in the garden, presumably because they are not too demanding on the soil. There are some varieties which prefer a richer soil, but generally speaking plums do very well in light or not too heavy soils. Half-standards are usually grown—for one thing it makes picking easier.

Sour or cooking cherries are usually planted either as bush-trees or fan-trained against a wall. The Morello will provide a regular fruit-crop even against a north wall. It dislikes wet soil, but is otherwise easy-going.

Peaches can be successfully grown in protected sites, usually against a south wall. The early spring blossom can be destroyed by late frosts and—no blossom no fruit—the wood would be damaged in exceptionally cold winters. But even if frost spoils the blossom two years out of three, the harvest in the third year is often surprisingly high: peaches require a warm deep soil, in the warmest, best-sheltered position possible. They are just not worth planting in heavy wet soils.

Apricots are even more demanding than peaches and can only be grown successfully on a sheltered south wall, preferably where they also benefit from reflected heat from a patio. When the tree does bear fruit, it will be of the most exquisite flavour. Often during the apricot's early blossom time there are a few if any bees in flight; so you need to transfer the pollen from one flower to another with a brush. Also, spraying with sugar water helps; the few bees that are about will then be more readily attracted to fly on to the blossoms. The quince can be used as a camouflage for the compost heap or it can be planted among other ornamental bushes. The blossom, beautiful foliage and rose and yellow, fleecy-skinned fruit give the tree a handsome appearance all the year round. The hazel, cob nut or filbert can also be considered an ornament to the garden, though it often grows too vigorously to be worthwhile in a small garden. Although cultivated varieties do not grow as vigorously as the common hazel *Coryllus avellana,* they yield much larger nuts. Unfortunately these are often raided by grey squirrels.

If you want hazel nuts and not merely to admire the beautiful catkins, you must plant at least two plants together: hazels are not self-fertile. A suitable pollinator is the wild hazel. All hazels prefer a strong, slightly damp, humus-rich soil.

FRUITS FOR THE LARGER GARDEN

To the above-mentioned species can be added the sweet cherry and the walnut.

The sweet cherry likes a deep, loamy, well aerated soil. In wet heavy soils the tree will soon suffer from gummosis and other diseases and so become liable to suffer damage in hard winters. In some cases whole branches and eventually a whole tree, may die. So this fruit should only be planted where conditions are favourable. A further disadvantage is that one can hardly harvest anything from full-standard trees because the top branches cannot be protected by nets from blackbirds and starlings, as is possible with a low-growing sour cherry bush.

The walnut is a magnificent tree, but far too majestic for the small to medium-sized garden. In the larger garden, however, it can play a dominant role. This tree, which children love climbing, lends itself to various other games as well: the sausage-like male catkins can be 'sold' or 'baked'. In addition there is the harvesting and cracking of the nuts.

The soil should preferably be warm, deep and open. When buying young walnut trees, always choose grafted plants of named varieties: the nuts of seedlings are very variable, both in size and flavour.

TREE FORMS AND PROPAGATION

Bush-trained fruit trees With a trunk height of only 60–90 cm/2–3 ft, this is certainly the tree form for modern requirements, at least as far as apples and pears are concerned. It is ideal for the small garden but equally usable in medium and larger gardens where a row of rich-yielding fruit bushes along the kitchen-garden fence may be required.

Fruit bushes are also excellent for allotments. Moreover, their low stature leaves most of the garden still in sunlight, even in later years when the bushes are fully grown.

There is little point in growing a full- or half-standard which will produce about 45 kg/100 lbs or more of fruit every year, especially if it all ripens at the same time. One soon becomes fed up with eating apples! The bush, however, bears only 10 kg/22 lbs, though quite often it may produce 20–30 kg/44–88 lbs or more. As they take up so little room, eight to ten different varieties can be planted in the same space as one standard or half-standard tree, with its big crown of branches. The different varieties will ripen successively, which

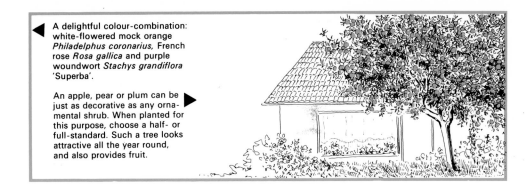

A delightful colour-combination: white-flowered mock orange *Philadelphus coronarius,* French rose *Rosa gallica* and purple woundwort *Stachys grandiflora* 'Superba'.

An apple, pear or plum can be just as decorative as any ornamental shrub. When planted for this purpose, choose a half- or full-standard. Such a tree looks attractive all the year round, and also provides fruit.

give you the chance to have both cookers and eaters, and to use them or preserve them as they ripen.

In most gardens one row of these miniature trees is enough, so that a gap of 2·5 m/8½ ft between each is sufficient. Since the bushes only grow to a height of 180–270 cm/6–9 ft all cultural work can be done comfortably: pruning, pest control and (most important) harvesting. The work becomes quite enjoyable—no ladder is necessary; and one can take care of these little trees almost in passing. And, at eye level, diseases and pests are quickly spotted, often not the case with taller trees.

It all depends on the stock   And so it does, but the following learned discourse on rootstocks is designed wholly for the benefit of British readers: American readers should skip this sub-section.

The correct root stock is vital for success with fruit bushes. Most fruit trees consist of two partners: the stock root and the scion (top growth). In many cases the stock is a seedling grown from an apple or pear pip. There are also the East Malling stocks, which are not grown from the pip but by vegetative propagation, and are known by an initial (M or EM plus a roman numeral indicating how dwarfing the root stock is). The offspring of a single plant with valuable characteristics, which has been selected from a mixture of seedlings, is planted out and afterwards cut back. The following spring a number of offshoots will grow out of this rootstock, and if these are earthed up they too will form roots. In the autumn these rooted offshoots are taken from their parent plant and re-

planted in rows. Every stick obtained by this method will inherit the same features as the parent plant.

On no account should the stock for a fruit bush be of vigorous growth, otherwise the distance of 2·5 m/8½ ft between plants would not be sufficient, and the result would be an almost unmanageable tangle of offshoots and branches. If a variety grows too large, it means the grafting was done on the wrong type-stock. Such trees cause more trouble than they are worth. Therefore, pay careful attention to the details on the label when buying trees.

Type-stocks for apples   M. IX is the smallest-growing stock known; scions grafted onto it are characterised by early and prolific fruit yield. They often bear fruit in the second year of planting. The fruit will be large, with a good colour and delicate flavour. However, fruit bushes on M. IX stock require the best soil conditions obtainable, and the addition of compost or peat is essential. Since the bushes have only small roots, they need permanent staking. This is the correct stock for all medium-to-strong-growing scions. With care, trees on type M. IX will grow for twenty years.

M. IV is more vigorous in growth, and is used where soil conditions are not so good, and above all in combination with weaker-growing scions. If these scions were grafted on the very dwarfing M. IX stock, growth would in many cases be too feeble to produce satisfactory crops. Those grafted on type M. IV have an early crop and they, too, always require staking.

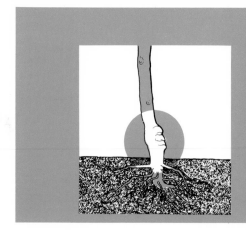

Fruit trees grafted on to dwarfing stocks must be planted with the graft a little above ground level. This must under no circumstances be forgotten when planting.

Even the beginner can easily recognise the grafting place: it is swollen. If this were completely buried, the scion itself might form roots and the tree grow too vigorously.

M. VII is used for weak-growing scions on poorer soil. The growth is middling, similar to M. IV.

Root stocks for pears Here only type A (Angiers quince) is important. Unfortunately this stock has some disadvantages: it will not unite properly with some pear varieties. It's main advantages are that it will yield soon after grafting, the crown of the bush will remain small, and the fruit will keep its fine flavour.

The fruit hedge Instead of a row of bushes, try instead, growing a fruit hedge. This provides an attractive screen and a delicious harvest, requiring but little space, since the larger branches are allowed to grow in two directions only. The same fruit bush plant material can be used, perferably two-year old scions on dwarfing stocks. Distance between trees should be 180–260 cm/6–8½ ft. Instead of stakes, use a trellis: place wooden posts (treated with preservative) or—still more durable —iron pipes set in concrete, at a distance of 14 m/ 15 ft. The espalier should be 150 cm/5 ft high. The first wire should be 60 cm/24 in. above the ground, with two more wires above it at 60 cm/24 in. intervals. Train the thicker branches that are to bear the fruit along the wires. By the summer, all branches should be trained horizontally or—if they are growing too thickly—taken out altogether. After the first year, cut back only the central branches until the required height is reached. The rest of the pruning is quite simple, since it is restricted to removing superfluous shoots.

An espalier against the house Pear, peach, apricot or sour cherry tree can be planted against a house wall. Among the pears, specially suitable varieties are 'Bon Chretien', 'Gute Luise', Alexander Lucas', and 'Madam Verte'.

The first requirement is a firm espalier, able to take the weight of the fruit-bearing branches. Next, a strip at least 90 cm/3 ft wide must be prepared in front of the wall, cultivated to a depth of 60 cm/ 2 ft and enriched with compost and peat. When building a new house, ensure that sufficient good topsoil is replaced along any wall intended for the espalier.

It is necessary to prepare the soil as deeply as that because a pear tree suitable for growing against a house wall is usually grafted on a vigorous, long-living seedling pear stock, whose roots go deep, certainly deeper than most named stocks. If on the other hand the pear is to grow against a shed, then it should be grafted on to a quince stock.

By suitable pruning of the central trunk and branches, a fan-shape can be obtained, with distance of 60 cm/2 ft between each branch in the case of pear trees, and 75 cm/2½ ft for peaches, apricots and sour cherries. Branches should be fastened to the espalier, and should produce a well-distributed array of fruit-bearing wood. Make sure the lower branches are allowed to grow longer than the top branches. For pruning instructions, see the section *Fruit Tree Pruning*.

Bush trees With a stem height of 60–150 cm/ 2–5 ft, this form of tree is recommended only for

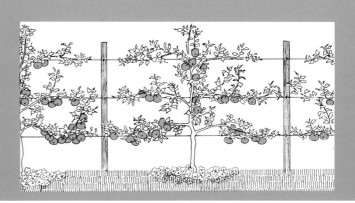

Fruit bushes can be fan-trained along the boundary between neighbouring gardens, making a sort of widely planted hedge. This takes up very little room, looks attractive, and both leaves and fruit get plenty of sunlight.

sour cherries and peaches. Both species keep a relatively small crown, so even in this form do not require much space. Both need a strict annual pruning, and this is made easier by their relatively low stature. This is an added advantage when it comes to protecting sour cherries from birds by means of nets. To ensure that the crown remains low, plant sour cherries that have been grafted on to dwarfing *Prunus mahaleb* stock. Trees grafted onto this stock will also grow quite well in poor, light soil.

It is not advisable to plant apples in bush tree form since their crown width of 4·5 m/15 ft takes up too much room, and it is not easy to walk under the tree as it is too low. It is much the same with the pear, but in this case, the bush tree is not quite so unsuitable, provided it is grown on seedling stock of a kind that encourages height rather than breadth.

Half and Full Standards The full standard, with a stem height of 1·5–2 m/5–7 ft is not so popular, since its height makes care difficult. It is the ideal form of tree, however, if an apple, pear or walnut is to be planted for ornamental purposes, near a patio or in some other conspicuous place. A full-standard plum can be grown as a shade tree—near the compost heap for example. In all these positions, the full standard has the advantage of being tall enough for people to move about comfortably under its branches.

Sometimes a half-standard with a stem height of 90–120 cm/3–4 ft will do for these purposes just

as well. It is the most popular form of tree for plums and greengages. Seedling stock should be used for full- and half-standard apples and pears. Unlike named stocks, seedlings are not of uniform features, but produce vigorous growth in the scion (top growth), as required for full- and half-standards. For plums and gages, the vegetatively propagated plum stocks are usually used.

SELECTION

To choose the right fruit varieties for your locality it is best to consult a professional gardener or some experienced member of the local horticultural society or allotments association. In this way many useful tips can be picked up for the advice of an old, experienced gardener cannot be rated too highly.

Always bear local varieties in mind. Obviously, these cannot be dealt with in this book, belonging as they do to particular localities where they have proved their worth for countless decades. These varieties are not usually of the highest quality, but are generally easy to grow and care for. Normally, you will find the local varieties are hardy and not easily prone to disease. Particularly if you should wish to plant a half- or full-standard tree as a feature in an ornamental garden, it is often best to choose one of these hardy varieties.

There is a large selection of proven fruit varieties: apple and pear are planted mainly as bushes; sour cherry, and peach as bush trees; plums and gages as half-standards.

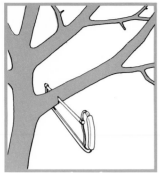
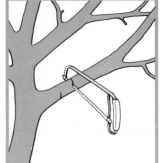
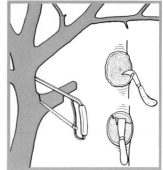

APPLES

For bushes, cordons and fan-trained plants use
MM 106 stock: for half-standards use M 25 stock.

Recommended varieties for the U.K.

'Cox's Orange Pippin'
'James Grive'
'Laxton's Superb'
'Golden Delicious'
'Bramley Seedling'
'Crispin Discovery'
'Egremont Russet'
'George Cave'
'Ellison's Orange'
'George Ross'
'Blenheim Orange'

Recommended varieties for the U.S.

'Rome Beauty'
'Winesap'
'Grimes Golden'

PEARS

Recommended varieties for the U.K.

Grow on Quince 'A' stock
'Conference'
'William's Bon Chretien'
'Doyenne du Comice'

Recommended varieties for the U.S.

'Beurre d'Anjou'
'Worden Seckel'
'Beurre Bosc'
'Comice'
'Bartlett'

PLUMS AND GAGES

Recommended varieties for the U.K.

'Victoria'
'Czar'
'Early Rivers'
'Cambridge Gage'
'Dennison's Superb Gage'

Recommended varieties for the U.S.

'Shropshire'
'Ozark Premier'

CHERRIES

Recommended varieties for the U.K.

'Morello'
'Cherry Gaucher'
'Napoleon Biggorau'
'Merton Glory'
'Merton Hert'

Strong branches must be sawn carefully to ensure a clean, straight cut and avoid bleeding. The best method is to begin sawing from the underside of the branch and saw about half way through. Then, a hand's breadth further along the branch, begin sawing again from the top. Only when the branch has been removed, begin sawing the remaining stump close to the trunk. The wound should be as clean and neat as possible so as to heal quickly. While it is healing, apply a coat of wound compound. Smoothing of the wound-edges with a pruning knife is not absolutely necessary.

Recommended varieties for the U.S.

'Montmorency'
'Royal Ann'
'Venus'

PEACHES

Recommended varieties for the U.K.

'Rochester'
'Amsden June'
'Duke of York'
'Hale's Early'
'Peregrine'

Recommended varieties for the U.S.

'Elberta'
'Reliance'

APRICOTS AND NECTARINES

'Hungarian Rose'
'John Rivers'
'Early Rivers'
'Lord Napier'

QUINCE

'Portugese Quince'
'Riesenquitte von Lescovac'
'Van Deman'
Very handy. In U.S. does best in zones 5 to 8.

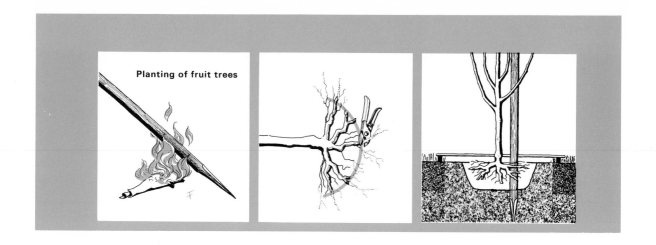

Planting of fruit trees

BUYING FROM THE NURSERY

As fruit trees have a long life span, plant only the best. Look out not only for general quality but for the strongest roots, a healthy straight trunk, and a vigorous-growing crown. Then check the root-stock. There is no point in buying strong and healthy-looking fruit bushes that have been grafted on to a too vigorous stock. This mistake is often made because bushes grafted on to the specially dwarfing M. IX and M. IV tend to have a meagre appearance.

Normally it is best to buy from the local nursery-man or garden centre. Or, just as good, order from a specialist nursery farther afield. The important thing is that the variety, stock and form of tree should suit your particular needs and that the plants should be healthy. Since the roots can easily dry out during transport, the tree should be unpacked immediately on arrival and stood in water for a few hours before planting. Buy from a reputable nursery or garden centre where the plants are properly labelled.

Of course, you may be tempted to buy too many plants. You may go in to buy only five roses, and finally emerge with two Omorika spruces, a grace-ful little birch and a walnut tree as well, having spent five times as much as you'd planned. And, what's worse, you don't have sufficient space any-way for these in your garden, which will be turned into a primaeval forest, without light and air and sun! So, like a good housewife, write out a shopping list of the items you really need. Then stick to it resolutely.

Plant and border distances

Distances between plants:

Apple—full/half standard	7·2–9·14 m/24–30 ft
Apple—bush tree	3·6–4·5 m/12–15 ft
Apple—bush	2·4 m/8 ft
Pear—full/half standard	5·4–7·2 m/18–24 ft
Pear—bush tree	3·6–4·5 m/12–15 ft
Pear—bush	2·4 m/8 ft
Plums—half/full standard	4·5–5·4 m/15–18 ft
Sweet cherry—full/half standard	7·3–9 m/24–30 ft
Sour cherry—bush tree	3·6–4·5 m/12–15 ft
Peach—bush tree	3·6–4·5 m/12–15 ft
Quince—bush	2·7–3·6 m/9–12 ft

The distances indicate the ultimate dimensions of the crowns of the trees concerned.

The minimum planting distances should not therefore be underestimated. The newly-planted trees often look too far apart when planted, which is why some gardeners deliberately plant a third tree between every two, intending to remove it later once there is no longer space for it. However, experience suggests that the extra tree will not be removed: the gardener won't have the heart to do it, so don't plant extra trees.

Just as important is the distance between the plant and the garden boundary. It happens time and again that a friendly relationship between neighbours is spoilt by shrubs and trees growing over into the next door garden. A good and simple rule is that the distance to the boundary should

be half that between plants, or half the expected spread of the tree. For example, the distance between dwarf apple trees should be 240 cm/8 ft; so the distance to the boundary should be at least 120 cm/4 ft. The spread of the sweet cherry, for instance, can be up to 7–9 m/24–30 ft if soil conditions are right. The branches will therefore grow over into the neighbouring garden after a few years, unless a generous space is left between it and the boundary.

PLANTING A FRUIT TREE

The most important thing when planting a fruit tree is to prepare the ground thoroughly. When planting bushes, which in the average garden are usually placed in rows, the whole area should be dug over, about 2 spits deep. Make sure the lower layers of soil remain below the top soil. Remove large stones and persistent weeds.

Apart from plenty of leaf-mould and compost, 1·5 kg/3 lb of a phosphate and 1·5 kg/3 lb of potash of magnesium per m²/sq yd should be spread and dug uniformly into both the top and lower layers of soil. It is best to have the soil analysed (see later) and to assess the quantities of fertilizers according to the results of the test.

For a single tree (standard or bush varieties) a hole 120 × 120 cm/4 × 4 ft wide, and 45 cm/18 in. deep should be dug, making sure that the top soil is kept separate from the lower layer. The soil at the bottom of the hole should be loosened with a fork, or if the soil is particularly heavy, use a pick. Mix 3–4 kilos/1½–2 lb of phosphate and 3–4 kilos/

1½–2 lb of potash of magnesium with the soil which has just been dug up and also mix some with the loosened soil at the bottom of the hole. When filling in the hole, care should be taken to replace the soil in the same order as it was removed. Except for a slight indentation round the actual plant, the hole should be completely filled in. The best times for planting are from mid-October until December or in spring as soon as the soil has dried out enough. When planting bushes, first drive a stake which has been treated with a timber preservative or hardened by fire into the hole. This stake should be 180–240 cm/6–8 ft long, and about 7·5 cm/3 in. thick; about 60 cm/2 ft of it should be hammered into the ground. It is then about the right height, so that the bush as it grows, can be tied to the stake round its stem as is necessary. Not all varieties of trees need staking, but a fruit bush will need one throughout its life, since it has been grafted on to a weak, shallow-rooting stock.

Before planting the bush, only a small hole need be dug in the prepared ground, just large enough for the roots. Roots which are either too long or have been damaged should be cut back to healthy growth. The soil should be mixed with a damp peat and/or leaf-mould. While one person is covering the roots with the soil mixture, another should shake the bush up and down to allow soil to fill all the spaces around and between the roots. Then the soil should be lightly trodden down round the trunk. The bush should then be watered generously; this ensures that moisture will penetrate right down to the finest roots. Finally, the earth surrounding the bush should be given a mulch of

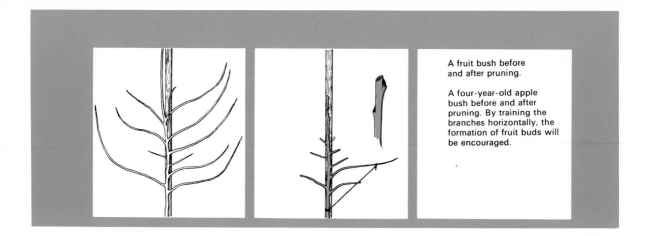

A fruit bush before and after pruning.

A four-year-old apple bush before and after pruning. By training the branches horizontally, the formation of fruit buds will be encouraged.

leaf-mould, half-rotted compost or stable manure to ensure moisture retention for as long as possible.

It is important to ensure that a tree or bush is planted no deeper than it was in the nursery. When it has settled in, the swollen join between stock and scion should still be visible. This is especially important for bushes which are grafted on to weak growing stocks. Therefore, deliberately plant the bush slightly higher in the soil to make sure that the graft is at the right height after the earth has settled.

Fruit bushes should be tied to the stake with tree-ties, stong coconut fibre or some similar material in the shape of a figure 8. There must be sufficient 'give' after tying to allow for the trees settling.

PRUNING A FRUIT TREE REQUIRES SOME SKILL

The pruning of spindle bushes The stem of the bush continues growing upwards. Young shoots that grow out from the main stem should be trained horizontally; these are the fruit-bearing branches. Only if there are too many of these side-shoots should some be removed. You want the side branches about 60 cm/24 in. apart.

If the tree is planted in autumn, prune the following spring; if planted in the spring, prune directly after planting. Along the length of the main stem several one-year offshoots will be found. Three to five of these shoots should be chosen. These shoots should be growing almost horizontally from the main stem, or only slightly upwards.

Branches growing at a steeper angle should be removed at the point of origin. And one of any two branches crossing each other should be cut away; also any that grow along the main stem or are very upright. All remaining branches will in the future bear fruit, and should be left. To ensure plenty of fruit-bearing wood, these branches should be trained horizontally. The central stem and three or four offshoots should be cut back quite severely. Depending upon the length of the branch, they should be cut back by two to four buds. The higher the branch, the shorter its length should be. The basic principle should be to prune so that the outer buds remain and the shoots can continue to grow outwards, allowing plenty of air and light to penetrate between the branches. The main stem should eventually be shortened to six to eight buds to make a pyramid shaped bush.

The young bush should be pruned again after one year. This pruning is to obtain the required shape. Firstly, any offshoot crossing another should be removed, regardless of whether it grows from the main stem or from a branch. Occasionally some of these crossing branches are in a better condition than the extended growth of the central stem or main branch, and in such a case the extension should be removed and the crossing branch left. All branches which are growing in an inward direction should be removed. Then the extended growth of the central stem should be shortened, as also the side shoots—the fruit-bearing branches —down to one bud (also known as an 'eye') growing on the outside of the branch. If the bush has developed strong branches the previous year,

about half of these should be removed. But if growth has been weak (i.e. since the last pruning the new shoots have only grown a few inches) then do not prune at all.

When shaping the bush, and when pruning, see to it that fruit-bearing branches are distributed in all directions from the stem. Fruit-bearing branches, which have grown further up on the central stem, should be allowed to develop in a gap between those already there. After the second year's pruning, the bush should again have a pyramid shape. Attention must be paid to the following points: when cutting branches growing across others or those growing inwards, all the others should be left, even if, owing to the lack of space, they are not to be used for bearing fruit. If not already growing horizontally, they should be tied with twine into a horizontal position. Under no circumstances—as opposed to fruit-bearing branches and the main stem—should these be shortened, since every pruning encourages growth. New shoots are only wanted on the fruit-bearing branches and the main stem. The other branches will soon become fruitful if left alone. On trees it will soon be noticed that the more horizontal a branch grows, the weaker it is, but the more it is inclined to blossom.

The following points apply to the pruning of fruit trees, as well as fruit bushes:

1 All branches needed for forming the shape of the tree (for the bush, the central stem and fruit-bearing branches) should be pruned annually. This results in the required strong growth of shoots and fruit bearing branches.

2 The upward growing branches and those crossing each other, and those growing too densely, should be removed.

3 All other branches should be left unpruned, but trained horizontally if necessary.

Proceed as follows: first remove the branches not required, then train those not needed for the formation of the top of the tree into a horizontal position, and lastly cut back the main stem and the fruit bearing branches as far as outward growing buds. The final shape of the fruit bush should be a pyramid. This is for practical reasons, not beauty: the branches growing higher up the main stem, will grow more strongly than those below. They must be kept shorter to prevent the lower fruit bearing branches becoming stunted.

The work described above can be done partly in summer. During the summer pruning in June or July the crossing branches and those not required for the crown should be removed. Also the horizontal training of branches not needed for forming the crown is easy now, when the young branches are still pliable. When trained into a horizontal position, growth ceases, and they become fruit-bearing. They will go on hardening until the autumn and will remain in a horizontal position.

If this summer work is done regularly every year, there will be hardly any pruning left to do in the winter; only the pruning of the main stem and fruit-bearing branches need be done in winter or early spring. As soon as a fruit bush has attained its final shape and size, only light pruning is necessary to keep it in shape.

133

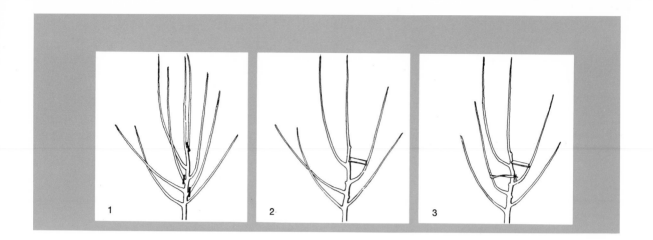

Annual pruning, combined with manuring and general plant care, should keep a tree healthy. The leader and fruit-bearing branches should be shortened every year or cut back to the young shoots.

Having provided as much fruit-bearing wood as possible by training some branches horizontally during the early years, some of the older, fruit-bearing wood must now be removed, to encourage new growth. To do this, remove the older, hanging branches or cut back to young shoots, growing from top side of the branch. As soon as this branch becomes fruitful, it will be weighed down by the fruit.

The pruning of the Semi-standard or Standard Tree The pruning of fruit bushes should really follow now, but since standard trees are grown much more often than the bushes, it is easier to deal with these first.

Unlike bushes, standards and semi-standards have, apart from the main trunk, only three main branches from which the fruit-bearing branches can later grow. Fruit-wood should grow well on all these strong branches and these should be given plenty of light. This applies to all varieties of fruits grown as standards.

Pruning Choose three strong branches from the crown, growing out of the trunk in good, well spaced positions. These three branches—later to be the main branches—should not come from the same point at the stem, but should be spaced over an extent of 60 cm/2 ft. This provides a good, sound basic structure for the head.

Should there not be three ideal main branches, then three of the most suitable should be chosen on a temporary basis, replacing them in following years with branches in better positions that will have developed by then. The angle of the three branches of the stem should be fairly small. Once they have grown away from the stem, they can develop at an angle of 45°. Branches growing at a steep angle to the stem, should not be used as main branches, since there is some danger of their splitting later.

All strong upright growing branches should be cut out of the crown, especially those crossing each other. Should one of the future main branches be too upright, then it should be trained to a lower angle; if the opposite applies, train to a higher angle.

Finally all branches forming the crown should be cut back. Start with the weakest shoots, after which the rest should be pruned accordingly. The weaker the branch, the more severely it should be pruned. In general, branches of the smaller stone-fruits should be cut back by two thirds; those of the larger stone-fruits even more severely. Only then will all the buds blossom and the main branches grow fruit-wood. Apart from that, a severe pruning encourages healthy, sturdy growth in future main branches. The more severe the pruning, the stronger the growth.

During planting a tree loses many of its roots. Those remaining are unable to provide enough water and nutrients for the crown, so by pruning one can restore the equilibrium between roots and upper growth.

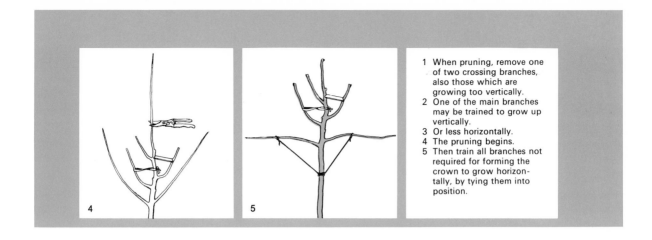

Pruning of the three lateral branches should be carried out so that one outward growing bud is left. All these branches should be the same length after pruning. Only if one of the branches is extremely strong, should it be cut back more severely. The leader should be about 15 cm/6 in. higher than the three lateral branches. The leader should be cut back to just above a bud which looks as if it will produce a fairly straight branch. Usually this bud will be found just above last year's cut. If you are exposed to a strong prevailing wind, the leader should be cut just above a bud which points away from the direction of the wind. Should the leader in a young tree be very weak, it should be cut back very short, so that the next branch can be tied to it with twine. As soon as this branch has assumed the position of the leader, the old leader should be cut away completely.

Apart from the three future main branches, a few weaker branches may be left in the crown. They should be trained horizontally and not pruned. They cannot then hinder the main branches by crossing them. They will develop in the spring into fruit-wood and, through their leaves, provide the young tree with additional nourishment.

In the spring of the second year, prune again to continue shaping the tree. Remove all props, stakes or strings used in training the tree during the previous year, so that this need not be done in the summer. After this choose three main branches.

If this was not possible when pruning in the previous year, make corrections now. Branches crossing each other, or those growing too close together, or growing upwards from the main branches, should be removed to their point of growth, to gain the required shape. All other new branches should be trained horizontally, unless already growing sideways.

Finally the leader and lateral branches should be pruned. The severity of pruning will depend on the growth of the tree. There is no need to prune strong-growing new branches now as severely as was done straight after planting. If, after the first pruning the tree did not grow healthily, producing only weak shoots, then it is better not to prune at all. In this case, the branches will grow from the healthy buds at the end of the shoots. To judge how severely to prune, the following should be borne in mind: the object of pruning the leader and lateral branches is to make new branches grow from all the buds left on the pruned branch. Supposing that a main branch is cut back insufficiently, then the buds towards the top will develop satisfactorily, but not those in the lower third of the tree. Consequently, the main branch will not develop sufficient fruit-wood and will remain weak and almost bare. If, however, pruning is too severe, all the buds will develop into branches, but more sturdily than required, so hardly any fruit-wood will grow; but instead, a great number of strong branches that will have to be removed because of their all too thick growth. Therefore, when pruning it is important to judge the growth of a tree correctly. The pruning of the leader and lateral branches should be severe enough for all buds to develop. There should, however, be only a few strong branches, with numerous weaker ones

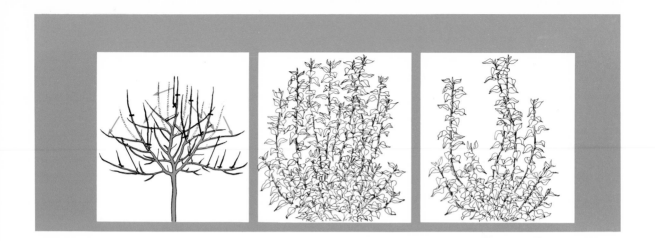

suitable for fruit-wood. This rule applies to fruit trees in general.

In the third and subsequent years, prune along the same lines. On the other hand, the growth of fruit-bearing branches, is a new development. Fruit branches should grow from the main branches, about 60–75 cm/2–2½ ft away from the trunk. They should of course be smaller than the main branches. After a further 60–75 cm/2–2½ ft another set of fruit-bearing branches could start growing; they should grow alternately along the branch.

There should also be a few fruit branches along the leader. They should be encouraged so as to fill a gap, and should not overshadow the existing branches.

To sum up, the most important points regarding pruning in the first years after planting are:

1 Bear in mind when new pruning is undertaken, the effects of any previous pruning. If the leader and main branches are bare underneath, then pruning must be more severe. Should however, strong offshoots be growing from all buds, pruning should be less severe.

2 Remove all props, and twine used during the previous pruning.

3 Remove all branches not required (crossing branches, branches growing on the upper side of the main branches and those which grow inwards towards the crown).

4 Choose fruit branches in the best positions.

5 Train all other branches horizontally, unless they are to become fruit-bearing branches or main branches. If they are already growing horizontally, then nothing further need be done.

6 Prune the leader and main branches.

The crown of a fully developed standard or semi-standard tree consists of:

1 Trunk or leader.

2 Three well distributed main branches. With the less sturdy stone fruits such as damsons, plums or sour cherries, there could be four branches.

3 Several well distributed fruit branches along the leader and main branches.

4 Fruit-wood, which is spread uniformly all over the crown. This should preferably grow horizontally, have sufficient light and always be developing new branches.

In the first years when a tree is becoming established, pruning should be done during the summer. All parts not required for the formation of the crown (e.g. crossing branches), should be pruned in June. The rest should be trained horizontally unless required for the crown. In this way all the nutrients taken in by the roots or absorbed by the leaves benefit all the branches in the crown. In winter or early spring, after summer pruning, only the leader and main branches need be cut back.

The advantages of this summer treatment are:

1 Growth of crown is accelerated.

2 Very little pruning need be done in the winter. Prune those branches growing too close together or tie branches into a horizontal position.

3 Scars heal more quickly, since the tree is still growing.

Extreme left: this standard was grown from three main branches out of which a well distributed series of fruit-branches and fruit-wood have grown. When pruning in winter, shorten only the leader and lateral branches. Branches that cross each other, shoots growing out of the top of a branch or those growing into the crown should be completely removed.

Centre and right: A young tree before and after summer pruning.

As soon as the crown is fully developed—after about six years—only slight pruning will be necessary to keep the tree in shape. It is important, as with the fruit bush, to make sure there is new fruit wood each year. In the following years, the crown should be kept clear and uncluttered. Therefore, any hanging fruit-bearing branches that are more than three years old should be removed or tied at a slight angle, to upwards growing branches. Superfluous young branches should be removed from the crown and the rest left as fruit-wood or to develop into fruit-wood.

One often sees in gardens, older pear, apple or plum trees that have been left for years. The crowns are too full and there is no fruit-wood at all in the interior of the crown. Instead, shoots have begun to grow at the ends of the sturdier branches, with the result that the dense foliage prevents light penetrating to the centre of the crown. In such cases, first cut all closely growing branches right back to their source, then remove the strong woody branches growing from the upper sides of branches. The best tool for this work is the multi-purpose tree saw. All cuts more than 25 mm/1 in. across should be treated with a proprietary wound healer.

The dense confused mass of branches towards the outer part of the crown, which has been neglected for years, should be cut with secateurs. Old, gnarled branches should be cut back to the younger branches that have grown from them. Crowns that have become too high should be tied down on to lower branches to make harvesting and pruning simpler. At the end of this thinning pro-cess the crown should have a truncated, pyramid shape.

SPECIAL HINTS ON PRUNING SPECIFIC FRUIT TREES

When pruning pears at planting, the leader should deliberately be kept short, and should be only a little taller than the main branches. This applies to the initial pruning, since pear trees grow strongly straight upwards in their centre. This can be prevented by careful pruning.

Sweet cherries grow strongly: it is therefore advisable to keep a greater distance than usual between the main branches. Once the crown is well developed, it should only need tidying up. The removal of old fruit-wood need not be done. A major pruning operation like the removal of the larger branches or the old wood in the crown should be carried out straight after harvesting the fruit. When removing the older branches, make sure that the larger branches are cut off near to younger shoots.

Plums and other stone fruits should be severly pruned after planting. Stone fruits are very sensi-tive to the sun on their main branches. For that reason the leader, the main and fruit branches should be well covered with fruit-wood. With these trees, more fruit-wood is left growing on the tree than on apple or pear trees. But the crown should be trained as described above. Instead of three main branches, four should be left.

Pruning Bush-trees As mentioned before, not

only sour cherries and peaches come as bush-trees. But whereas with apple and pear bushes, all pruning can be done as for the standards, sour cherries and peaches must be treated differently.

Sour cherries are mainly planted as one-year-old grafted plants, with a trunk about 40 cm/16 in. high. The so-called early branches are those that in summer grow only from one year old branches (i.e. those grown in the same year). It is advisable to cut the lower branches after planting so as to keep a stem height of about 60 cm/2 ft. This facilitates the later working of the soil beneath the plant. On this stem of 60 cm/2 ft three to four early branches should be left, and they should be shortened to about 2 or 3 eyes. These too, should be severely pruned.

The stem should be cut back to about 15 cm/6 in., just above a strong bud. If there is no bud—only early branches—after the stem has been cut, the central stem should be cut back to an early branch and this branch shortened to its lowest bud.

After this severe pruning, the tree should grow strongly. The following spring, three of the best positioned branches should be selected, and these should be cut back to one third of their length. Further development is as for a standard tree.

The Morello cherry only bears fruit on one-year-old branches. If the treatment of fruit-wood is neglected, then the branches will grow very little. On this short new growth, blossom and fruit will appear in the following year and the rest of the branch will be bare.

Older Morellos that have not been carefully treated look like weeping willows. The fruit on the short, weak growths will become noticeably smaller.

To prevent this, after harvesting the fruit, cut fruit-bearing branches right back to the young branches that have grown near to strong crown parts such as the stem or main branches. These young branches should not be shortened, since they yield most blossom and fruit on the upper third of the branch. This continual fruit-wood renewal after harvest will keep a Morello cherry vigorous and healthy. Numerous new branches will grow every year; and the fruits will be considerably bigger than on untreated trees.

Old Morello cherries that resemble weeping willows should have the trailing branches removed and the remaining branches in the crown shortened by about one third. Next, remove most of the long whip-like branches. As far as possible, bare branches should be cut back to young branches that have grown from the lower third. A Morello cherry will look very bare after this rigorous treatment, but the result will be strong growth from its trunk and all its branches. The peach is planted mainly as a one-year-old grafted plant. Pruning after planting should be carried out as with the sour cherry. Instead of a pyramid-shaped crown with leader, main and fruit branches, fan shaped crowns can be formed. When pruning the following year to obtain the shape, leave three well spaced main branches and cut out the leader. The further formation of main and fruit branches is as for ordinary fruit tree crowns.

The peach tends naturally to grow strongly upwards so that the lower parts of the crown tend

From left to right: Sour cherry and peach trees should be pruned severely. The fruit-bearing branches of the Morello cherry should be cut back to new shoots after the fruit has been gathered.

This is how to restore an old Morello cherry tree that looks like a weeping willow.

Peaches: on true fruit-bearing branches there should be one leaf bud between two rounded fruit buds.
False fruit-bearing branches will have only fruit buds (centre right) and non-fruit bearing-branches will have only leaf buds (bottom right).

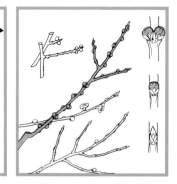

to become bare unless the tree is constantly severely pruned. Like the Morello cherry, the peach yields fruit on wood of the previous season's growth. This is why, by correct pruning, new shoots must be encouraged to grow annually. The most beautiful fruit is grown on the so-called 'true' fruit branches. These are about as thick as a pencil, and 60 cm/2 ft or more in length. Mostly, the three buds will grow side by side; between two round blossom buds will be one pointed 'leaf' bud. These 'real' fruit branches should be shortened to half their length. This produces outstanding fruit and in addition strong new shoots are 'true' fruit branches in the following year.

'False' fruit branches, which are considerably weaker, shorter and bear almost exclusively blossom buds, should be cut hard back, to one or two buds. These branches will hardly ever yield any fruit. However, the severe pruning will provide for growth of new branches. Branches covered with nothing but long pointed wood buds should be shortened if they are needed as extentions of main or minor branches. If not required, they should be completely removed. A peach tree carries very short 'bouquet' branches, that will be covered with many blossoms. These should not be cut off.

It is advisable to carry out a summer pruning on peach trees. At the beginning of June, all crossing branches, those growing too closely together, or others growing inwards, should be cut away.

The pruning of these branches and 'true' and 'false' fruit branches can be carried out during or after blossoming. The latter is generally preferred, especially in colder areas where peach blossom can

be touched by frost. Once the blossom or young fruit has been affected by frost, not only the 'false' but also 'true' fruit branches should be cut hard back. Since it would not in any case be possible to harvest any fruit, in such a year, healthy, strong new shoots can be encouraged to grow by pruning the tree very vigorously, to encourage the growth of numerous 'true' fruit branches in the following year. Peaches can be damaged in a very severe winter. If the crown is injured in this way, all dead parts should be cut back to lower, healthy, young branches, from which a new young crown can develop.

If a peach bush is bare low down, pruning should be carried out preferably in summer, after the fruit has been gathered, to encourage new growth. The main branches, and fruit branches, growing from them, should be cut back severely, removing the old wood. Care should be taken to cut back at points where young branches are growing that will simply become extensions of the newly shortened branches. It is specially important to treat all larger cuts on a peach tree with a proprietary wound-healer.

IMPORTANT POINTS ON PLANT CARE

Fruit bushes with shallow roots are usually only successful if planted in open ground. It has proved a good idea to mulch the ground under bushes during the summer; grass mowings, leaf-mould or other green matter should be spread to a depth of about 15 cm/6 in. to shade the soil and keep it damp.

From January onwards tree trunks can be protected from snow damage by placing planks around them.

Trees that are unsatisfactory either in yield or quality can have a new crown grafted on to them. This is only sensible if the tree concerned is still relatively young and vigorous. Otherwise it is better to pull it out by the roots and plant a completely new tree.

In the winter before grafting, the whole crown should be severely cut back into the old wood. The stronger branches should be only about 90–120 cm/3–4 ft long; the crown should look like a roof (at an angle of 100°–120°). The branches should not be thicker than 10 cm/4 in. where they are cut; their grafts otherwise would take too long to heal. Some of the weaker, hanging branches should be left untreated. As soon as the bark can be loosened easily, in May, grafting can be carried out. Shortly before that the shoots to be grafted should be cut back to 15–25 cm/6–10 in. in length.

The scion should be cut back to between three and five buds just before grafting, and an incision made in it. The bark of the stock should also be cut into. The bark on either side of the incision is then lifted and the scion is pushed into place between the two parts. The join should then be bound with raffia and treated with wax. The top of the stock and the scion should also be treated with wax.

The pencil-thick, one-year-old scions, should be cut in January and February from a high yielding tree of the required variety and should be embedded in deep soil or damp sand at the north side of the house, or in a cool cellar. The care and treatment of the tree after grafting and during the following years is very important. The grafted trees should subsequently be pruned as described for fruit trees. Grafting, like pruning, can only be learnt through experience.

One of the most important factors of fruit cultivation is manuring. The regularity and amount of the yield depends on this. The application of organic matter to the soil is very important for the development of the fruit tree. For that reason compost, well rotted stable manure or leaf-mould should be added every year. In accordance with recent practice, artificial fertilizer should be applied in November or December, when the roots were still able to absorb nourishment. Some roots grow very deep into the ground, so it is a good idea to leave nutrients already in the soil by winter, so that they can be washed down through the soil to the deeper roots by winter rain.

As a general rule, spread about one third of the total amount of required fertilizer in late autumn: about one handful of artificial fertilizer per m^2 square yard. At least 90 cm/1 yd beyond the spread of the tree should be covered in fertilizer, since the roots spread a fair distance. Where there is a row of fruit bushes, the entire area should be treated. Another handful of artificial fertilizer should be applied in the March of the following year, and possibly again in May or June; altogether two to three handfuls per m^2/sq yd in a year. It is worth pointing out that these recommendations, though only general, have been proven in practice. Precise knowledge concerning the nutrients needed for a given soil can only be obtained by soil analysis.

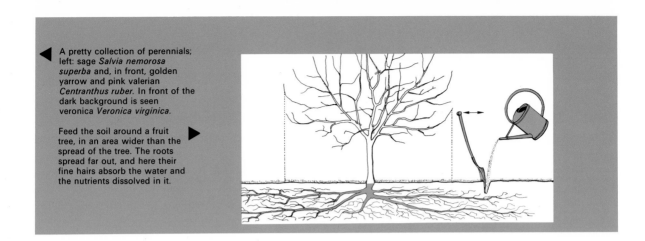

A pretty collection of perennials; left: sage *Salvia nemorosa superba* and, in front, golden yarrow and pink valerian *Centranthus ruber*. In front of the dark background is seen veronica *Veronica virginica*.

Feed the soil around a fruit tree, in an area wider than the spread of the tree. The roots spread far out, and here their fine hairs absorb the water and the nutrients dissolved in it.

Instead of adding some form of fertilizer in late autumn and spring, it is possible to use a liquid manure once a year only, in February or March. Dissolve 0·5 kilos/1 lb of an inorganic fertilizer in 10 litres/10 quarts of water in a watering can or bucket, and sprinkle 2 litres/12 quarts per square yard or square metre over the root areas. To make sure that the roots of bushes, standard and semi-standard trees absorb the fertilizers as quickly as possible, drive a spade into the soil two or three times per square yard or square metre, moving the spade to and fro to form a wedge-shaped crack into which the fertilizer can be poured. On a lawn the spade need only be driven into the earth and moved to one side, the solution being poured into the exposed soil. Thus, the liquid fertilizer is immediately taken to the roots. This method is not advisable with shallow rooted fruit bushes since this could have an adverse effect on the plants—it can cause damage to roots. The fertilizer should be spread evenly in the ground. If these simple rules are followed, the fruit trees will yield fruit and also form shoots and fruit buds for the following year, while developing strong, healthy new branches.

HARVESTING AND STORING

If you want to enjoy the fruits of your labours at their best, it is important to harvest at the right time. The colour, quality and ability to last in storage are all greatly influenced by this.

Early varieties of apples and pears are gathered when fully ripe. Since the fruits do not all ripen simultaneously they must be picked when individually ripe—i.e. at different times from the same tree. If left on the tree too long, apples will become floury, pears overripe. Autumn varieties should be left on the tree until completely ripe (e.g. 'James Grieve' or 'Worcester Pearmain'). The colour must be well defined and the fruit easily loosened from the branch when twisted slightly. Later varieties of apple such as 'Cox's Orange Pippin', 'Laxton's Superb', 'Granny Smiths', 'Winesaps' and 'Northern Spys' should be picked shortly before they are fully ripe, as this will improve their keeping ability when stored. This should be done in late autumn. Late pear varieties such as 'Winter Nelis' and other pears that can be stored, should be gathered when not quite ripe from November to January. If harvested too soon there is a danger of their not developing their true flavours—they can even taste like carrots. A slight frost during the night will not damage these fruits at all, as long as they are not touched straight after a cold night.

Quinces should not be left to ripen on the bush. They should be picked at the time of the first frosts and left to ripen indoors. However, they should not be left too long before eating or using. To know whether stone fruits are ready for gathering, they must be hand tried. Or if some fruits begin to fall, this is a sign that they are ready for picking. Damsons can be harvested by shaking the tree, whereas plums and gages would bruise easily using this method, so should be picked by hand. Later varieties of plums should be left on the tree for as long as possible, and only when the A slight night frost will not harm the fruit.

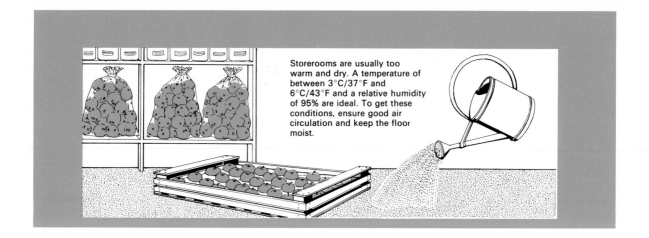

Storerooms are usually too warm and dry. A temperature of between 3°C/37°F and 6°C/43°F and a relative humidity of 95% are ideal. To get these conditions, ensure good air circulation and keep the floor moist.

All varieties of fruit should be gathered as carefully as possible. Place apples and pears that bruise easily in plastic buckets or baskets lined with some cushioning material. Apples and pears that bruise less easily can be gathered into larger, lined wicker baskets or fruit boxes. Cherries and plums should go into larger plywood baskets. Ripe apples, pears and peaches should be grasped with the whole hand. By twisting and lifting slightly the fruit may easily be loosened from the branch. Sweet cherries should be harvested with their stalks attached; they should be nipped from the branch or twisted off with the fingernails. Particularly juicy varieties should be cut off with scissors. Varieties of sour cherries that are fairly difficult to loosen should also be gathered with scissors. For domestic consumption, most sour cherries may be picked without their stalks. Walnuts must be harvested when fully ripe. This usually occurs in September or the beginning of October. Under no circumstances should they be knocked down with a stick.

Whereas berry fruits and cherries may be stored in the deep freeze, late fruits often present storage problems. If no special storage room is available for the fruit, other satisfactory means must be found. In rooms which are too dry and warm, the fruit will soon start to shrivel, especially the coarse skinned varieties. It is best to store fruit in the cellar or in some similar cool room. The most favourable temperature is between 3°C/37°F and 6°C/43°F, and should not be higher than 8°C/48°F under any circumstances. The relative humidity should be 80 per cent–90 per cent,

ideally 95 per cent. If the cellar is too dry, then water should be sprinkled on to the floor.

Before storing, the cellar should be well cleaned and if possible it is a good idea to whitewash the walls. A disinfectant can be added to the whitewash. The storage racks should be cleaned with disinfectant.

Apples and pears are best stored in proper fruit trays, normally available from any greengrocers. They should be piled up so as to make the best use of the space available. In such shallow trays the fruit can be easily inspected. Only healthy fruit should be stored, and the storeroom should be checked regularly each week. Any rotting fruit must immediately be thrown out.

If one is obliged to store later varieties of fruit for long periods in a room that is too dry or warm, damp leaf-mould can be used. Wrap each fruit in tissue paper and place on 5 cm/2 in. of leaf-mould in the bottom of the tray; then add alternate layers of fruit and leaf-mould, using only the very best apples and pears.

To extend the storage period, it is possible to put a layer of foil in the bottom of the tray, then when it is filled with fruit, the ends of the foil are wrapped around the fruit. This reduces the amount of evaporation.

The storage time may also be extended by using plastic bags. This is only advisable for medium sized, completely healthy fruits. After filling the bags with fruit, leave them open for two to three days to ensure that the temperature inside and outside the bags is identical. Only then can the bags be closed.

6 Soft Fruits

SOFT FRUITS IN THE GARDEN

A garden without soft fruits is almost unthinkable. However limited in extent, try to make room for some currant bushes and strawberries.

It is not surprising that soft fruits are so popular. For one thing, these versatile plants can adapt themselves to most situations; for another, they can usually be relied on to yield a good harvest. Even if other fruit blossoms are caught by frost, soft fruits manage to come through unscathed. They are adaptable both to soil and climate, and it saves money to grow one's own, as these fruits have become very expensive in the shops. And what pleasure it is to gather them fully ripe, for immediate eating.

It is most important to buy plants only from recognised nurseries where the fruit is grown under strictly controlled conditions. Years of experience have proved beyond doubt that, next to the variety, the origin and health of the plants when bought determine future yields.

As for choosing varieties, go for those with most flavour. After all, you don't have to worry too much about how they will travel, how they will store or how long their shelf-life is as commercial growers do—and these factors are often inconsistent with the best flavour.

STRAWBERRIES

These are probably the most popular of all soft fruits, and can be grown in even the smallest gardens.

Culture If there is already one of the newer, heavy-cropping varieties in the garden, check individual plants at the beginning of harvesting and note the healthiest and most prolific. Your choice can hardly be too strict.

After harvesting, inferior plants should be uprooted and discarded. Put down peat between the healthy plants, which will have the effect of loosening the surface soil. In dry weather, the plants should be watered. This will give the runners a loose, damp soil in which they can quickly root. These are usually ready for planting out towards the end of July to mid-August.

Runners can also be pegged down into little clay or peat pots sunk into the soil. After new roots have been made, the daughter plants can be severed and planted elsewhere. There are several good methods—each gardener can choose the one he finds simplest and best.

The bed to receive the new plants should be dug over with a fork, at the same time introducing compost or rotted stable manure into the upper layer. Damp peat can also be mixed with the soil if you don't have any compost. To complete the nutritional requirements of a new strawberry bed, one and a half handfuls per square metre/square yard of a chloride-free mixed fertilizer should be dug in. Under no circumstances should fertilizer be put in the actual drills.

With most varieties, it is usual to plant three rows in a bed 120 cm/4 ft wide. If the bed is to be retained, the middle row can be removed after the first harvest to allow the remaining plants sufficient room to spread. A distance of 30 cm/12 in. should

Detaching the runners

Strawberry propagation

Pricking-out under plastic

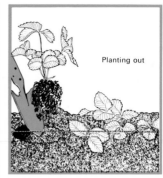

Planting out

be kept between rows. A few days beforehand, the parent plant with the rooted runners should be well watered. The young plants should be lifted out with a trowel without disturbing the fibrous roots, then immediately planted in a freshly-prepared bed where they can grow without further interference.

Every plant should be given a thorough watering, using the watering-can without the rose, and this should be repeated as necessary during the next weeks. Planting should be done from the end of July to mid-August. By late autumn the young plants will have developed so vigorously they can be used for a two-year culture.

It is a mistake to apply too much fertilizer. Some gardeners use extra quantities and are very proud of the well-developed strawberry plants that result —but in fact these never bear extra quantities of fruit. On the contrary the harvest in such cases is very poor because the foliage grows too well, and the fruits are prone to mildew.

In the following spring the newly-planted bed will need hardly any manure, unless the plants have suffered in a hard winter and show only poor growth. In this case, scatter half a handful of mixed fertilizer per square metre/square yard in March.

At the June harvesting, follow the procedure already described: selection; get rid of poor croppers; improve soil between remaining parent plants; between the end of July and mid-August put the rooted young plants into a new bed. In this way fresh beds are made yearly, resulting in larger fruit that also ripens a little earlier. However, the main advantage is that the plants, since they have

not developed excessive foliage, dry quickly after rain, so avoiding the danger of mildew. This disease can be combatted by spraying, but you want to avoid doing this if you can. For this reason the one-year system of cultivation is generally best.

If, however, you want to keep a bed for a second year, the runners must be severed immediately after the harvest and the middle row of plants removed, so that the remaining ones have sufficient room. If the leaves become affected by leaf spot disease, cut off the foliage. The surface soil between the strawberries must be loosened and any weeds pulled out, then $1\frac{1}{2}$–2 handfuls of a chloride-free mixed fertilizer per square metre/square yard lightly dug in. Compost should, of course, also be dug in, and the bed watered frequently in dry weather. Everything will then have been done to prepare the bed for next year's harvest.

Under no circumstances should a bed be kept longer than four years; and the propagation of strawberry plants should not be continued after the third or fourth year. Then new plants should be bought; the modern varieties not only bear prolifically but also deteriorate quickly.

Plants ordered from a nursery often do not arrive until late August or even September, and if they are planted so late the following year's harvest will be poor. Therefore one should not plant harvest beds with plants delivered late, but carry on the old strawberry culture for cropping, while the new plants are establishing themselves in an other bed. In this way one need order only a fifth of the plants needed for the harvest bed.

The yield next year will be limited, but the

To keep the fruit from rotting, surround the plants with straw or plastic wool before the harvest. Runners will root well if peat is applied to the bed.

Top U.K. strawberry varieties:
'Royal Sovereign' is still prime favourite in the amateur's garden. Heavy cropper, and still the finest flavoured. Mid-season 'Cambridge Vigour' and 'Cambridge Rival' ripen early and are delicate in flavour. 'Huxley Grant' and 'Hummi Grundi' are late varieties from the Continent with a rich, aromatic flavour.
Top U.S. strawberry varieties:
'Bean' and 'Streamliner', both everbearing. 'Vesper', late bearing.

runners will grow much earlier. You can expect five, well rooted young plants per parent plant, and these can be planted as described above, from the end of July to mid-August. In this way the planting can be renewed every three or four years with relatively little expense, and at the same time the quality of the fruits kept at a high level.

A few more tips: in order to protect the ripening fruit from decay, wood shavings can be put underneath the plant. Better—unfortunately more expensive—are polystyrene shavings, since this material dries out more quickly after rain. Another efficient method is to put rings of cardboard or polystyrene round the plants. Low wires stretched alongside the rows, on which the ripening stems of fruit can be laid, are also practical. The fruit can dry quickly after rain and hardly ever gets dirty. Nylon nets make the best protection against the increasing number of blackbirds and starlings.

One occasionally sees strawberry beds covered with black plastic sheeting. If you wish to keep the plants in the bed for two or three years, this method has certain advantages: no weed trouble, protection from evaporation, no mud splashes on the fruit, higher yield and earlier harvest. The disadvantages are higher cost, increased labour in preparation, and no rooted young plants. The fact that one cannot obtain new rooted plants every year is a specially big disadvantage.

To make a good-sized fruit, strawberries need plenty of water during harvest-time. Watering should not, however, be left until the late evening, as this might encourage mildew—damp leaves should be able to dry quickly.

Perpetual strawberries are well worth a try. These strawberries fruit from July to October. The flavour is delicious, and the berries are equally suited for eating fresh or cooking.

It is quite simple to raise one's own plants from seed. Seeds should be sown in pots or trays from April onwards. The seeds should be lightly covered with sieved soil, then put in the shade and kept permanently moist. The seedlings must not dry out.

As soon as the seedlings have formed their first true leaves they should be pricked out 5 cm/2 in. apart. When the plants are sufficiently strong they can be planted out, either in a bed or as edgings along a path.

CURRANTS

Only strong, healthy specimens from a reliable nursery should be planted, preferably in late autumn. The same is true of all bush fruits. Planting can of course take place in spring, but should not be left too late because the bushes start sprouting very early. Bush fruits are generally planted in rows.

Black currants 180 cm/6 ft apart.
Red currants—vigorous varieties 150 cm/5 ft apart.
Smaller varieties 120 cm/4 ft apart.
White currants 120 cm/4 ft apart.

It is possible to grow your own plants from cuttings, but this should only be done when the parent plant is known to be a heavy cropper of a good variety. With cuttings, you know from the start what can be expected, because the outstanding characteristics of yield and quality are transmitted unchanged by vegetative propagation.

Having selected a high quality bush as parent plant, take from it at the beginning of October several straight and well-ripened one-year shoots, cutting them to a length of about 20 cm/8 in. The base of each cutting should always be severed just below the bud. The cuttings are then put into a slanting trench, deep enough for only one or two buds to be visible.

The next autumn the rooted cuttings are dug up and their roots and new shoots cut back. The one-year-old shoots should be shortened by about two-thirds of their previous length. The rooted cuttings are then transplanted to 45 cm/18 in. apart, and by the following autumn they will have developed sufficiently to be planted in their permanent positions.

The soil preparation for bush fruits has already been discussed. Four handfuls of potassium nitrate mixed with a similar amount of phosphate per bush, are added to the soil, care being taken that this fertilizer does not come into direct contact with the roots of the newly-planted bush.

Black currant bushes are planted a hand's breadth deeper than they were growing in the nursery. This encourages the development of young shoots. The black currant should be allowed to branch out freely from the base, producing vigorous new growth every year.

The advice given on the planting of fruit trees, ornamental shrubs, roses and perennials also applies here. Should you be unable to plant the

bushes until a few days after their arrival, they should be kept side by side in a shallow trench, the roots being covered with earth or damp peat.

After planting, prune the bushes. Not more than five sturdy, evenly-distributed shoots should be left. The branches should be cut back by two-thirds. As with fruit tree pruning, the more severly you cut back, the more vigorous the growth will be. Early pruning is carried out in the same way for both red and black currants, but there are differences in the pruning of established bushes.

Firstly, the pruning of red currants. One year after planting, all shoots too closely crowded together must be removed. The remaining shoots are cut back by about a third of their length to make sure they will branch out well. This structuring is all the bush requires, because there is no need for more than eight strong, evenly-distributed and well-branched leaders. Those eight leaders need all the available space to themselves.

Any further pruning is limited to an annual thinning-out. It is no longer necessary to cut back the well-branched leaders of vigorously growing varieties. However, the more demanding small-growing types such as 'Red Lake' will continue to need pruning in subsequent years; the leaders will have to be cut back to a third or a half of their length each year. This is the only way to achieve strong leaders with plenty of lateral growth. Without pruning, however, the branches of weak-growing varieties tend to spread and rest partially on the ground.

Whether the bush is of feeble or vigorous growth, the branches of red currants should not be

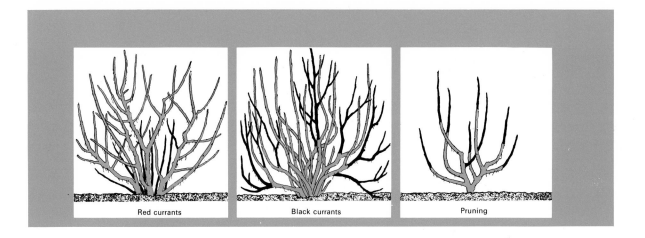

Red currants   Black currants   Pruning

allowed to remain on the plant more than four or five years. As required, cut out one or two of the older branches every year—they can be recognised by the darker wood—and leave the same number of strong shoots that have grown up from the ground. All other offshoots, however, must be cut out. This ensures that the bush remains light and open.

Quite often one sees currant bushes with thirty, forty, or even more thin, spindly-looking branches. The fruit is always small and sour, and harvesting is no pleasure. Instead, open out the bushes with some vigorous pruning. With neglected bushes that have been allowed to grow far too dense, the most important thing is to remove the thin, aged and prostrate branches. The remaining branches then have enough space, and with a good supply of humus and fertilizer the bushes should soon become rejuvenated.

Although currant bushes will grow in semi-shade, it is better to plant them in full sun if possible, because vitamin and sugar content become poorer in shaded areas.

In the case of all bush fruits, the work of pruning can and indeed should be done directly after harvesting. If all older and useless branches are removed in the summer, the growth of the remaining branches is greatly encouraged and the leaves are better supplied with light. Pruning can, if necessary, also be done in autumn or winter, but as bush fruits make new growth very early in spring, pruning must be finished by that time.

Black currants bear their best crops on one-year-old branches; in other words, on strong young wood developed in the previous year. Pruning is, therefore, different from that of red currants. Immediately after harvesting cut back all branches that have borne fruit, leaving only the new ones. If the offshoots growing out of the rootstock have enough space and are not too weak, they can be left as well. This method ensures that the bushes consist of hardly anything else but young branches, which, after the summer pruning, will continue developing into the autumn, and be capable of bearing a good crop in the following year.

Obviously this means that black currant bushes have far more than eight branches, but since they are only one year old they will make little lateral growth and so have plenty of room. If branches occasionally happen to be too close together, they should be cut off close to the ground.

It is helpful to be able to harvest and prune at the same time; the fruit-bearing branches are cut, leaving the young ones. The fruit can then be plucked at one's ease.

It would be wrong to cut back the vigorous young branches left on the bush. This would reduce the harvest because the top third of one-year-old branches bears the most fruit. Only a few young branches, well distributed through the entire bush, should be cut back by one-third in order to promote new growth.

Soil preparation is of the utmost importance for all bush fruit. Above, all, perennial weeds such as bindweed, couch grass, and so on must be eradicated. Once these have taken hold, it is almost impossible to disentangle them completely from the roots of a fruit bush.

Bush fruits have shallow feeding roots, going only to a depth of 15–21 cm/6–8 in., so shallow soil cultivation is all that is needed. It is not advisable, under any circumstances, to dig between the bushes during autumn; in so doing quantities of root fibres, essential for the absorption of water and nutrients, would be cut off. Nor is it advisable to plant fruit bushes in grass: they will remain puny-looking specimens.

Feeding the soil is very important. Humus in the form of compost, rotted stable manure or peat should be spread lavishly and worked in just below the surface. In addition, at the end of February/beginning of March apply a chloride-free mixed fertilizer, two handfuls per m²/sq yd. Should the soil lack potash and phosphorus (which can be ascertained by a soil analysis), add this in the form of potassium nitrate in the autumn.

Gooseberries Planting, soil preparation and feeding should be carried out as for currants. The distance between bushes should be a good 3 m/4 ft, though 2·5 m/3½ ft is sufficient between standards. Again, pruning influences growth, yield and quality of fruit. The same rules apply here as for currants: branches that are too weak, awkwardly positioned or drooping to the ground should be removed, the rest shortened by more than half their length.

Next spring, all offshoots coming through the soil that are not required to fill out the bush should be removed. Any young branches that prevent light penetrating the bush should also be cut out. It is sufficient to have eight strong, well spread branches with vigorous side growths or spurs. The tops of these eight leaders are cut back by about a third.

After this pruning, numerous young shoots will grow in the following season out of these eight pruned leaders, and out of the soil. At the following winter pruning, the offshoots from the soil should be cut out, all except two to four of the strongest, which should be kept to fill up any gaps. These should be shortened by one-third, while the remaining branches can be left as they are, unless they show signs of mildew at the tips.

This pruning should be repeated every year in order to encourage the development of one-year-old branches, which produce the best harvest.

It is also possible to prune immediately after harvesting. After the prickly experiences of gathering the gooseberries one may feel all the more inclined to thin the bushes thoroughly!

Once the bushes are established, the rule in later years should be to retain the young branches—provided there is no overcrowding—and remove the older wood, recognisable by its darker colour.

In many gardens one sees neglected and decrepit bushes with a dense tangle of branches. These can be given a new lease of life. Directly after harvesting, which on account of tiny berries and scratched fingers is more of a nuisance than a pleasure, the bush must be thoroughly rejuvenated. No more than five well spread older branches should be left, and the rest cut off close to the ground.

Next spring, apply compost (or other organic material) and a mineral fertilizer, as with black currants.

Choose about eight of the strongest existing long shoots and shorten them in the winter by one third of their length. Further maintenance of the revitalised bush proceeds as already described.

A few remarks about standard gooseberries, which have rightly become very popular in many gardens. These are grown in nurseries by grafting gooseberry scions on to the 90 cm/3 ft stocks of yellow currant, which grows very upright. Standards do not have as long a life as bushes, but this form does have the advantage of being easier to harvest, since no stooping is necessary.

In the case of standards, it is important to support both the stem and the heavy branches, using a stake (treated with wood preservative) that reaches right up into the crown. Even better is a triangle of three stakes joined at the top with laths, on which the fruit-laden crown can rest. The stem need only be tied to one of the three stakes.

Pruning is similar to that for the bush. At the time of planting, the branches should be cut well back. In the following years the crown must be kept clear in order to allow the long young branches room to grow and bear a rich crop of delicious fruit. Overcrowded young branches must be thinned out in early summer, so that all remaining parts—and eventually the fruit—receive sufficient light.

RASPBERRIES

Raspberries do not keep well or travel well—a good reason for growing one's own. The fruit should be left until completely ripe before picking, so as to develop its flavour to the full.

One disadvantage of the raspberry bush is that innumerable side shoots will grow up where they aren't wanted. Often, however, two neighbours can agree to grow raspberries along the boundary between their gardens and then, however vigorously the bushes grow, there need be no 'border incidents'. If one neighbour will not agree to this, the other can build a wall of 5 cm/2 in. thick concrete, 45 cm/18 in. deep in the ground along the boundary, through which the shoots cannot penetrate.

Garden raspberries are usually planted in a row, with a distance of 60 cm/24 in. between each plant. Plant autumn or spring. Crucial for success is the variety and origin of the plant, so one must first of all be satisfied as to the quality and fruitfulness of the mother plant. Only really healthy raspberry canes should be bought, as they are prone to virus diseases, such as mosaic virus, which shows as yellowish-green mottling and crinkling of the leaves.

Propagation is simple: offshoots can be dug out and replanted elsewhere. The soil is prepared as for other soft fruits. In addition, raspberry canes need a simple support: wooden posts treated with preservative should be driven about 60 cm/2 ft into the ground at about 4·5 m/15 ft apart; they should stand about 120 cm/4 ft above ground. Two wires should be stretched tight between the posts, the bottom one at 75 cm/2½ ft above ground level and the second 30 cm/1 ft higher up. The canes can then be tied to these with raffia. Another method is to provide parallel wires between which the canes can grow, attaching the taut wires to two wooden

cross-pieces nailed to the posts at each end.

Directly after planting, cut back the canes to within 30 cm/1 ft of the ground. This will encourage the production of fruiting spurs lower down the canes, and prevent the plant exhausting its energy on overlong growths.

It also helps to cover the soil with compost, grass-cuttings or peat during the summer, thus providing similar conditions to those under which wild raspberries grow in the woods, and therefore encourage the varieties to thrive. This mulching is also very important as a preventive measure against disease. Besides copious applications of humus, give two handfuls of a chloride-free mixed fertilizer per m²/sq yd in spring.

Pruning is simple: immediately after harvest, remove all canes that have fruited and any that are weak, so that each plant consists of about six strong, evenly distributed young canes.

BLACKBERRIES

What keeps many gardeners from planting the raspberry is the fact that it spreads; with the blackberry it is the prickly confusion of its branches. Yet the blackberry, with its wonderful fragrance and flavour, is among the best of fruits.

Good varieties to choose from are the early fruiting 'Bedford Giant', mid-season 'Himalaya Giant' or later-fruiting 'John Innes'. All are self-fertile and heavy yielding. The distance between each plant should be 3·6–5 m/12–16 ft, and if more than one row is grown, allow 180–270 cm/6–8 ft between rows.

Here too, support is necessary. At 5 m/16 ft intervals wooden posts, treated with preservative should be driven into the ground, leaving 1·80 m/ 6 ft above for support (or iron pipes may be concreted in. The first wire should be stretched at 45 cm/1½ ft above the soil, and there should be five subsequent wires with 25 cm/10 in. between each.

When planting in spring, damaged roots should be pruned. Of the shoots, only one should be left, and this cut back to a stub of 10 cm/4 in. The lowest bud should be covered with soil when planting.

As the branches grow in the summer, they should be tied to the wires. Shoots formed in the axils between stem and side shoots should be pinched back to one leaf. In the first winter after planting, remove all but three of the strongest branches, which should be shortened by half. In the second year after planting there will be a great number of young shoots growing out of the root stock. The six strongest should be retained and tied to the wires left and right.

The most important cultural task is summer pruning. If this is omitted, the stems will grow into a tangle almost impossible to sort out. This pruning is simple: the so-called premature shoots that have sprouted out of the leaf axils of young stems are cut back to one leaf as soon as they have reached a length of about 45 cm/18 in. In autumn the young shoots are laid on the soil and covered.

Winter pruning should be done after the frosts have finished virtually in springtime. All canes

With espalier vines, the shoots of the previous year are cut back to two buds in spring. The cut should be made slightly above the bud, so that a short stub of stem remains. Summer treatment consists of pruning the tops of the longer young branches, and pinching back the precocious shoots formed in the axils—the angles between leaf and stem.

that fruited the previous year are removed. Of the young canes, only the six strongest are retained, and tied to the wires on either side. Very long canes can be trained to bend over in an arch.

While the tied canes are bearing fruit, new shoots are growing out of the rootstock. Of these, once again the six strongest should be chosen and tied to the wires that are still free.

A good method of training is in one year to tie the six new canes right and left of the plant centre to the first, third and fifth wires, and the young shoots that will make next year's growth to the second, fourth and sixth wires. The fruit-bearing branches thus occur on alternate wires in any year. The summer pruning of the young shoots must be seen to each year.

Leave harvesting until the fruit is black and fully ripe, otherwise the taste is sour and lacks the true aromatic flavour. Leave the harvested branches over the winter so as to give the young canes shelter; cut them in the following spring.

Give a top dressing of compost or peat in the spring, together with one to one-and-a-half handfuls of mixed fertilizer per square yard/square metre.

CRANBERRIES/BILBERRIES

Under whichever name, these have been a major commercial and home garden crop in the U.S.A. It is only very recently that they have been tried in the U.K., either as commercial crops or in home gardens.

The most important success factor is a very acid soil (pH-value 3·5–5). The peaty, humus-rich soil of heaths and moors are what they are used to. In all other types of soil it is necessary to dig out a trench measuring 90 cm/3 ft wide and 45 cm/18 in deep, and fill it with damp peat. It should be watered with soft water (i.e. rain water, not tap water, which contains a considerable amount of lime) and only a lime-free fertilizer used. In addition, a handful of chloride-free mixed fertilizer can be supplied in spring.

When planting, shorten the long shoots by one third of their length. Further pruning should be limited to thinning out the old wood. The berries ripen one after the other, and during the fruiting season the bushes should be protected with nylon nets from birds. Useful varieties for garden cultivation are 'Blue Ray' (early), 'Berkeley' (mid-season), and 'Colville' (late). At least two different varieties should be planted, to ensure pollination.

THE GRAPE VINE

In most gardens grape vines are of minor importance, and if planted at all they are grown more for ornament than for their fruit. Yet how delightful is is to gather one's own ripe grapes.

The right place for a vine is on the south or south-west side of a house, or spreading over an open arbour. Vines can thrive in quite inclement regions, so long as the plant is sheltered, and is roofed over with glass to make best use of the summer sunshine to enable the grapes to ripen in our climate. Watering will, of course, be necessary.

After planting, leave only one vigorous branch,

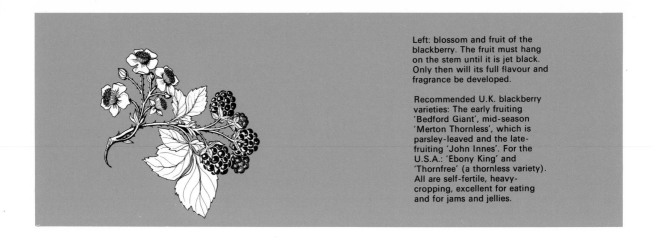

Left: blossom and fruit of the blackberry. The fruit must hang on the stem until it is jet black. Only then will its full flavour and fragrance be developed.

Recommended U.K. blackberry varieties: The early fruiting 'Bedford Giant', mid-season 'Merton Thornless', which is parsley-leaved and the late-fruiting 'John Innes'. For the U.S.A.: 'Ebony King' and 'Thornfree' (a thornless variety). All are self-fertile, heavy-cropping, excellent for eating and for jams and jellies.

and cut this back to two buds. During the summer two shoots should grow out of these buds, and the weaker of the two should be pruned at the tip after the growth of several leaves. This enables the stronger shoot to develop more vigorously.

The following spring, the weaker shoot should be removed altogether and the stronger cut back by half. When pruning the vine, as opposed to all other fruits, a little stub 2·5 cm/1 in. long is left above the bud. This prevents the sensitive bud from bleeding dry. The topmost bud of this shoot lengthens to form the leader, which is tied securely to the espalier to ensure an upright centre for the vine. The other buds will produce lateral shoots at intervals of about 15–18 cm/6–8 in.

If the vine has to cover a large area, lateral shoots can be allowed to grow out further at intervals and are tied to the espalier. The aim is to make these sideshoots develop into strong branches that will produce fruiting wood, as will the central branch. The extension shoots should be cut back every spring.

As in the case of fruit trees, with the vine a framework of stronger branches is created, from which grow numerous lateral shoots that will bear fruit. These side shoots, which occur at a distance of about 18 cm/8 in. from each other, should be tied to the espalier.

At the winter pruning, done when the worst of the cold weather is over, these lateral shoots should be cut back to two buds, again leaving a little stub above the end bud. Out of these buds will grow two young shoots, which will of course need treatment in summer. At the end of May, young shoots that are too close are taken out, especially those growing out of old wood. On any branch keep only the two strongest shoots, training the vine so as to produce a compact shape for flowering and fruiting.

When the vine is in flower—about June—the young shoots are tied to the trellis with raffia, so as to cover the wall evenly. The tips should be pruned from any shoots that are longer than 2·5 m/8½ ft. Premature shoots growing out of an axil are shortened back to one leaf. This work continues throughout the summer. In August the fruit-bearing branches should be cut back to about five leaves above the topmost bunch (see diagram).

At the subsequent winter pruning, of the two young shoots that have grown out of last year's stubs, the outer one with the old stub portion is cut off. The other is retained, and again cut back to two buds.

In late winter, give two handfuls of a chloride-free mixed fertilizer per square yard/square metre.

7 The Vegetable Garden

IS VEGETABLE GROWING WORTHWHILE?

The growing of vegetables today at home or in an allotment is worthwhile for many reasons. Firstly, one can produce a veritable feast of vegetables of all kinds, different sorts of radish, tomato, peas and so on at a fraction of what it would cost to buy them in the shops. Secondly, the chemicals used are under your own control. However, if you have to use sprays and powders, then you can use the least poisonous and least persistent preparations. By using any chemicals as early in the season as possible, you can ensure that all traces have disappeared long before the plants are gathered.

SOIL-CULTIVATION AND FEEDING

In most gardens the vegetable plot should be dug over roughly with a spade in autumn. This is particularly necessary on heavy soils and in newly laid-out gardens, because then the frost will break up any wet, heavy clods and by spring the soil will be easier to work. However, soils that have for years been under cultivation and are richly supplied with humus, can dispense with this. Soils such as these come through the winter better if they are covered by a crop of some sort—spinach, for example—or a mixture of, say, rye and vetch sown in the autumn for green manuring.

Nature sets the right example in this matter, for no piece of ground is ever left uncovered for long. The green mantle of plant life protects the precious friable soil-structure from erosion by sun and rain. The organic activity of the soil is promoted and its nutrients are enhanced and retained. Experiments have shown that far fewer food materials are washed out of the soil if a crop is growing on it, another advantage being that humus is added to the soil.

In spring the green manure crop can be dug into the soil or put on to the compost heap. Only areas that it is intended to till very early require no autumn sowing of green manure.

In spring, before laying out the vegetable beds, the soil should be generally worked over with cultivator or rake, to loosen it ready for sowing or planting.

Summer soil cultivation starts as soon as the beds are sown and consists of frequent superficial loosening of the ground with a hoe or cultivator. As soon as the surface soil has dried out after rainfall or a thorough watering, the bed should be given a shallow hoeing. This prevents a hard crust forming, and so enables oxygen to reach the roots and the carbon dioxide given off in this activity to escape. It also protects the lower soil from undue evaporation: when the upper inch or so is loosened, the tiny capillary tubes through which water rises to the surface of the soil and evporates are disturbed, and moisture is conserved.

Another method of moisture conservation is mulching, particularly valuable for crops requiring a great deal of water, and for those where it is desirable to keep the undersides of leaves dry to avoid outbreaks of fungus diseases. Lawnmowings, for example, can be spread 10 cm/4 in.

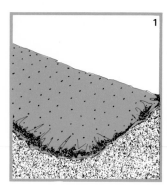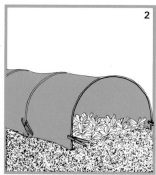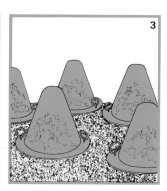

thick between celery plants, tomatoes and other crops. Under the blanket of mulch the soil remains moist and cool; most weeds give up the struggle to push through; and the crops so treated look a picture of health.

The bed can also be covered with a thick layer of newspaper. The innumerable organisms in the soil cause the paper to decompose and the printer's ink does no damage whatever to the plants. Of course, a vegetable plot carpeted with newsprint doesn't look very attractive, so the paper can be covered with a little earth.

How to prepare a vegetable plot   In March or April, as soon as the soil has dried out, loosen it with a cultivator, drag-hoe or digging-fork, then level it with a wooden or iron rake. The customary width for a vegetable bed is 120 cm/4 ft. In smaller areas, where the beds have to be short in length, the width could be 75–90 cm/24–36 in., which would give better proportions. The boundary of the bed is marked off with a garden-line; a path of about 30 cm/1 ft wide is trodden out; then mark out the rest of the beds, each with a walk between, until the whole plot has been divided up. Then a layer of compost or peat at least 2·5 cm/1 in. deep is put down, together with a chloride-free mixed fertilizer—two handfuls for the roots, which then soon 'take hold'.

If the bed has to be watered during dry spells, this should be done very thoroughly and repeated as necessary. Give the plants a real drenching, then let them become dryish before watering again. That is far better than the 'little and often'

approach. You can use a watering-can, hose or sprinkler, it makes no difference. If a hose is used, the spray should be as fine as possible, the droplets warming themselves in the air. A fine spray is less likely to clog the soil particles together than a sharp jet of water.

The best time to water is in the evening. The water can soak in overnight, with scarcely any evaporation, and by next morning the plants look as though they've been given a new lease of life; thanks to absorbtion their cells are refilled with water. Watering can also be done in the early morning, but never in the heat of the day.

Vegetables that have to stay in the beds for a long time, particularly cabbage, clery, leeks, tomatoes and cucumbers, should be given a top dressing of a chloride-free fertilizer once or twice during the growing period; in this way they will always have plenty of food to sustain even and continuous growth. When applying top or side dressings, never let the nutrient salts touch the foliage of the plants, otherwise scorching will follow.

The fertilizer should be spread under the foliage or between the rows and then watered in. It is even better to apply the fertilizer in solution, for then the nutrients will be more quickly available to the plants. Use one handful per 10 litres/10 qts of water, which will be enough for 1–2 sq m/1–2 sq yds of ground.

How much fertilizer to use   For most kinds of vegetables one handful is sufficient before planting or sowing; radishes and lettuces requiring a

Encouraging an early crop

1 Perforated plastic.
2 Rigid plastic cloche: the ends should sometimes be closed.
3 Plastic pots are ideal for bringing on early crops of cucumbers and beans.
4 Home-made frames, the sides made mainly of glass.
5 A thermostatically controlled frame.

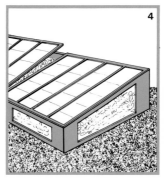

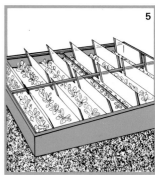

scant handful only. Exceptions are: Cauliflower— one handful before planting, then half a handful at fortnightly intervals, two or three times.

Celery—one handful before planting, one handful four to six weeks later; in both July and August half a handful each of nitrate and potash or, failing that, of mixed fertilizer.

Leeks—one handful before planting, a half handful at four-weekly intervals, two or three times.

Carrots—one half handful before sowing, followed by one handful four to six weeks later.

Radish—one-and-a-half handfuls before planting out.

Tomatoes—one-and-a-half handfuls before planting, one handful in June/July.

Cucumber—one scant handful before culture, a half handful in June.

Beans—one-and-a-half handfuls before sowing.

Rhubarb—two handfuls in spring and one half handful in June after gathering.

Asparagus—two to three handfuls in two doses after cutting has ended.

Early potatoes—one-and-a-half handfuls before planting out.

Where possible, the same crop should not be grown on a particular bed two years running. This rotation of crops, as it is called, is particularly valuable when it involves a change from shallow— to deep-rooted vegetables. If for example a shallow-rooted plant like cucumber is rotated with a deep-rooted plant such as leeks or spinach, then nutrients that have been washed down to deeper layers can be utilized, and all soil layers are enriched with humus residue from the roots. The soil structure is improved, the danger of transmitting diseases and pests is lessened, and the balance of nutrients maintained.

If stable manure is readily available (which nowadays is only the case in country districts), it is possible to divide up the kitchen garden and each year manure a different part with it.

1 Directly after applying the rotted stable manure, plant vegetables which are tolerant of this fertilizer: members of the cabage family (except kohl-rabi), cucumbers, celery and leeks.

2 One year later plant those vegetables intolerant of stable manure: kohl-rabi, tomatoes, such leaf vegetables as lettuce and spinach, root vegetables such as carrots, radishes and pulses such as beans and peas, also onions.

One is often obliged to mix the limited amount of stable manure obtainable with other garden and kitchen waste on the compost heap, and when all has been properly rotted down to put this compost on to the garden.

Winter is the time for making a plan of the vegetable garden. Sketch out the beds on a sheet of paper, and write in the individual sections the work involved before planting, during growth, and after cropping. This will depend on personal taste, the size of one's family, and climatic conditions; and every cultivation plan will be different. The various catch-crops should also be noted.

There are bound to be a few mistakes at the first attempt—too many of one sort of vegetable and not enough of another. One must learn by experience, and write down one's discoveries. A record

157

of this kind will be of great help when drawing up a plan of cultivation for the following year.

One more thing: the bed should not be left empty for long after one crop has been harvested. The sooner the soil has the protection of another crop, the better.

AIDS FOR EARLY HARVESTING

The traditional forcing frame with lights needs no further description here. The important thing is that there should be a slope of from 5–10 cm/2–4 in. from north to south, and for early cultivation, that it should not stand too high from the ground, so that heat loss is reduced.

Forcing frames can very easily be made out of wood, using boards that have previously been treated with a proprietary wood preservative that is harmless to plants.

A concrete frame is much more durable. For years it has been possible for the amateur gardener to buy a pre-fabricated frame of concrete or composition (which weighs less), to be assembled in its permanent position.

For the gardener whose occupation leaves him little free time, or for an allotment situated far from one's home the self-ventilating frame is a boon. The framework is made of a light alloy. Its uses are practically unlimited. Each light consists of six panes, which slide along and have no putty round them. If one pane breaks it can be replaced by another on either side.

The self-regulating opening and closing of the light is brought about by an oil-filled thermostat, which lifts or lowers the panes at a pre-arranged temperature. The panes can also be raised by hand, separately. It is advantageous to have a frame for two or three lights, of which one is self-ventilating.

Cultivation can start at the beginning of mid-March. At this early time of the year even the thermostatically controlled frames should be covered with straw matting or planks in the evenings, to keep in the warmth for as long as possible. The use of plastic sheeting as a means of obtaining an early harvest has become increasingly popular in recent years. The simplest method is to spread a 0·05 mm thick sheet of plastic film over the seed bed, digging the sides into the earth, and weighting them with earth or bricks. As soon as germination is complete and the seedlings are visible, remove the plastic sheeting. By this means radishes can be harvested ten to twelve days earlier than would be possible otherwise.

Plants can also be covered with plastic sheeting without using any particular structure, but this can be done for short periods only. If lettuce is covered in March or April, this should be for ten days only unless it is unusually cold, when the plastic sheeting can remain over the plants for up to three weeks. The fact that the plants will be covered and pressed down on to the ground does not matter. As soon as the lettuces have grown the plastic sheeting must be removed.

This method has also proved satisfactory with early cauliflowers and cabbages, since this encourages root growth. For all these plants, perforated plastic sheeting should be used, which has

Left: As soon as soil crusts over after rainfall or repeated waterings, loosen the surface; but this is unnecessary where the surface has been well mulched with a layer of compost or peat.

Right: Mulching keeps the soil moist and protected from undue evaporation. Lawn-cuttings are very suitable for this purpose.

◀

Aster tongolensis 'Apollo' an early aster with fragrant, lilac flowers, blooming May/June.

up to now not been available on the market. You can make the perforations yourself. A whole roll of cheap plastic sheeting, 0·05 mm thick, can be bought and holes made in it with an electric drill about 10–12 mm diameter—about 15 cm/6 in. apart. This must be done slowly in order to make perfect holes. The plastic sheeting should always be new, since only then will condensation form on it. It is this thin layer of moisture that protects the plants from frosts.

Vegetables can be induced to produce early crops by using cloches, these again being made by the amateur gardener. A stronger plastic sheeting, 1 mm thick, is needed for this.

The following is the easiest and cheapest method: buy a roll of wire 0·5 m thick, and cut from it lengths of about 120 cm/4 ft. These lengths are already curved—since the wire was in a roll—and they can be placed in the ground on the seed bed 45 cm/1½ ft apart. The distance between the two wire hoops should not be more than 45 cm/18 in. otherwise hollows will form in the plastic sheeting, when it rains or snows, and this will press down on to the plants. The hoops should be placed securely in the ground, and it will only be necessary to spread the plastic sheeting over them, fastening it down tightly at the ends by weighting with earth or stones. The plastic is attached to the wire hoops with washing pegs. It thus is easy on warm days to allow the air to circulate. This is a cheap and practical method.

Experiments have proved that lettuces may be harvested fourteen to seventeen days earlier by using this kind of ventilated cloche. Of course, a wooden frame can also be used, and plastic sheeting 0·1 to 0·2 mm thick, spread over it. This can be used over nursery beds and over seed boxes. The plants in a nursery bed are thus protected and vegetables can be brought on to an early havest.

According to the size of the wooden frame some nylon threads can be tied across so that the plastic sheeting will not hang loosely. The plastic sheeting should be spread tautly across the wooden frame and fastened down on the underside of the battens with large-headed galvanised nails. Before doing this, it is best to place a piece of plastic along the underside of the frame, into which the nails can be hammered, so making the frame longer-lasting.

These are only a few suggestions: every gardener can be his own inventor. But care should be taken when making such structures that they are not only practical but not too much of an eyesore. Rigid plastic cloches do not, unfortunately, add to the beauty of a garden.

SOME USEFUL VEGETABLES

First a quick look at the sorts of vegetables mentioned under this heading:

Leaf vegetables: Varieties of lettuce, endive, chicory, spinach.

Fruit vegetables: Corn, cucumber, pumpkin, squashes and tomatoes.

Legumes or pulses: Bush or dwarf beans, peas, broad beans, runner or pole beans, lima beans.

161

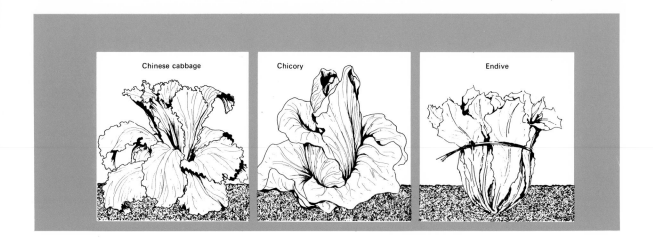

Chinese cabbage · Chicory · Endive

Brassicas: Cauliflower, kohl-rabi, white cabbage, red cabbage, Chinese cabbage, savoy, brussel sprouts, kale.

Root vegetables: carrots, radishes, beet, celeriac.

Bulb crops: Shallots, leeks, onions.

Also: Asparagus rhubarb.

Less familiar vegetables: Courgettes, cardoon.

Herbs: Dill, cress, parsley, chervil, mint, chives, marjoram.

Leaf vegetables

Lettuce One can never eat too much lettuce; on the contrary a bowl filled with fresh green lettuce leaves gives an edge to the appetite, especially if slices of tomato and radishes are mixed in. All lettuce varieties like a moist soil, rich in humus.

Leaf vegetables should be washed immediately after picking, so that the leaves remain crisp. They should, therefore, be watered well and often, and the soil aerated and fed frequently. Lettuce leaves must not touch the soil during growth; otherwise they will rot easily and the heads remain small.

Lettuce can be grown from spring through to autumn, and since they require so little space they can be planted anywhere and harvested continuously. The first plants should be bought from a reputable nursery, but from then onwards lettuce seeds can be sown in a small bed at intervals of two to three weeks. From the middle of March lettuces can be planted in cold frames or under plastic sheeting about 25 cm/10 in. apart, with 25 cm/10 in. between rows. From the beginning of April they can be planted in the open ground. Finally at the end of August, a cold frame or plastic sheeting can again be used. Lettuces take six to eight weeks from planting to harvest.

Top U.K. varieties For early spring sowing, there are 'Attractive', 'Trocadero Improved' and 'May King'. For spring or summer sowing choose 'All the Year Round', 'Continuity', 'Feltham King' and 'Unrivalled'. For late summer sowing, to winter outdoors, 'Arctic King', 'Imperial' and 'Stanstead Park'.

Top U.S. varieties 'Curled Simpson', 45 days, an early harvest leaf lettuce. 'Salad Bowl', 48 days, heat resistant leaf lettuce. 'Oak Leaf', 40 days, semi-weeding top quality. 'Bibb', 57 days, very famous semi-heading dark green. 'Butler King', 70 days, large headed, good crisp leaf texture.

Cabbage lettuce This forms large cabbage-like heads, surrounded by large spreading outer leaves. Because of their size, and the length of time they take to develop—they normally need ten days longer than the ordinary lettuce. They are very hardy, and do not mind heat and dryness; and the heads when they are fully grown can remain in the garden for two-three weeks without running to seed. Ice lettuce can be sown in the seed bed from April to July. They should be planted out 25 cm/ 10 in. apart. They appear to be very coarse, but are in fact tender and are pleasantly crisp. When preparing the lettuce the leaves should be cut into 2·5 cm/1 in. wide strips.

Endive Winter endives should be sown sparsely, in nursery seed beds from mid-June to mid-July, so that sturdy plants can develop. Pricking out is not absolutely necessary. Cultivation takes about 4 to 5 weeks, so from the middle of July they can be planted out in beds about 20–25 cm/8–10 in. apart. As for lettuces, spread one handful of artificial fertilizer per m² or sq yd before planting, and lightly rake in. Since the plant has long leaves, these should be shortened by one third, and the roots as well. This will restrict evaporation in unusually hot summers, and make planting easier, as well as harvesting.

Endives are often damaged by caterpillars. Their presence is easily recognised by the shrivelled and withered leaves. The dirty grey caterpillar can readily be found by gently removing the soil by hand from around the withered plant. The caterpillar should immediately be destroyed. This is a good reason for keeping a few extra plants in the seed bed, to take the place of affected plants.

It takes eight weeks from planting to harvesting. The fully developed plants should be gathered together with twine or a rubber band during dry weather to prevent rotting, and to blanch the leaves. Every ten days a new lot must be gathered together. They can stay in the beds until Decem-ber, as they can withstand temperatures as low as 4°C. After December the endives should be placed in sandy soil in the cellar.

Chinese cabbage This is used in salads, like endives or savoy, in the U.K. but in America is cooked at high heat in Chinese dishes. It may not be to everyone's taste, so try just a few sample plants. Has a very mild un-cabbagy taste. The best U.S. variety is 'Bok Choi'.

Sow from mid-July to August, but under no circumstances earlier, otherwise the plant will run to seed without developing a head. It is best to sow Chinese cabbage directly onto a prepared bed, because in August it will need a long time to root and grow. It should be planted with 45 cm/18 in. between rows. Later, thin to 45 cm/18 in. between the plants. If sown in a seed bed, then the plants need only be transplanted from the middle of August to the beginning of September.

Lamb's lettuce (or corn salad) A very popular species with a pleasing flavour. When picking the lettuce the whole plant should be cut—including the heart—very close to the ground, and should be prepared as soon after picking as possible. Sow mid-August to mid-September with 12–15 cm/5–6 in. between each row and 8 to 10 rows to a bed. If the ground is completely weed-free it is preferable to broadcast the seed. It is best to sow in two sessions, so that the harvesting time is as prolonged as possible. Sow the seed sparsely otherwise the hearts will be small and many yellow leaves will drop off.

Extreme left: Only in warm, damp climates will cucumbers grow abundantly. They should therefore, be covered with cloches since great variations in temperature during summer rainy periods will often harm the plants, and may cause them to die.

Right: Cucumber plants carry both male and female flowers (the latter forming the cucumbers).

Spinach This tastes best when freshly picked and furthermore, if grown in your own garden, you know how it has been fed. This is important, because if spinach is given too much nitrate large leaves will develop that are very hard to digest.

To germinate well, spinach needs a well aerated soil that is, however, firm on the surface. The soil should therefore be pressed down with a board after sowing. Sow seed in drills 20 cm/8 in. apart. There will be about six in the average bed rows.

Before sowing, one small handful of artificial fertilizer per m²/sq yd should be worked into the soil. When sowing winter spinach, spread an additional handful of the artificial fertilizer in spring. When sown in spring (March–April), it can be harvested in April or May. When sown in mid to end of August, the crop can be harvested from October to November. Winter spinach is sown from mid to late September and harvested in the March or April of the following year.

It is not worth growing spinach in summer because the plant will immediately run to seed. This temporal gap may be closed by sowing 'New Zealand' spinach, which can be sown from the end of March, in clay or peat pots in a frame or on a windowsill. Put only one seed in a pot. After mid-May plant only one row in the bed with 45 cm/ 18 in. between each plant. Five plants are sufficient for one family. From the end of June until October, as soon as the shoots are 15 cm/6 in. long they and the leaves should be harvested. The plant will continue to grow fresh shoots. Because of its great mass of foliage, New Zealand spinach requires a great deal of water and nourishment.

FRUIT VEGETABLES

Corn Anyone who has tasted corn-on-the-cob boiled in salt water then spread with butter, will surely have enjoyed this North American speciality and will want to try growing it.

These plants need a humus-rich soil, well-fed but with only moderate amounts of nitrogen. Give as long a summer growing period as possible. In the British climate, sow in March/April under glass (temp. 15.5°C, 60°F) in peat pots. Plant out late April/early May, in blocks of three or four, 22–30 cm/9–12 in. apart. Water in dry weather.

Harvesting will take place in August as soon as the silky tassels turn brown and wither. The surface of the cobs should be slightly soft to the touch. The plants should be harvested often.

Cucumbers These can be planted from the end of April in cloches or under glass, using one plant per m²/square yard. The plants can be either bought from a nursery or grown from seed in pots of peat or clay at the beginning of April. Sow two seeds per pot and later discard the weaker plant. Where the cucumber is to be planted, the ground should be given a good deal of compost or manure and liberally covered with soil. The plants are placed at an angle to ensure that the roots do not grow too deep.

A good variety for raising under glass or cloches is 'Improved Telegraph'.

If you do not plant in a cloche or under glass, plant from mid-May, one row in the middle of the bed. Before that the bed should be well prepared with compost; or a shallow trench about

Successful cucumber varieties 'Bedfordshire Prize Ridge', 'Stockwood Ridge', and 'Carter's Greenline'—all excellent for salads. 'Short Prickly' and 'Small Paris Gherkins' are small cucumbers suitable for pickling. Right: With tomatoes, the ancillary shoots growing at the leaf axils should always be removed. Leave only five clusters of blossom, which will develop into fruit. Cut the rest as soon as they become visible, since it is not possible for too many fruits to ripen in our climate. This will promote the growth of the fruits already developing.

45 cm/18 in. wide should be dug, filled with well rotted stable manure or compost, then covered over with earth. The cucumber seeds should be sown in this central area about 10 cm/4 in. apart. The seedlings should be thinned out to 45 cm/18 in. apart.

If a cold frame is available, the seeds can be sown in pots (two seeds to a pot) in the middle of April, and from mid-May the seedlings can be planted out in a central row in the bed, about 60 cm/2 ft apart. The plants can also be bought from a nursery. It is very important that these have a good root growth.

In areas where there are great changes in temperature, cucumbers should be planted under a cloche. Only then can a luxuriant growth be encouraged. If the weather is very changeable—alternating between hot, dry and cool, rainy weather—the cucumbers will soon become diseased and die. Water frequently during growth with warmed water, since cucumbers like warm and moist conditions. It is a good idea to keep a watering can full of water standing near the cucumber bed so that it will become warm on sunny days.

Harvesting begins early in July and reaches its climax in mid-August. Salad cucumbers should be picked when they reach a weight of 500 grams. Cucumbers for pickling should not be more than 12 cm/5 in. long. If they are allowed to become bigger or heavier, their flavour will be affected.

Pumpkins One plant is normally sufficient for most families. They can be planted either under glass or in a pot on the window ledge (in April), then transplanted into open ground in mid-May, or they can be planted straight into the ground from the beginning of May. Pumpkins grow best on the compost heap. When fully ripe, these giants should be pickled with spices, vinegar, sugar and salt or made into pumpkin pie. Among the best varieties—all of them American—are 'Straight Eight' (66 days), 'Smoothie' (63 days), 'Burpless' (65 days) and, just for pickling, 'Ever bearing'.

Tomatoes Although rather difficult to grow in the garden, the taste of splendid bright red tomatoes makes all one's work worthwhile. If you decide to grow plants from seed, then these must be sown in a frame or in a room, up to the end of March. As soon as the seedlings have two seed-leaves, replant them into pots containing peat or clay (Jiffy pots) and put these pots into the frame. The pots will soon have to be moved away from each other so that the plants can develop sturdily.

Planting out should take place from the middle to the end of May; preferably in one row in the middle of the bed, with 40 cm/16 in. between the plants. If possible, a row should be planted against a south wall, or some other sheltered place. If there are two rows in one bed, the plants should be 60 cm/2 ft apart with 45 cm/18 in. between each row. It has been satisfactorily proved that covering tomatoes with plastic sheeting gives not only an earlier and longer harvest, but also protects the plant against mildew and blight. The plastic sheeting should be about 45 cm/18 in. from the ground to allow free circulation of air.

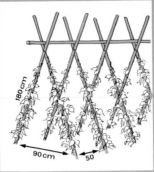

Left: Dwarf beans started in pots should be planted out in the open 60 cm/16 in. apart.

Right: Bed of runner beans. Recommended varieties of runner beans, in addition to those already mentioned are the early cropping 'Kelvedon Marvel' and 'Princeps', both growing 1·5–1·8 m/5–6 ft in height.

Each plant should be staked. It is possible to drive in stakes at the end of each row of tomatoes, so deep that about 1·6 m/4½ ft shows above the earth. Then stretch a wire between the two stakes and attach each plant to a cane tied to the wire. Canes are easily stored. Pay special attention to the following points: plants must be securely attached to stake or wire. Buds at leaf axils should be pinched out regularly. This must be done early, while the shoots are still soft. Your thumb and index finger are all you need for this job. Leaves growing close to the ground must also be removed, to prevent the spread of disease, which contact with the earth could encourage.

Retain only five good trusses. Remove all the others with a sharp knife, but do not cut the top of the plant. The leaves should be spared, as they produce nourishment for the plant. Water the soil but do not allow the leaves to become wet.

Healthy but unripe tomatoes, which must be picked in the autumn because of the damage that frosts could cause, can be ripened in the house or in shallow boxes in an empty frame.

Top U.K. varieties that have proved their worth include 'Ailsa Craig', 'Early Market', 'Harbinger' and 'Moneymaker'. The F₁ hybrids are proving reliably trouble-free; these include 'Hertford Cross', 'Kelvedon Cross' and 'Ware Cross'. Particularly good for outdoor growing are 'Outdoor Girl', 'Primabel' and 'Amateur'.

Top U.S. varieties are 'Park's Whopper 75' (75 days), 'Better Boy' (75 days), 'Beefsteak' (80 days), 'Rutgers' (73 days)—justly famous for its reliability—'Reina' (76 days)—with small, pear-shaped fuits.

Dwarf or Bush Beans Since these are so tender to eat, they are in great demand, especially as they are suitable for deep-freezing, and loose none of their quality in the process.

They are sown from mid-May to mid-July; five seeds are placed into holes 2·5 cm/1 in. deep and 40 cm/16 in. apart. These should be covered with compost so that the young seedling can quickly push its way up through the earth. Harvest begins 8–10 weeks after sowing and it is advisable to cover the dwarf beans for a short time with plastic sheeting because they grow quickly and need a lot of warmth during germination. It is also possible to sow in 11 cm/4 in. pots (5 seeds to a pot), and plant out after the middle of May.

Runner or Pole Beans Many gardeners admire the distinctive flavour of runner beans, which are harvested at the end of July. Start sowing from mid-May to the end of June, two rows per bed. Place the canes into the ground first and plant six to eight beans in a semi-circle round each cane 40–50 cm/1½–2 in. in deep; never too deeply. If wires are preferred to canes for training the beans, then at each end of the bed, drive a stake 1·8–2 m/ 6–8 ft high into the ground, then span a wire between them. Firmly attach steel wires to this main wire.

Varieties 'Sutton's Scarlet' is a good cropper

As soon as the cauliflower is about the size of a man's fist the inner leaves should be bent over the flower.
Good varieties of peas: 'Feltham First', 'Foremost' and 'Kelvedon Monarch'. But as there are so many other good and newer varieties, it is best to consult reliable catalogues.
If only a small amount of space is available the dwarf varieties should be planted. Recommended varieties of Kohl-rabi: 'Earliest White', 'Early Purple' and 'Model Green'.
Good U.K. cabbage varieties are: early, 'First and Best'; mid-season, 'Monarch F'; autumn-winter, 'Winter Keeper', 'January King'. Good U.S. varieties are 'Golden Acre' (58 days) and 'Savoy King' (90 days). Red cabbage, good U.K. varieties: 'Red Blood'; 'Red Drumhead'. Savoys: early, 'Best of All', late, 'Sutton's New Year'. Good U.S. varieties: 'Mammoth Red Rock' (100 days) and 'Red Acre' (76 days).
A reliable cauliflower for the U.K. is 'All the Year Round'. Best for the U.S. are: 'Snow King' (50 days) and 'Snow Queen' (60 days).

and deservedly popular; and 'Streamline' is another good scarlet runner. 'Prizewinner' is healthy and a good cropper. It's beautiful red flowers make it particularly suitable for training up fences or arbours. The wires should be $1 \cdot 2$ m $\times 75$ cm/ 4 ft $\times 2\frac{1}{2}$ ft apart. Since this bean is a slow grower it should be planted by the middle or end of May.

Broad beans   Sow in March, 2 to 3 beans in each hole $1 \cdot 8$–$2 \cdot 5$ cm/$\frac{3}{4}$–1 in. deep and 20 cm/8 in. apart with 60 cm/2 ft between rows. After germination, leave only one plant per hole. As soon as the plants are 15 cm/6 in. high, build up the soil at their base to ensure that the plants do not fall over. Harvesting lasts from the end of May until the end of June. The crop should be picked at least once a week as the shell of the bean should be green with milk-white beans inside.

Peas   Sow pea seeds in mid-April in $3 \cdot 7$ cm/$1\frac{1}{2}$ in. drills, 40 cm/16 in. between drills, leaving approximately $2 \cdot 5$ cm/1 in. between each sown pea. Harvesting can take place at the end of June, the yield being about 1 kilo/2 lbs per m^2/sq yd. The pods should be full but still green. The ripe peas should be picked several times a week, to ensure they do not over-ripen. Two particularly delicious varieties are 'Mange Tout' and 'Dwarf Sugar' peas.

BRASSICAS

Kohl-rabi   A plant that grows quickly and re-quires little space. The plants should first be placed in frames or under cloches in mid-March and transplanted into open ground at the beginning of April. If you want a late summer or early autumn crop, then the seeds can be planted in a nursery bed between mid-May and the end of July. Plant them for an early crop 30 $\times$ 30 cm/1 $\times$ 1 ft otherwise 30–40 cm/1 ft–16 in. apart.

Kohl-rabi takes about ten days longer than lettuce to mature. The blue varieties grow more slowly than the white, but remain tender longer.

Cauliflower   This brassica is very popular for the small garden, not least because it is attractive to see the white head appearing through the green of the leaves; it is also ideal for deep-freezing. The first batch should be planted in the open in mid-April. In most cases, it is best to buy the plants from a nursery but if you want a later harvest cauliflowers can be grown from seed in an open bed. They should be planted at latest by mid to late July. Sow the seed 40 cm/16 in. apart, in rows 45 cm/18 in. apart; sow only three rows per bed. Harvest after seven to nine weeks.

Cauliflowers need constant attention; lack of fertilizer or water will lead to stunted growth, and the flower will develop early and remain small. Beside the initial manuring when preparing the ground, two or three other dressings of an artificial fertilizer should be given during the growing period. As soon as the plant is the size of a man's fist, bend the outer leaves over the flower for increased protection. Without this added protection the flower can become yellowed.

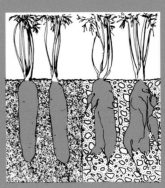

Left: Carrots can only grow to full size if there is at least 5 cm/2 in between each plant, even at a very early stage in their development.

Right: Carrots require deep well loosened soil; in stony soil the root spreads out at too shallow a depth and divides. Some varieties have already been mentioned in the text.

White cabbage, red cabbage and savoy It is possible to deal with the cultivation of these types together as their requirements are so similar. But these vegetables are of only minor importance in the small garden. Far better to use your limited garden space for more interesting plants and buy cabbages from the shops. Only the early varieties are worth growing: these should be planted in the open in April in three rows per bed, leaving 40 cm/16 in. between each plant and 45 cm/18 in. between each row. White cabbage and Savoy take eight weeks to grow and red cabbage eleven weeks.

Brussels sprouts and kale These are really worth growing and don't need too much attention. They can share a bed with other varieties.

Sow at the end of April and plant out at the beginning of June. Brussels sprouts should be 45 cm/18 in. apart in rows and kale 40 × 45 cm/16 × 18 in. Do not harvest before mid-November as frost on these varieties will much improve their flavour. By contrast with Brussels sprouts, kale can be left in the beds all through the winter. Harvest the leaves as required, starting at the bottom of the plant.

Sprouts can be left in the bed without any damage during a mild winter; the leaves around the sprouts will be sufficient protection against the frost. The best method is to pick the sprouts in December and to freeze the crop. They can also be placed in shallow trays and stored in a cool room for several weeks. Should there be a lack of space kale can also be sown directly into the bed in early

August in rows 20 cm/8 in. apart. The leaves can be harvested from November until the end of the winter. Kale is not very demanding and will even grow in semi-shade.

VARIETIES

U.K. best Brussels sprouts: 'Continuity', 'Ormskirk Giant', 'King of the Lates'.

U.S. best 'Jade Cross Hybrid' (85 days), 'Long Island' (90 days).

Kale: 'Cottager's Kale', 'Hungry Gap' and 'Ormskirk Hearting'.

ROOT CROPS

Carrots Varieties have recently been developed in which the carotene content is twice as high as before, and the colour has become much brighter. Early varieties can be sown at the beginning of March and can also be sown as successive crops until mid-July. Sow later varieties from April until the end of May.

Early varieties should be sown in rows 20 cm/8 in. apart; later varieties, 25 cm/10 in. apart. The harvest should yield approximately 5 kilo per m²/11 lb per sq yd. Early varieties can be harvested from the end of June and later varieties and successive plantings of early varieties from the middle of October until the end of November. If there is a bed with early varieties that can be harvested at the end of June or the beginning of July, it is not neces-

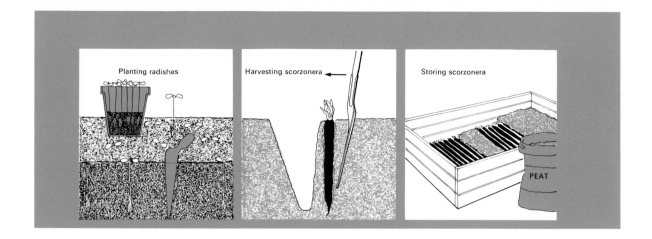

Planting radishes | Harvesting scorzonera | Storing scorzonera

PEAT

sary to pick the crop all at once; dig up as required.

Carrot seeds will only germinate after a period of three to four weeks. In the meantime, to aerate the soil, some radish and lettuce seeds can be sown with them since these germinate comparatively quickly and so will be easily distinguishable. Like all vegetables, carrots require an aerated soil but one with a firm surface. After using a rake to cover the drills with earth, press the soil down firmly with the back of the rake or a board. Good carrots will only be produced if the plants are sufficiently far apart. Therefore, even in a very young state, the carrot plants should be thinned out to 5–6.7 cm/2–2½ in. apart.

Later varieties will keep well if stored in a garden clamp. As soon as there is a nice warm day in winter, the carrots needed for the next few weeks are removed from the clamp and stored in the cellar until required.

Varieties The well known 'Early Nantes' ripens early and yields well. Two good later varieties with high carotene (Vitamin A) content are 'Chantenay' and 'Autumn King'. Another excellent variety, is the long-rooted 'Long Red Surrey' which to develop to its full capacity, needs a soil that is well and deeply dug.

Radish It is important that radishes grow quickly, so that they remain tender and their flavour does not become too sharp. They may be planted in March in the cold frame or under plastic sheeting. The early varieties should be sown in April, summer varieties in May or June, and the winter radish towards the end of July. If radishes are to be planted in beds that have already been harvested in mid-August, the early and summer varieties should be used. Make holes in the soil with the finger to a depth of 0.6–1.2 cm/¼–½ in. and plant two or three seeds to a hole at 20 cm/8 in. intervals and in rows 20 cm/8 in. apart. As soon as the first leaves show, all superfluous plants are discarded, leaving only one plant in each position. Harvest after eight to ten weeks, winter varieties after fifteen weeks. Radishes may also be sown at fortnightly intervals throughout the summer in the seed bed. When the seedlings have grown at least two leaves, transplant, on a dull, rainy day to the permanent bed. If radishes are woody, this is due to a lack of water, excessive heat or the fact that they have remained too long in the bed; frequent watering is therefore important.

VARIETIES

U.K. best Early: the long-rooted 'Wood's Early Frame' and 'White Icicle' and the round-rooted 'Saxa' and 'Scarlet Globe'. There are also the oval-rooted 'French Breakfast' and 'Sutton's Succulent'. Winter radishes: 'Black Spanish' and 'China Rose'.

U.S. best 'Champion' (28 days), 'Cherry Belle' (22 days), 'White Icicle' (28 days)—a summer grower. 'Black Spanish'—plant July, harvest winter: 'The White Prince' (26 days)—very large, white.

169

Left: Leeks are planted deeply, and covered with earth several times during growth, as this will provide long, pale stems, whereas lettuce (centre) endive and celery are deliberately planted deeply to blanch them.

Asparagus (right) is harvested as soon as the tips show 15–20 cm/6–8 in above the surface, before the asparagus leaf buds open.

Small red radishes are more suitable for growing in very small gardens. Because of their bright red colour they are attractive for garnishing salads and other dishes. They taste best when picked fresh from the garden. They can be sown from mid-spring to early September continuously. There is enough room for 150–200 plants per square metre/ square yard, but they are not usually sown in beds of their own, but often mixed with other plants which have longer lives. They should be sown in drills at a depth of 1·2 cm/$\frac{1}{2}$ in. After germination the plants should be thinned out to 3·5–5 cm/$1\frac{1}{2}$–2 in. between each plant in the row, then the round radishes can be successfully garnered. The use of cloches will produce an earlier spring harvest and lengthen the autumn harvest. Make sure that there is adequate ventilation in the cloches in warm weather so that the plants do not grow too long. They can be harvested after six weeks' growth in the spring and four to five weeks in summer. As mentioned above, tender radishes are achieved by watering frequently and keeping the soil loosened to achieve quick growth.

Beetroot This only requires a small space of 1–2 square metres/square yards, and this could be in the shade. Salads made from these lovely red vegetables not only taste delicious, but are also eye-catching. They are sown from mid-May to the end of June in the open ground—or in the seed bed, and then transplanted. If sown too early the cold weather will stunt their growth. Space 15 × 30 cm/6 × 12 in. apart and have 5 rows in every bed. Allow about twelve to fifteen weeks

from sowing to harvesting. In late autumn beet-roots may be stored in a clamp, and in this way kept fresh until spring.

U.K. varieties 'Globe' which is round and dark red, and is an early cropper; 'Exhibition', which has a very long root.

U.S. variety 'Summer Pascal' (120 days) grown unblanched.

Celery and Celeriac A successful crop of celeriac is as good for the reputation of the amateur gardener as a marvellous white cauliflower or an enormous cucumber. Not only the globe shaped root, but also the spicy foliage, is used in cooking. So as not to miss its delicious spicy flavour, even in winter, celeriac leaves can be cut up and put in the deep freeze. Sturdy plants are usually bought from a nursery and should be planted in beds from the end of May. Celeriac seeds can also be sown up to the beginning of July, but under no circumstances before the middle of May.

Celery should be planted 40 cm/16 in. apart, in rows 40 cm/16 in. apart, and as shallow as possible, otherwise many side roots will grow from the bulbous root and this will affect the taste. It is wrong to cut off the lower leaves because the chlorophyll in these is necessary for the natural growth of the plant. One may cut a few leaves now and then for use in the kitchen, but if larger amounts are required then extra plants should be grown for that purpose. Celery requires ample water and fertilizer. The ground should be well

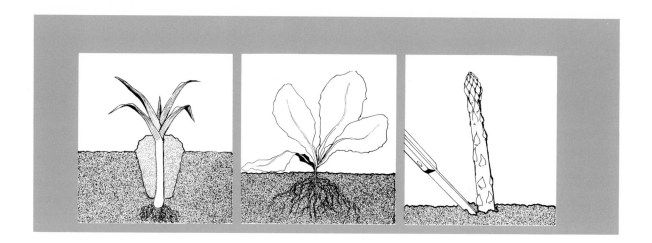

fed before planting, and then dressed three times at five weekly intervals.

Scorzonera or Black Salsify This is a vegetable that tastes particularly good in winter and is really something special for the gourmet. A disadvantage is simply the hard work needed to grow it well. To keep it a delicacy, one bed of 2 square metres/square yards is sufficient.

The seed does not germinate easily. Sow relatively densely, therefore, in rows 30 cm/1 ft apart, in March or April. The plants should be thinned out to 5–8 cm/2–3 in. apart. Plants can be harvested at the end of October, and will produce as much as 2 kilos/4 lbs per square metre/ square yard.

It is important to aerate the soil well and deeply, otherwise the roots will become quite small and split. Scorzonera may be stored during the winter if they are placed in a fruit box in alternating layers of roots and damp leaf-mould. In addition to this one may cover the container with plastic sheeting, which will go over the top layer of leaf-mould.

BULB CROPS

Onions Onions are needed throughout the whole year for cooking and it is an advantage to be able to pick them half-ripe in summer, together with their tasty leaves. Begin sowing from mid-March to the beginning of April in rows 20 cm/8 in. apart. They should then be thinned out so that there is 5 cm/2 in. between each plant. Spring onions should be sown in August or September and are grown 4 cm/1½ in. apart. During summer every alternate plant should be pulled out for use in the kitchen, to give enough growing space for the remainder.

Onion sets, which are most popular in the average garden, should be planted in April, 5 cm/ 2 in. apart, in rows 25 cm/10 in. apart. In early summer, every alternate plant should be pulled out for cooking, to allow sufficient room, 10 cm/4 in. between plants. The smaller the onion set the less the danger of sprouting. They should be about 0·6–1·8 cm/¼–¾ in. in size.

The onions from sets should be harvested in July or August; those that were grown from seed will be harvested in August or September; and spring onions, harvested in May or June.

Recommended U.K. varieties 'A.1', 'Improved Reading'. 'Ailsa Craig' and 'Unwin's Reliance'.

U.S. variety 'Southport Red Globe' (110 days). Keep until March.

'White Spanish' or 'White Lisbon' are good varieties for sowing in the autumn for spring onions.

For the U.S. 'Crystal Wax' (95 days). White Bermuda type.

Good pickling onions are 'Paris Silverskin', 'White Portugal' and 'The Queen'.

Leeks Leeks prepared as a salad are a real

Extreme left: Broccoli ready to be picked.
Right: A courgette or zucchini with blossom and fruit.

1 The fully developed cardoon looks very attractive.
2 The leaves are gathered together like this and blanched as required.
3 For this purpose corrugated cardboard or black foil or straw is tied around the plant and earth is heaped up round the plant.

delicacy. They are also most delicious for soups or sauces, or served as a vegetable.

Leeks are thoroughly hardy. Sow in the open from March to June, in drills 1·5 cm/½ in. deep. Plant out seedlings late May–early August, in shallow trenches or in holes 15–22 cm/6–9 in. deep, 30 cm/12 in. apart. Before planting out the long leaves and roots should be shortened.

In contrast with lettuce and celery, leeks should be planted preferably in fairly deep trenches and earthed up as they grow. This will provide a long, white stem. The leek is very demanding as far as water, feeding and soil aeration is concerned. The white roots will push their way up through the soil, draining it of moisture, thereby loosening the soil and leaving it in a friable condition for growing other plants later.

To provide sufficient supplies for the kitchen throughout the summer, some leeks can be planted in a row in the kitchen garden, some one or two metres/yards in length, to be picked as required.

YEAR-ROUND CROPS

Rhubarb This is a hardy perennial that will grow well in semi-shade. The clump-like plants should be planted in autumn or spring, one plant per square metre/yard. For average family, 2 or 4 plants are sufficient. Before planting the soil should be well loosened and improved with humus. After planting, cover the buds with 5–10 cm/1–2 in. of soil. No stalks should be cut in the first year because the leaves are needed for strengthening the growing roots. As soon as the yield deteriorates

(after approximately 8 years) the plant should be divided into several parts and replanted. In order to give the plant opportunity to gain strength for the following year, cease gathering the stalks by the end of June. The stalks should not be cut, but twisted and pulled from the plant. Do not take more than four stems from one plant at a time, to allow it time to recover. The thick heads of blossom should be cut as soon as they appear. The leaves are not edible: they contain oxalic acid, but they can be laid under the plant to prevent evaporation from the soil after some of the stalks have been cut. To grow strong rhubarb, substantial amounts of water and nutrient are required. During growth, spread half a handful of artificial fertilizer round each plant each month.

Recommended varieties for growing in the garden are: early, 'Prince Albert'; maincrop, 'Sutton'; and late, 'Victoria'.

Green asparagus This is the original form of asparagus cultivation, and has been handed down from the 17th century, whereas white asparagus has only been cultivated since the 19th century. Now the green asparagus has returned to us from America, and is increasing in popularity. It tastes slightly sharper than the white variety, but is better for you because it contains more minerals and vitamins and, what's more, is easier to cultivate. Green asparagus can be grown in any good garden soil, even on clay, and decorates the garden in summer with its fine green colouring. It should preferably be grown in a warm, sunny spot.

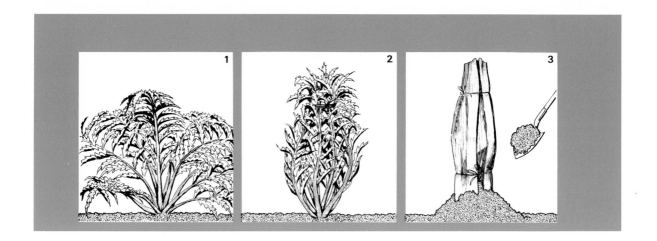

Buy one-year-old plants from a nursery. There should be about five buds on each, and long thick roots. One row should be planted per bed and there should be 40–50 cm/16–20 in. between each plant. A wide, but shallow trench about 15 cm/6 in. deep should be dug in the middle of the bed and the crowns should be planted so that the roots are arranged in a fanlike fashion. They are covered with 5 cm/2 in. of soil. When shoots appear the hollow should then be filled in, and covered with compost or stable manure.

Harvesting is simple: as soon as the plant shows 15–25 cm/6–10 in. above the soil cut it with a knife to just below ground level. It must be harvested before the leaf buds open. Like the tender white asparagus, harvest only after the third year, up to the beginning of June; and after four years, until the 21st June.

Feed heavily immediately after the harvest to ensure that the root stock under ground remains strong and able to produce numerous stems the following year. A dressing of 2–3 handfuls of artificial fertilizer per m²/square yard should be spread in two sessions four weeks apart. And in summer the asparagus rows should be covered with compost, rotted stable manure or leaf-mould.

LESS WELL KNOWN VEGETABLES

Courgettes or Zucchini There are various possibilities for preparing these vegetables. This recipe is recommended: peel and cut into slices 0·6 cm/¼ in. thick; sprinkle with salt, pepper and lemon juice and allow to stand for one hour; pour off the juice, dry the slices lightly and turn them in flour. Fry in hot fat and serve at once. Like cucumbers, they are cultivated in pots from mid-April. The small plants should be planted on the compost heap, 45 cm/18 in. apart. 2 or 3 plants are quite sufficient. If watered well and occasionally given a dressing of an artificial fertilizer, they will grow surprisingly quickly and luxuriantly. They are more hardy then cucumbers and keep growing even when the weather is cool and damp. As soon as the courgettes are 25–37 cm/10–15 in. long, they should be gathered and prepared as mentioned above. Expect six to eight to a plant.

Broccoli This is a brassica that thrives in the garden without any trouble at all, and is in many ways similar to cauliflower. In July, heads sprout in the centre of the plant and unlike the cauliflowers, are blue-green and growing on stalks 15–30 cm/6–12 in. long. Shortly before flowering, the firm heads, with the stalks, should be cut. Peel the stalks, cut into 2–3 cm/1–1¼ in. lengths and boil with the heads in salt water until tender (5–10 minutes). Strain and serve with butter. Or they can be served cold in a salad. An interesting fact is that new shoots continue to grow from the leaf axils after the harvest, so it is possible to harvest again and again right into the autumn. This procedure will only be stopped by a hard frost. This is why six to eight plants are sufficient for an average family, since broccoli will not usually be eaten more than once a week. It should be sown in April in an open seed bed and transplanted at the end of May, 50–60 cm/20–24 in. apart. A handful

of artificial fertilizer per m²/square yard and occasional watering is all that is necessary since the plant thrives in both damp and dry summers.

THE HERB GARDEN

There are annual and long lasting kitchen herbs. The latter are treated as perennials. This must be taken into account when cultivating them. In this section, only those herbs that add particular flavour to dishes are dealt with. For the winter they are cut shortly before they bloom, preferably in the morning as soon as they are dry. They should then be dried in a shady, well ventilated place. Never dry herbs in blazing sunlight as they will lose some of their effective and essential oils. They all require a humus-rich soil and a sunny position.

Savory   The leaves can be used for flavouring dwarf beans and runner beans, broad beans and sausages as well as in potato salad and mushroom dishes. Sow in April in the herb garden. Seedlings should be thinned out to 20 cm/ 8 in. apart.

Borage   The finely chopped leaves can be added to lettuce and spread on bread and butter, or whole sprigs decorate and give a pleasant cucumber-like tang to long summer drinks. Sow from the beginning of April onwards, at staggered intervals since borage should only be used when still young and fresh. Once sown in the garden it seeds itself and continues growing.

Dill   Should be sown from April onwards, as the leaves should only be used when young and tender. Dill is very good for flavouring salads, preparing a dill sauce and for fish dishes. The seeds of fully grown plants are used in pickling gherkins. For use in winter, dry the plant before it goes to seed, and store in closed containers.

Garden Cress   Sow in rows with 10 cm/4 in. between each row. As soon as the leaves can be seen they should be harvested by cutting the cress just above the surface. Successive sowings enable cress to be gathered continuously.

Cress can be grown during the winter on the window sill in a warm room. Packets with fresh seedlings can be bought from nurseries and stores and planted according to instructions on the packet. These packets consist of a container, four layers of wadding and seeds of the large leaved variety of cress. These are ready for use—without any earth—in only one week.

Tarragon   The young tips of this grey-leaved herb can be used in salads, sauces, soups, and for pickling gherkins. It can also be used along with other herbs in Tarragon vinegar. Propagation is by dividing one plant and replanting. One plant is usually sufficient for a family's requirements.

Chervil   Sow only a small amount at ten-day intervals. The plants can be harvested once only, after which they should be dug in. Suitable for potato and spring vegetable soup, sauces, salads, roasted meats and cottage cheese. Not suitable for drying.

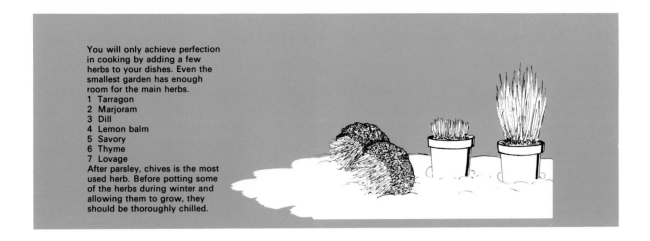

You will only achieve perfection in cooking by adding a few herbs to your dishes. Even the smallest garden has enough room for the main herbs.
1 Tarragon
2 Marjoram
3 Dill
4 Lemon balm
5 Savory
6 Thyme
7 Lovage
After parsley, chives is the most used herb. Before potting some of the herbs during winter and allowing them to grow, they should be thoroughly chilled.

Garlic The bulbs or cloves (similar to onion sets) should be planted in March, 15 cm/6 in. apart in rows with 15 cm/6 in. between. As the smell is so pungent, it is enough for salads just to rub the bowl with a clove of garlic. One or two cloves cut up finely and added to meat or fish before cooking give a delicious flavour to many dishes.

Lovage The aromatic roots and leaves can easily be dried. Use very sparingly in soups and gravies. One plant is sufficient.

Marjoram This should be grown in a nursery bed, or in pots in a room, before planting out. Plant in mid-May, four plants together in rows 45 cm/18 in. apart, leaving 35 cm/14 in. between each plant. Marjoram requires lots of sun, warmth and a well-fed soil. The plant can be harvested for drying shortly before it blooms. The aromatic leaves are used for flavouring roasts, poultry, sauces, liver and potato dishes.

Parsley This herb, full of vitamins, is the most frequently used in the kitchen. Sow at the beginning of March in rows 38 cm/15 in. apart. Later the plants should be thinned to 3·7–5 cm/1½–2 in. apart. Some parsley roots can be planted in pots during the autumn and placed near a window that is not too warm. The other roots can be stored in a box filled with damp sand, in the cellar, after the roots and leaves have been slightly shortened. In this way there is greenery for soups and sauces throughout the winter. Smooth-leaved parsley, or a variety with well-curled leaves can be sown early. The bed used for parsley should be changed each year, as the plants will react adversely— shrivelling up and turning yellow—if planted more than once in the same place.

Chives Probably the most popular herb of all, chives require strong, damp soil, and a lot of sun. Sow in rows in the open during spring. To ensure that the roots develop strongly do not cut in the first year. In the autumn the plants should be dug up in clumps and planted in their final bed. Chives should be divided every couple of years and replanted. The flowers should be removed.

In November, a few plants, complete with roots, are taken out of the soil and left in the garden for a few weeks. A frost is good for them. After this preparation, plant in narrow pots with only a little soil and stand on the window-sill. If one plant dies, there is always another to take its place. Water frequently.

Thyme An attractive looking plant, suitable for use in herbaceous borders and as an edging plant. Sow in April in nursery beds and plant out in mid-May 20 cm/8 in. between plants and in rows 20 cm/8 in. apart. After three years, the plants should be divided and replanted.

Lemon balm The citrus-smelling leaves are used in salads, roast meats and in fish and mushroom dishes. The plants can be bought from a nursery. One plant is usually sufficient.

8 Feeding Your Plants

HOW THE SOIL IS FORMED

Soil is formed by the weathering of rocks. This process, which has been going on for millions of years, has still not stopped. Large rocks are reduced in size by frost, changes in temperature, water and other agents. Algae, fungi, lichens and mosses growing on rocks, contribute to their disintegration. Finally the taller plants establish themselves on this material, and their roots accelerate the process of forming soil. Most people have certainly noticed, in the mountains or in quarries, how the roots of the stronger trees thrust through and open up the deeper rock strata.

If decomposition has proceeded far enough, then a fair number of different plants will grow on originally barren ground. When their foliage dies down its decomposition is aided by a multitude of living organisms in the ground to form a fertile humus, which serves as a foundation for the new plants. The minerals released by the disintegration of the rocks, are used as food by the wild plants. Despite the previous long period of time the fertile layer of humus-bearing soil is at most only 20–30 cm/8–12 in. deep; it undergoes constant erosion. When building a house, precautions should be taken that the site of the future garden retains this dark layer of rich topsoil.

Why must a fertilizer be used? A glance behind the scenes of plant life showed that plants take in a large amount of their nutriment from organic food and minerals in the soil. From these, and in combination with photosynthesis through the green leaves, the plant builds up its roots, shoots, leaves, flowers and fruits. A great number of important nutrients are extracted from the garden soil each year through this intensive absorption. Rain and snow also wash some of these vital foods away from the deeper layers. So in the course of years the soil becomes depleted of nutrients, crops become poorer and the plants soon make a very poor show.

To make up the loss of plant nutrients from the soil, it must be fed, either with organic or artificial fertilizers. The nutrients will only be effective again if the soil is healthy, and harbours a rich bacterial life. By digging in loads of compost, leaf-mould or rotted farmyard manure, this important need is fulfilled. The cost of the fertilizer plays a minimal role in comparison with its great benefit in the garden; the increased yield will prove this many times over.

It can be well meant, but it is never right to over-manure. Beyond a certain point, adding manure would no longer increase the yield, since every variety and type of plant has its upper limit of the amount it can produce. If too much manure is added, the point would soon be reached where it could even be harmful; the plants would be more prone to disease, and the durability and taste of the fruits would suffer; or they could 'burn up' completely.

The question is often asked why a plant can grow well in the wild, without any form of added fertilizer. In the wild, plants feed on the materials produced by the decomposition of rocks and the formation of humus. Nothing is taken away from

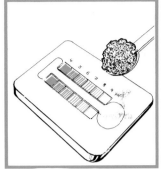

With the pH-meter the alkali content of the soil can easily be measured. The earth sample is placed in the bowl of the instrument and a drop of the indicating solution added. The solution then runs down the channel, and by noting the change of colour on a colour scale the pH value can be exactly established.

under a free standing tree. The plants round its base die down and produce humus, the foliage remains lying there and rots, and thus the cycle continues.

As soon as man steps in, producing several crops from one area in a year, and growing highly cultivated and productive varieties, the nutrients produced by nature are not sufficient. In areas used a great deal, natural humus cannot be formed, since the parts of the plants that would be used for this purpose are harvested—e.g., the roots of radish or celery; the leaves of lettuce or spinach; or the fruits of apples or tomatoes.

For this reason care must be taken that humus is added to the soil, also nutrients in reasonable amounts, if highly cultivated fruits, vegetables and flowers are to be grown. The soil's fertility must be maintained.

SOIL ANALYSIS

If a piece of land is bought or rented, it will be done with many different points of view in mind. It is very unlikely the decision will be greatly influenced by the type and condition of the soil. In other words, the ground is accepted for what it is, and experience proves that a quite productive garden can be created from almost any soil. In extreme cases one has to add a great deal of peat, leaf-mould or compost to create favourable growing conditions.

If you want to find out what kind of soil you have, which nutrients it contains or lacks, and which and how much fertilizer you should use, the pH value should be taken. Most local authorities or State Horticultural Experimental stations have a soil analysis service or you can test the soil yourself with one of the many soil-testing kits on the market. Since the pH value of your soil will change as you cultivate it, you ought to re-test it every 3 or 4 years. For the purpose of analysis about ten samples should be taken from different parts of the garden, at about one spit down. Half a handful is enough from each place, and should then be placed in a bucket and thoroughly mixed together. From this overall sample $\frac{1}{2}$ kg/1 lb should be placed in a plastic container, well packed, and sent to the horticultural advisor for analysis.

So that there can be no muddle, the sample should be carefully labelled. Once the sample has been tested, you will know a lot about your soil: its type, its acid reaction, the phosphate content; even a recommendation as to how the soil should be manured and improved. If further information is wanted as to the organic substances and trace elements, this can be asked for too, when sending the sample for analysis.

The pH value is merely a scale for determining whether the soil is acid, alkaline or neutral. The pH scale is a scale of values (1–14), in which pH0 is extremely acid, (hydrochloric acid); pH14 is extremely alkaline (caustic soda); between these two extremes is pH7, which is neutral.

Most garden plants prefer a slightly acid-to-slightly alkaline soil (about pH6–7·2). Only rhododendrons, camellias, garden bilberries and a few other plants allergic to alkalis, need an acid soil of about pH4·5.

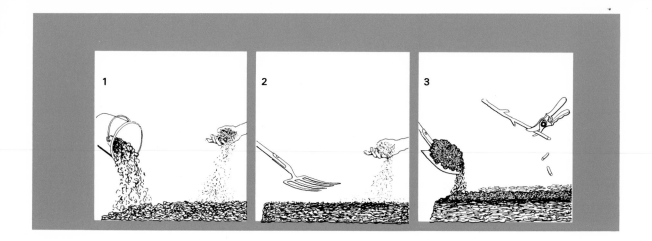

You can add lime to an acid soil to make it less acid, and flowers of sulphur to a chalky soil to make it more acid.

HUMUS, HUMUS AND STILL MORE HUMUS

It's impossible to give too much organic material to the garden. It is the very basis of the soil's productivity. Soil will remain healthy and fertile through constant additions of humus: large pieces of humus are tit-bits for its organisms. The bacteria in the soil are absolutely essential to its fertility. They turn the nutrients into a form acceptable to the plants, and create at the same time that vitally important decomposition of the soil which produces a perfectly friable structure, and prevents it from becoming clogged or crusted. Through the breathing of the numerous tiny living creatures in the soil, carbonic acid gas is produced, which will benefit the plant while growing and aid photosynthesis.

The most important producer of humus is the garden itself. It creates all the materials that are needed for the compost heap. Only parts of the plant with stubborn diseases (e.g. clubroot) should be omitted from the compost heap. But many diseased plants can go on to it, since the bacteria in the heap would soon biologically destroy almost all diseases.

The positioning of a compost heap is simple. It should be placed in the shade of a tree or building. All vegetable matter from the garden or house can be used to form a compost heap, be it lettuce leaves or potato peelings, dead heads or lawn mowings; even old newspapers. Wood ash, soot, foliage, grass, are also suitable. To make use of kitchen waste—e.g. eggshells, potato peelings, cucumber and orange peelings, other vegetable waste—a bucket with a lid can be placed in the cupboard under the sink, or some similar position, which can be emptied on to the compost heap. The heap should be so positioned that it can be about 1·2–1·4 m/3½–4 ft wide. The length does not matter, as that will depend on the place. When it is completely full up it should be about 1·4 m/4 ft high.

Here's the best way of making a compost heap. First spread a layer of waste materials about 20 cm/8 in. thick on the ground, and lightly sprinkle it with powdered lime. On top of that sprinkle four handfuls to the m^2/sq yd of hoof-and-horn or bonemeal. These organic fertilizers, slow to take effect, are good food for bacteria, and the compost will be enriched with nitrogen and phosphoric acid.

At the same time a few shovelfuls of already completed compost mixed with earth obtained from another compost heap, are added to the top layer. In this way the fresh compost material is injected with an abundance of bacteria that can begin working at once! Then the whole lot is well watered, and the next layer added, and treated in the same way.

Between each layer come twigs and weak branches from cutting fruit trees and hedges. These should be cut into small pieces. If a handful of this loose material is added to each layer it will

Preparation of compost heap
1 Organic waste is spread out to a depth of 20 cm/8 in, and hoof-and-horn or bonemeal scattered over it.
2 Lightly sprinkle chalk over this, and mix in slightly with a fork.
3 Scatter some half-rotted compost, and cover with twigs to allow aeration.
4 Thus layer is added upon layer, until the heap is complete.

aid in the decomposition of the compost heap, as more oxygen can get at the material, and thus accelerate the rotting process.

During dry weather the piled-up compost heap should be well watered from time to time. The materials should be kept damp, but not wet. Oxygen and moisture are absolutely crucial for quick decay.

If these directions are followed the heap should be sufficiently rotted to be ready for use in six months, less in summer. The compost should then be passed through a coarse sieve, so that woody pieces can be removed; they can be used when making a new heap. By using this method, without any special constructions and with the minimum of time, really effective compost is produced.

It would be wrong to leave the heap for three years or so, as used to be done. For the soil and crops, humus formed of large rotted particles is the most valuable.

Compost should be spread over the ground where needed and worked into the surface soil—it would be a waste to dig it in deeply. It is only when it is on or near the surface that it feeds the plants and helps the soil. When thoroughly dressed with such compost the plants grow sturdily and become more resistant to diseases and pests. So compost is an absolute essential to plants, both as a growing and a protective medium.

Because of the quick cycle of the compost heap, not much space need be allocated to it. It is important that the appearance of the compost area should be neat, especially in the smaller garden.

There are a number of compost-containers on the market. A container needs to be practical, i.e. it must allow sufficient air to get to the rotting material, and should be easy to dismantle. Heavy concrete constructions should be avoided for that reason—besides which they do not look particularly attractive. A good-looking container is one made of rounded logs treated with preservative. Another consists of wooden boards between concrete posts. A built-in concrete container is not suitable since it does not allow the air to circulate freely, and so the refuse does not form a loose friable humus but merely rots.

Not much need be said about farmyard manure. If obtainable, it is most valuable. It should be added to the heap, together with peat, in 20 cm/ 8 in. layers. The heap should be kept moist, and after a few months it should be turned twice, so that the peat and rotted manure are well mixed.

As soon as the heap has rotted sufficiently, the dark, crumbly mass should be taken to the beds and worked into the surface soil. Manure can be dug in deeply in the autumn, if there is some to spare. Chalk should not be added at the same time.

PEAT CAN PLAY A MAJOR PART IN PROVIDING HUMUS FOR THE GARDEN

Peat consists of nothing but an enormous number of minute moss plants, which in marshy areas, over thousands of years have become humus, or peat as it is called.

Instead of using peat and a mineral fertilizer

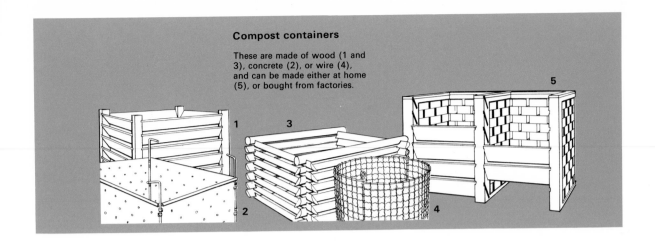

Compost containers

These are made of wood (1 and 3), concrete (2), or wire (4), and can be made either at home (5), or bought from factories.

separately on the garden, a mixture could be used, which in the right quantities would save time. This is especially to be recommended for a new garden, which needs to be made productive in as short a time as possible. Compost can hardly be added here, since there won't have been time to establish a compost heap.

The contents of two sacks of peat should be well moistened with water, and mixed with 5 kg/2½ lbs of calcium nitrate (bought in plastic bags), 7 kg/3½ lbs of calcium phosphate and 7 kg/3½ lbs of potash of magnesium, placed in a heap and covered with an 20 cm/8 in. layer of earth. After about four weeks, the heap should be turned over, and covered with another layer. After another four weeks, this 'quick compost' is ready, and can be put on to the vegetable or flower garden, wherever it is needed, and worked into the top spit.

If this quick compost is required even sooner than mentioned above, two sacks of peat can be mixed with 10 kg/5 lbs of artificial manure and well moistened. This is then ready for use immediately.

Complete peat-based fertilizers can be bought under various proprietary names from garden centres and nurseries. They should be used according to the instructions on the package.

THE IMPORTANT PLANT NUTRIENTS

Nitrogen (N) furthers the growth of the plant. The leaves grow luxuriantly, and with plenty of nitrogen are dark green. A lack of nitrogen shows itself in lesser growth than usual, in pale, unhealthy looking leaves; the fruits on fruit trees are small, as are the 'flowers' of cauliflowers and the roots of turnips and other vegetables. Nitrogen is very essential to growth.

Nitrates should be added, except for vegetables and annual flowers, only at the end of June. Otherwise if it is added too early, growth would be stimulated once again, and fruit, roses and so on, would not mature. By feeding too late the danger of frost damage would be increased. Too high a nitrogen content must be avoided, since this promotes rank coarse growth. And vegetables might then give off a bad odour while being cooked.

Phosphorous (P) benefits the formation of flowers and fruits. Plants that bloom or bear fruit particularly need this nutrient.

Potash (Potassium) (K) helps form the sugar and energy. The plants become sturdy and hardy; their resistance to cold and disease is favourably influenced.

Calcium (Ca) has a special job to do among the plant nutrients. It aerates the soil, promotes friability and neutralises acids. So it is an essential plant nutrient.

Magnesium (MG) is the fifth of the important plant nutrients. Apple trees, beetroot, French beans and many others extract as much magnesium as phosphate from the soil. Magnesium is an important constituent of chlorophyll—and a deficiency of magnesium will offset the green colouring of the leaf.

Besides these main nutrients the plants also need other chemical elements like boron, manganese, copper, zinc and cobalt. Others, such as iron, chlorine, sodium, sulphur and silisium are usually already plentiful in the soil. These chemicals are just as important to the plant as are the main nutrients, but only in smaller amounts.

A COMPLETE FERTILIZER MAKES WORK A LOT EASIER

Garden work should be made as easy as possible. That is why only chloride-free complete fertilizers are mentioned for the individual cultivations, since they contain in a balanced form, all the essential main and subsidiary nutrients.

As a measure, the author has always taken the human hand which can hold about 50 g/$1\frac{3}{4}$ oz, since scales on which 60 or 80 g/2 or 3 oz can be exactly weighed out are not always available in the garden. Anyway, such exactitude is much too fussy. If one's hand is larger or smaller, or if a few grammes more or less are taken, it's not so very crucial. It is only important that approximately the right amount is taken. All the complicated tables and calculations are deliberately waived! Dressing the garden with a fertilizer should not remain a mystery to the man who gardens in his spare time, but should give him as much pleasure as sowing, planting and harvesting.

Despite the artificial feeding of plants with the necessary nutrients, it can happen that over the years the soil becomes deficient in one of the essential nutrients, or on the other hand it could have built up too high a concentration of another. The occasional soil analysis will give all necessary information, so that faults can be remedied as early as possible.

The nutrient content in a complete artificial fertilizer is always the same, and in the correct amounts: 1 Nitrogen (N); 2 Phosphoric acid (P_2O_5); 3 Potash (K_2O); Magnesium (MgO). The calcium content amounts to about 8–10 per cent.

Instead of the practical complete artificial manures, separate fertilizers can be used. When the soil is dug in the autumn, phosphoric acid in the form of calcium phosphate (10 kg per 84 m^2/ 5 lbs per 100 sq yd) and potash in the form of potash of magnesium (8 kg per 84 m^2/4 lbs per 100 sq yd) can be added. In order to provide the soil with nitrogen, calcium nitrate can be added (5 kg per 84 m^2/$2\frac{1}{2}$ lbs per 100 sq yd). The above mentioned nutrients are sufficient for the average garden. If necessary during growth, a liquid manure could be used in a weak solution. If, however, it is discovered that one particular nutrient is missing from the soil or is over-concentrated, this can be corrected by using fertilizers balanced to remedy this fault.

9 Killing Bugs and Curing Diseases

PLANTS MUST HAVE PROTECTION

Unfortunately, our green paradise is frequently invaded by pests and diseases. We must protect it if we want to achieve good results.

Some garden-lovers may ask: 'What's the point of spraying? We have done without it in the past! Well, plants have suffered from pests and diseases since time immemorial. We have only to recall the 'seven lean years' in the Bible story. Locust plagues often occurred in ancient Egypt, and there are age-old accounts of invasions of mice. Many fungus diseases seem new to us simply because the microscope has been available only a comparatively short time for the scientific detection of plant diseases.

Although the quality and yield of fruit and vegetable varieties have been much improved by constant selection and inbreeding their susceptibility to pests and diseases has also sometimes increased proportionately. The gardener who looks for choice fruit and vegetables at harvest-time, or who dislikes the sight of blighted roses withering on the stem before summer is over, cannot afford to be without some measure of plant protection.

PREVENTION IS BETTER THAN CURE

Needless to say, chemical preparations should be used in the garden only when absolutely necessary. We shall therefore consider what can be done to prevent the spread of pests and diseases, and how to keep them down to the minimum.

The most important measure is to keep the soil in good health by a constant supply of humus, and to provide the plants with well-balanced nourishment. Pruning is very important in the case of top fruit trees and soft fruit bushes, which of course must also be planted out at appropriate distances. Free-standing fruit trees with their branches thinned out are less likely to become affected by scab than trees which have not been pruned. Parasitic fungi need moisture and warmth in order to thrive. If this basic need is denied them—and well-pruned plants dry quickly after rain—the attack can often be repelled. We can also guard against pests and diseases by choosing the right kind of plant and setting it in a suitable place in the garden—otherwise poor growth will be the result.

ALLIES IN THE STRUGGLE AGAINST PESTS

Although only a portion of garden pests are destroyed by birds, they do eat a great many injurious insects, particularly while rearing their young. Even on mild winter days the ever-lively titmice can be seen darting from tree to tree and hopping about on the branches in search of food, no doubt consuming many hibernating pests in the process. Research shows that the diet of the great tit, the blue tit and the coal tit consists of up to 60 per cent of insect pests, and that of the skylark, warbler and hedge-sparrow of up to almost 70 per cent. Since, on the whole they are so beneficial, let us encourage them by providing them with nest-boxes and bird-baths, and with food during the winter. A very useful ally of the gardener is the

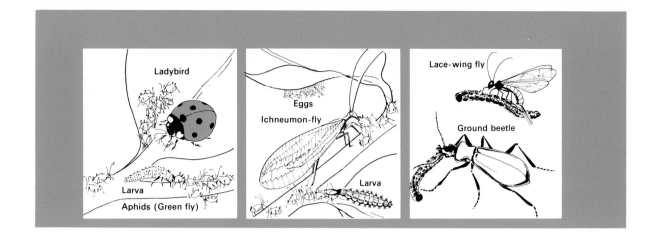

Ladybird
Larva
Aphids (Green fly)
Eggs
Ichneumon-fly
Larva
Lace-wing fly
Ground beetle

hedgehog. It eats cockchafer grubs, caterpillars, wireworms and snails. Unfortunately it also eats a few earthworms, which are very important for introducing humus into the soil.

Another benefactor of the gardener and natural enemy of pests is the ladybird and its larvae, which eagerly devour aphids (green fly), scale-insects, woolly aphis and suchlike pests in great quantities. The lacewing-fly has a light-green body, translucent greenish wings and long feelers. Its favourite dish, and that of its active grubs, also consists of aphids. In the autumn this insect is occasionally found indoors.

Hover-flies too are very beneficial, and lay their eggs on plants where there are likely to be colonies of aphids. A mature hover-fly maggot can destroy up to 40 aphids daily. In addition, various other kinds of predacious and parasitic insects, including ground-beetles and ichneumon-flies (which lay their eggs inside the bodies of other insects, usually caterpillars), help to keep down pests. Many other insects are beneficial.

We should never automatically start spraying without first satisfying ourselves as to whether aphids and other pests are on the increase, or whether their numbers are being effectively kept down by ladybirds and other natural agencies.

CHEMICAL CONTROL OF PESTS AND DISEASES—SOME USEFUL PESTICIDES

In spite of the preventive measures we may have taken, and the usefulness of some beneficial birds and insects in the fight against pests and diseases, some will keep recurring and can only be fought by chemical means.

Here are a few preparations, some old and some new, which are being used successfully in gardens and which are recommended for the individual pests and diseases mentioned on the following pages. They are well-known pesticides and can be obtained at most horticultural stores, garden centres, and the horticultural departments of some chemists shops. These chemicals are manufactured by different firms under a variety of brand names, and care should be taken to use them with all due safety precautions, at the rates recommended for the product. Where possible, use pesticides which carry the seal of government approval. The container of such chemicals bears a bold letter A surmounted by a crown and the words 'Agricultural Chemicals Approval Scheme'.

In England and Wales, amateurs may obtain advice on plant health problems from Horticultural Advisers employed by the County Councils or from Local Authority Farm and Horticultural Institutes: in the U.S.A. from the local State Horticultural Experimental Station. There is no general, advisory service on plant health problems for amateurs in Scotland but advice may be obtained from the Parks Department of their Local Authority, or, in some instances from the horticultural advisers of the Agricultural Colleges.

Basically pesticides fall into three groups, (a) insecticides, (b) fungicides and (c) herbicides. On the whole their activities are different, and only a few fungicides have marked insecticidal action or vice versa.

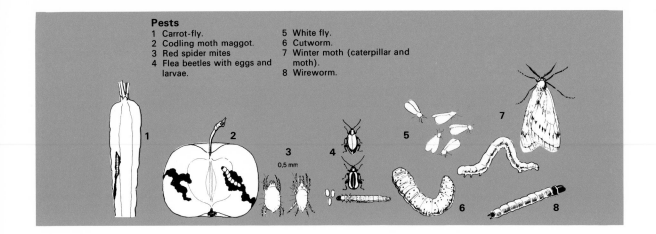

Pests
1 Carrot-fly.
2 Codling moth maggot.
3 Red spider mites
4 Flea beetles with eggs and larvae.
5 White fly.
6 Cutworm.
7 Winter moth (caterpillar and moth).
8 Wireworm.

FUNGICIDES

Benomyl   A systemic fungicide formulated as a wettable powder. Applied as a spray it is effective against *Botrytis* on a wide range of fruit and vegetable crops, and pot plants and against powdery mildews on apple, soft fruits, pot plants and outdoor roses. Scab on apple and other diseases are also controlled. Tolerance to benomyl has been found in certain strains of *Botrytis*, and the fungicide may not be effective against them.

Captan   Supplied as a wettable powder. Reduces scab infection of apples and pears, and grey mould on strawberries. It also helps to control black spot on roses. Also available as a seed dressing combined with BHC against damping-off of seedlings.

Copper compounds (e.g. oxide, oxychloride, etc.)   Supplied as dusts, wettable powders or colloidal suspensions. Also available combined with maneb. Useful against many common leaf and fruit diseases of top fruit (e.g. apple canker) and soft fruit (e.g. leafspot on blackcurrant, rust on gooseberry). Some products can be used for controlling damping-off of seedlings. Copper can cause damage to leaves and fruits if safeners are not added. Harmless to bees.

Dichlofluanid   Available as a wettable powder, and particularly useful against *Botrytis* on various soft fruits, (e.g. strawberry, currants, gooseberry, etc.). Do not use on strawberries under glass or polythene. Brassica seedlings can be protected from downy mildew with dichlofluanid. Minimum

interval before harvest for most soft fruits is 3 weeks (strawberries and raspberries 2 weeks). No effect on bees.

Dinocap   Formulated as liquids and wettable powders specifically useful against powdery mildews, but also suppresses red spider mites. Waiting time on outdoor edible crops is 1 week and on indoor crops is 2 days. Some varieties of chrysanthemum are sensitive to dinocap.

Lime sulphur and sulphur preparations Formulated as wettable powders or 'cols', and as dusts (sulphur). Particularly active against powdery mildews. Be careful as some varieties of fruit trees and bushes may be damaged by sulphur.

Quinomethionate   Formulated as a wettable powder and as smokes (not yet available to amateurs), particularly useful against powdery mildews, it also gives control of red spider mite on a wide variety of crops. Before spraying blackcurrants for control of leafspot, check on label that variety will not be damaged.
   Waiting time on apples is 3 weeks, on blackcurrants, gooseberries and strawberries is 2 weeks, on marrows is 1 week, and on cucumber and tomatoes under glass is only 2 days.

Quintozene   As a dust incorporated into the surface soil it is extremely useful against *Rhizoctonia* infection of seedlings and young plants of various crops including brassicas, lettuce, tomatoes and some flower crops. It should not be

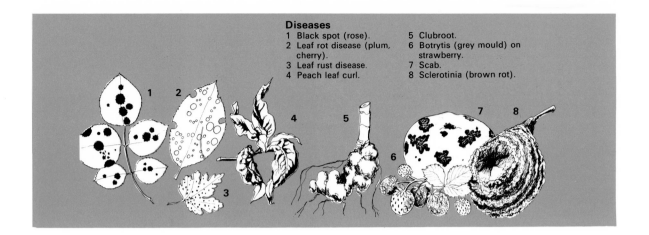

Diseases
1. Black spot (rose).
2. Leaf rot disease (plum, cherry).
3. Leaf rust disease.
4. Peach leaf curl.
5. Clubroot.
6. Botrytis (grey mould) on strawberry.
7. Scab.
8. Sclerotinia (brown rot).

necessary if clean soil is used in the seed boxes or seed bed. Quintozene is also available as a wettable powder for watering on turf to control grass diseases. Do not plant cucurbits or tomatoes in recently treated soil.

Thiram Wettable powders and 'col' formulations are useful against *Botrytis* on lettuce and strawberry, and a number of other diseases (e.g. cane spot of raspberry).

Zineb and Mancozeb Available as wettable powders, either alone or in combination. The combination is effective against such diseases as scab on apples and pears, black-spot on roses, leafspot on blackcurrant, and rusts on various ornamentals (e.g. roses, carnations, geraniums). Useful against downy mildew on lettuces. Allow at least a week between last application and harvest.

INSECTICIDES

BHC Used as dusts, smokes, sprays and seed dressings to control a wide range of chewing insects on foliage and in the soil. May cause taint in carrots and potatoes (see instructions on container). Pure g-BHC (Lindane) does not cause taint. Harmful to bees. Waiting period between application and harvest 2 weeks.

Bromophos Applied as a spray against sucking insects and against biting insects. It can also be used from a watering-can against carrot fly, onion fly and cabbage root fly on cabbages and radishes.

Bromophos also comes in powder form, and can be used against vegetable flies as well as soil pests such as wireworms, cockchafer larvae and cutworms. Also quite effective against fruit maggots.

Demeton-S-Methyl A systemic organophosphorous insecticide very effective as a spray against aphids and mites. This is a **VERY TOXIC** substance and care must be taken to observe all recommended precautions in use. It may be phytotoxic to some plants. There must be a waiting period of 3 weeks between treatment and harvesting of edible crops. It is a systemic insecticide, i.e. it is carried in the sap of the conducting tissue of the plant and renders it toxic to sucking pests. Harmful to bees.

Derris and Pyrethrum There preparations are made from vegetable raw materials and may be used together or singly. The active agent pyrethrum comes from the buds of a type of chrysanthemum grown in Kenya, Tanganyika and New Guinea. Derris is prepared from the root of a tropical leguminous plant. They are effective against insects of all kinds. Pyrethrum has a quick knockdown activity but is short lived—it requires the addition of derris or other insecticides finally to kill the pests. Both are short-lived, harmless to warm blooded animals and bees. Derris is very toxic to fish. Sold as aerosols, dust and sprays. Edible crops may be harvested 24 hours after treatment.

Malathion Sprays and dusts used for the

185

control of aphids, thrips, caterpillars, beetles and mites. Not toxic to warm blooded animals but harmful to bees and fish. Waiting period between applications and harvest 1–4 days.

Metaldehyde Active against slugs and snails used as solid tablets, as sprays or in bait pellets. The chemical anaesthetises the pests preventing them from returning to shelter and exposing them to desiccation. Toxic to warm blooded animals.

Methiocarb A new carbamate chemical giving good control of slugs and snails when used as bait pellets. Harmful to earthworms.

Propoxur Available as smokes. Effective against sucking and biting insects, can also be used against maggots in fruit. Harmful to bees.

WEEDKILLERS

Lawns and Paths A herbicide containing ioxynil is effective against weeds in freshly sown lawns, whereas in the case of older lawns materials containing mecaprop or mecaprop with 2, 4-D can be used. A number of herbicides, particularly atrazine, bromacil, chlorthiamid, paraquat and simazine, are available for weed control on pathways and drives.

Cultivated areas (for larger gardens only) Weeds between ornamental shrubs or roses, on garden paths, etc., can be controlled with paraquat, following the directions for use on the packet.

A splash screen must be used to prevent the preparation being blown on to neighbouring beds and borders. The spraying mixture kills off all green parts of plants that come into contact with it (but does not harm tree trunks or the woody parts of bushes). In the soil paraquat immediately becomes inactive, so that only two days after spraying the treated areas can safely be planted.

In addition, numerous other weedkilling preparations are available nowadays, designed for specific treatments and cultivations. These doubtless play a big role in commercial market-gardening, as time-savers, but are generally unnecessary for the amateur. For one thing most of them are unavailable to the amateur, and for another, we should welcome plenty of exercise in our own garden, as a healthy change from an often sedentary occupational routine.

WOUND HEALING PRODUCT

Arbrex 805 (trade name) Protective dressings for fruit tree wounds should also be kept.

WHEN HANDLING PESTICIDES

This much is certain: so far, accidents with pesticides have only occurred through wrong handling. Used correctly they are a benefit, just like electricity, gas, transport, and many other things without which our life nowadays would be unthinkable. But all these things can become dangerous if handled wrongly.

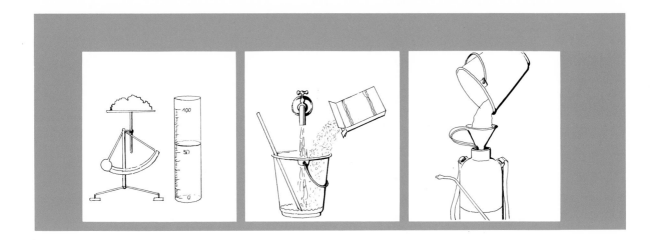

IF A CASE OF POISONING OCCURS A DOCTOR OR THE NEAREST HOSPITAL SHOULD BE CONTACTED IMMEDIATELY.

To avoid accidental poisoning, it is very important that the following points should be observed:

★ Preparations must not be stored in living quarters.

★ Contents must never be transferred from the original packages to other containers (bottles, bags, cans, etc.).

★ At all times preparations should be stored in a locked cupboard, out of reach of children.

★ Never prepare spraying mixtures in the house, and always use special containers meant for the purpose.

★ On no account leave the prepared mixtures unattended—(they are a danger to children!). Residues of spraying mixtures which are no longer needed must never be emptied where they can endanger the health of humans, animals or other plants (e.g. on a gravel path).

★ Protective clothing (overalls, gumboots, gloves, etc.) should be worn when spraying. Never spray or dust in bathing trunks.

★ Never attempt to spray against the wind. No spraying or dusting should be carried out in strong winds, which might blow the preparations on to surrounding cultivated areas or neighbouring gardens where it could do damage.

★ Do not spray while bees are on the wing. The best time is in the evening.

★ No smoking, eating or drinking during the spraying operation. The use of alcohol before, during or after spraying can be dangerous.

★ Do not use the mouth to free the spraying nozzle.

★ Wash thoroughly after the work is done.

WAITING PERIODS

The waiting period is the interval which must be allowed between the last application of a particular pesticide to a crop and its harvest. When using any pesticide check what is the minimum waiting period.

PROTECTION OF BEES

Some chemicals are dangerous or harmful to bees, and every precaution should be taken to avoid harming them. For this reason, certain pesticides should not be applied at flowering time, when the bees are particularly vulnerable. If crops in flower have to be sprayed, then neighbouring bee keepers should be given advanced warning in order that they may retain the bees in the hives. Crop protection chemicals which are harmful to bees may carry a printed warning on the package.

HINTS ON APPLYING CROP PROTECTION CHEMICALS

★ For spring spraying when buds are bursting and for winter spraying if needed, use a wide outlet nozzle giving a fairly coarse spray. Wash trees and shrubs thoroughly.

187

★ When spraying vegetation with fungicides use a fairly fine nozzle. The finer the spray, the better the cover of the plant with chemical and the more effective will the protection be.

★ Liquid sprays (emulsions) must be accurately measured out in a measuring-cup marked out in cm^3. Some firms supply such a measure with their product, by marking out the closure cap in cm^3. An overdose may cause damage, while too small a dose may have little or no effect.

★ For sprays in powder form, weigh out the quantity required for, say, 2 gallons (9 litres) water on a pair of scales, tip it into a plastic beaker and mark the level on the outside. Use a different beaker and mark it for each individual preparation, labelling each beaker on the outside with the name of the product. In this way there is no need to use the scale every time you are about to prepare a spraying mixture. **DO NOT USE SCALES THAT MAY BE USED LATER IN THE KITCHEN FOR WEIGHING FOOD.**

★ It is best, particularly in the case of wettable powders, to mix the formulation with a little water in a bucket (mix powders to a paste) before diluting the mixture to obtain the required concentration. Keep the mixture well stirred or agitated in the container so that the chemical does not settle out and the concentration does not vary during spraying.

★ Most modern pesticides contain surfactants which aid wetting and spreading of the chemical on the leaves. For some crops with waxy foliage (e.g. onions, bassicas, etc.) there may be insufficient in the products for satisfactory wetting, and additional wetter must be added. Several wetting agents are available from horticultural suppliers.

★ When using dusts, the best time to apply them is in the early morning, when the dust will cling to the dew-drenched leaves.

IMPORTANT COMMON PESTS

Aphids Distorted curled-up leaves and stunted shoots. Control is obtained by preventative winter spraying of fruit trees when the buds are dormant with DNOC/Petroleum Oil to kill eggs. Spring sprays (at green cluster stage) with demeton-S-methyl, dimethoate or malathion to kill the newly hatched aphids. In cases of severe attacks during vegetative growth, spray with similar materials.

Scale insects Weakened growth; countless small scales form a crust on wood, sooty moulds disfigure leaves and stems. Control: preventive spraying as for aphids.

Red Spider Mites Minute red mites feeding on the under surface of leaves, which become mottled with small whitish spots and may turn from grey to rusty brown. Fruit crops, cucumbers, beans, strawberries, roses and many others are attacked. In severe cases spray with demeton-S-methyl or a specific treatment (dicofol for example).

Caterpillars Appear on bush fruits, vegetable and ornamental plants. Cut off nests of caterpillars, or pick off the caterpillars themselves. Ward off severe attacks with BHC.

Slugs and snails Holes of irregular shape on the leaf-surface, trails of slime. Plants are particularly vulnerable during prolonged warm wet weather. Control; slug pellets containing metaldehyde or methiocarb.

Soil pests (wireworms, cockchafer larvae) They chew roots and tubers and shoots of a variety of plants. Pick out and destroy these grubs while working over the soil. Pull up withering plants and squash the grubs which are often lurking nearby. For severe attacks (new garden) work BHC, carbaryl or nexion dust into the top 4 inches of soil before sowing or planting.

Voles Plants are chewed off underground. The heaps of earth they dig up are shallow and irregular in shape, intermingled with grass and pieces of root, quite different in appearance from the high rounded shape of mole hills. Control: open up the hole; if still inhabited, one often finds it blocked up with earth again after only 10 minutes. The well-tried hinged spring-trap is still one of the best methods of catching them. Another method of destruction is by gassing with smokes or the exhaust fumes of an engine piped into the hole.

Birds (blackbirds, starlings) The best defence against the ravages of bird-pests is netting, either synthetic fibre or fishnet.

Hares Keep young fruit trees from being gnawed and nibbled by game in the winter, by wrapping with wire or synthetic fibre netting.

PESTS AND DISEASES OF FRUIT TREES

Type of fruit	Description of damage	Pest or disease	Control measures
APPLE & PEAR	Dark brown marks on leaves and fruit	Scab	Spray with benomyl, captan or mancozeb-with-zineb at bud burst and at regular intervals before and after blossoming
APPLE & PEAR (& PLUM)	Young shoots stunted and covered in sticky deposits followed by sooty mould. Small insects visible	Aphids and other leaf suckers	Use winter sprays of DNOC/petroleum oil, and following bud break use sprays of demeton-S-methyl dimethoate or melathion
APPLE	Fruit contains holes and small grubs in core	Codling moth and Tortrix moths	Spray in mid-June and 4 weeks later with malathion or carbaryl (Care bees!)
	White powdery growth on surface of shoots and leaves	Powdery mildew	Spray with dinocap, benomyl or lime sulphur from flowering to mid-July or later. Check for sulphur 'shy' varieties
	Initially sunken areas on branch, enlarge and become swollen. Wood discoloured and branch may die if ringed by canker. White pustules may be seen in winter and red ones in summer	Canker	Remove badly affected shoots. Cut away less severe cankers and paint with Arbrex 805 or paint direct on canker with organomercury paint during winter

Type of fruit	Description of damage	Pest or disease	Control measures
PLUM AND CHERRY	Leaves yellowish sometimes with pale spots which turn brown and drop out leaving 'shot holes'. Cankers on trunk on branches; young trees may die	Bacterial canker	Prune diseased branches during May–August. Spray at petal fall with copper fungicide, and also at 3-week intervals from end of August
PLUM AND DAMSON	Dark brown pustules on underside of leaves. Trees may be prematurely defoliated	Plum rust	Sprays with mancozeb-with-zineb at 2–3 week intervals from July to September. 1 week waiting time
PLUM AND DAMSON	Young fruit falls off soon after blossom. c.v. Czar very susceptible	Plum sawfly	Spray after petal fall with demeton-S-methyl or dimethoate (Care bees!)
PEACH	Leaves curled with whitish-green to reddish thickened areas. Premature defoliation	Peach leaf curl	Spray with copper fungicide or lime sulphur just as the buds begin to swell and again before leaf fall in the autumn

PESTS AND DISEASES OF BUSH FRUITS

Type of fruit	Description of damage	Pest or disease	Control measures
GOOSEBERRY AND RED CURRANT	Dark spots on leaves which turn yellowish and drop off	Leafspot	Spray at early stage and at 14-day intervals with benomyl, or according to makers instructions with mancozeb-with-zineb. Also apply one spray of benomyl or mancozeb-with-zineb after harvest

Type of fruit	Description of damage	Pest or disease	Control measures
BLACK-CURRANT	Yellowish powdery appearance on underside of leaves	Rust	Spray with copper fungicides after harvest, or with mancozeb-with-zineb according to makers instructions
GOOSEBERRY	Leaves, shoots and berries covered with whitish mealy, felt-like layer	American gooseberry mildew	Prune to obtain open growth. Do not delay until too late in year. Burn all prunings. *Either* spray with dinocap at first sign of disease and repeat twice at 14-day intervals, *or* with benomyl at grape stage and three times subsequently at 14-day intervals Also spray with dinocap or benomyl after picking complete, and repeat if necessary at 14-day intervals
	Rapid defoliation by blackspotted green caterpillars	Gooseberry sawfly larvae	Examine bushes May–June—spray with derris or malathion
RASPBERRY	Purple spots on young canes in early summer, later becoming grey with purple borders. Tips of canes may be killed	Cane spot	Clear the soil and remove old canes. To prevent infection, spray with benomyl, copper fungicide, dichlofluanid or thiram, when buds 1 cm long and continue at 14-day intervals to end of blossom

Type of fruit	Description of damage	Pest or disease	Control measures
BLACKBERRY	Purplish blotches appear on the young canes during summer	Purple blotch	Cut out severely affected canes. Spray with copper fungicide once or twice before the fruit swells
STRAWBERRY	Smoky grey fur on rotting fruit	Botrytis	Give sufficient space between plants. Spray at 10-day intervals from early flowering to harvest with dichlofluanid, benomyl, captan or thiram. Check on waiting period
	Young central leaves wrinkled and brown. Worst in hot summers	Strawberry mite	Remove damaged leaves. Spray prior to flowering and after fruiting with dicofol

PESTS AND DISEASES OF VEGETABLES

Type of vegetable	Description of damage	Pests or disease	Control measures
BEANS	Damage to seedlings. Brown tracks on seed leaves due to larvae feeding	Bean fly	Purchase insecticide-treated seed and sow when soil sufficiently warm to give rapid growth
BRASSICAS (cabbage, cauliflower, brussels sprouts, etc.)	Stunted, wilting plants with discoloured leaves. Plants easily removed from soil. White maggots visible on root	Cabbage root fly	Purchase insecticide-treated seed. Protect transplants by root dip of calomel and drenches or granules of diazinon or g-BHC dusts or drenches

Type of fruit	Description of damage	Pest or disease	Control measures
	Young stems stunted and coiled with feeding mites and small grubs	Cabbage weevil	Dust the rows of young seedlings with g-BHC
	Plants stunted and poorly developed. Wilt on warm days. Irregular swellings and knotted distortion of roots	Clubroot	If possible avoid growing brassicas continuously on same ground. Do not dig clubbed roots back in the ground or put on compost heap. Check soil pH—if less than pH7, and particularly if infected with clubroot, add lime. Check transplants are not infected before planting. Dip transplant roots in calomel suspension (57 g/ 2 oz pure calomel to 0·5 litre/1 pint water) before planting
	Holes in leaves and stems. Worst in dry weather (also occurs in radish and turnips)	Flea beetles	Use seed treated with g-BHC and if severe use g-BHC spray on seedlings
CARROTS (also parsnips and parsley)	Tops yellow and wilted. Small white maggots in tunnels in root (also on parsley and parsnips)	Carrot fly	Use seed treated with g-BHC. Protect seedlings with diazinon granules
CELERY	Rusty brown spots on leaves and stalks; the leaves gradually wilt and die	Leafspot	Use thiram-soaked seed if available. Spray seedlings in the seed box with copper fungicide or benomyl. If the disease is seen in the field spray at 2–3 week intervals until August

Type of fruit	Description of damage	Pest or disease	Control measures
TOMATOES	Grey-green spots on foliage, which dies off. Fruit bears brown marbled areas, and rots (mainly on outdoor plants, or in cold glass)	Blight	Repeated sprays with copper fungicide or mancozeb-with-zineb at 10–14 day intervals from end of July onwards, particularly if blight seen on potatoes
ONIONS	Whitish grubs eat into bulb, leaves wilt and turn yellow. Seedlings die off	Onion fly	Use seed treated with insecticide. Also apply g-BHC dust on to rows of seedlings at 'loop' stage
	Leaves die back from tips. Grey or purplish growth on foliage. Later dead leaves turn black	Onion downy mildew	Choose open site with well-drained soil for growing. Repeated sprays with zineb from early June onwards
VARIOUS VEGETABLES	Roots and stems chewed or eaten through	Soil pests: cock-chafer larvae, cut-worms, wireworms etc.	Apply g-BHC dust and work into soil
	Foliage and stems with ragged holes	Slugs and snails	Use slug pellets containing metaldehyde or methiocarb, or use sprays of above

PESTS AND DISEASES OF ORNAMENTALS

Type of flower	Description of damage	Pest or disease	Control measures
ASTERS	Plants wilt and die	Aster wilt	Do not compost diseased plants. Grow resistant varieties
	Crinkling of leaves, shoot tips withered. Aphids visible	Aphids	Spray with malathion, dimethoate pirimicarb, demeton-S-methyl or other aphicides

Type of fruit	Description of damage	Pest or disease	Control measures
GLADIOLI	White or grey streaks on leaves, and mottled patches on blooms. Pest feeds on stored corms	Gladiolus thrips	Protect stored corms by dusting with g-BHC. Spray growing plants with g-BHC or malathion
TULIPS	Dry bulbs may bear surface crater-like spots. Leaves distorted and scorched; petals and leaves may show clear or brownish spots. Flowers may rot	Fire	When purchasing, reject bulbs with brown spots. In spring, spray young emerging leaves with dichlofluanid, mancozeb-with-zineb, thiram or captan. Before storing in autumn, dust bulbs with quintozene, or soak for 30 min in 0·1 per cent benomyl and dry
ROSES	Leaves show ragged-edged black spots, later turn yellow and fall prematurely	Blackspot	At first sign of disease, pick off infected leaves when dry and burn. Spray with captan, zineb, or mancozeb-with-zineb, at 10–14 day intervals throughout season
	Whitish powder on leaves, stems and flower calyces	Powdery mildew	Spray at 10-day intervals with benomyl or dinocap
	Foliage stunted and distorted with much honeydew. Aphids visible	Aphids	Spray several times as directed with demeton-S-methyl, dimethoate, malathion or pirimicarb
	Yellow spotting on foliage. Small jumping insects on underside	Rose leaf-hopper	Spray at intervals with malathion

A SPRAY TIMING CHART FOR THE YEAR

This chart is meant merely as a rough guide, an aid to memory, for pesticides should only be used when absolutely necessary. The chart is designed as an adjunct to personal observation in the garden, and the advice obtainable from current articles in gardening magazines.

Spray	*Pest or disease*	*Pesticide spray*
Winter spray		
While buds on fruit trees are dormant	Aphids, scale insects, red spider mites	DNOC/petroleum oil or tar oil
	Moss or lichens on trunks and branches	Tar oil
Early sprays		
Between swelling and bursting of the buds. Exception: Peach—spray just as buds begin to swell	Aphids, scale insects, leaf suckers, blossom weevil, caterpillars	Demeton-S-methyl, dimethoate, malathion
	Peach leaf curl	Proprietary copper compound or lime sulphur
	The insecticidal treatments can also be applied to bush fruits and ornamental shrubs, including pines. Cover any flowers or vegetables growing underneath with polythene sheet while spraying with DNOC/petroleum oil or tar oil	
After bud blast		
Do not spray when bees are flying	If apple or pear scab seems likely	Benomyl, captan or mancozeb-with-zineb
	Apple mildew	Dinocap, benomyl or lime sulphur

Spray *Winter spray*	Pest or disease	Pesticide spray
After flowering 1 Immediately after petal fall	Aphids, red spider mites, sawflies etc.	Demeton-S-methyl, dimethoate, malathion
	Scab on apple and pear	Benomyl, captan or mancozeb-with-zineb
	Apple mildew	Dinocap, benomyl or lime sulphur
	Bacterial canker of plums, cherries, peach and almond	Proprietory copper compound
2 About mid-June and again in early to mid-July	Fruit maggots	Malathion
	Plum sawfly	Dimethoate
	Scab on apple and pear	Benomyl, captan, mancozeb-with-zineb
	Apple mildew	Dinocap, benomyl or lime sulphur
3 Mid-July	Plum rust	Mancozeb-with-zineb
	Bacterial canker of plums, cherries, peach and almond	Proprietory copper compound
Pre-storage spray Mid-August, to mid-September, with late varieties	Scab and other rots of apple (developing later in store)	Benomyl, captan
Leaf-fall spray In autumn. Particularly effective as a spray at start of leaf-fall, followed by another 2–3 weeks later	Bacterial canker of plums, cherries, peach and almond Peach leaf curl	Proprietory copper compound. Lime sulphur can also be used against peach leaf curl
	Canker on apple	Lesions should be painted with organomercury paints during winter, or cut out and painted with Arbrex 805

Appendix

Factors for the conversion of imperial to metric units

1 inch (in)	= 2.540 centimetres (cm)
1 foot (ft) (= 12 in)	= 30.48 cm
1 yard (yd) (= 3 ft)	= 0.9144 metre (m)
1 square yard (sq yd)	= 0.8361 sq m
1 acre (= 4840 sq yd)	= 0.4047 hectare (ha)
1 ounce (oz)	= 28.35 grams (g)
1 pound (lb)	= 0.4536 kilogram (kg)
1 hundredweight (cwt) (= 112 lb)	= 50.80 kg
1 ton (= 2240 lb)	= 1016 kg = 1.016 metric tons (tonnes) (t)
1 pint	= 0.5682 litre (l)
1 gallon (gal.) (= 8 pints)	= 4.546 litres
1 fluid ounce = 1/20 pint	= 0.02841 litre = 28.41 ml
1 cubic foot	= 28.32 litres

To Convert	*Multiply by*
oz/acre to g/ha	70.06
lb/acre to kg/ha	1.121
cwt/acre to kg/ha	125.5
cwt/acre to tonnes/ha	0.1255
tons/acre to kg/ha	2511
tons/acre to tonnes/ha	2.511
gal/acre to litre/ha	11.233

The following factors are accurate to about 2 parts in 100 :

1 lb/acre	= 1.1 kg/ha
1 gal/acre	= 11 litres/ha
1 ton/acre	= 2.5 tonnes/ha
1 lb	= 0.5 kg
1 lb/acre	= 1 kg/ha

Temperatures

To convert °F into °C subtract 32 and multiply by 5/9th (0.556)
To convert °C into °F multiply by 9/5th (1.8) and add 32

Factors for the conversion of metric to imperial units

1 centimetre (cm)	= 0.3937 inch (in) = 0.03281 ft
1 metre (m)	= 1.094 yards (yd)
1 square metre (sq m)	= 1.196 square yards (sq yd)
1 hectare (ha)	= 2.471 acres
1 gram (g)	= 0.03527 ounce (oz)
1 kilogram (kg)	= 2.205 pounds (lb)
1 kg	= 0.01968 hundredweight (cwt) = 0.0009842 ton
1 metric ton (tonne) (t)	= 0.9842 ton
1 litre	= 1.760 pints = 0.2200 gallon (gal)
1 litre = 1000 millilitres (ml)	= 35.20 fluid ounces = 0.03531 cubic foot

To Convert	Multiply by
g/ha to oz/acre	0.01427
kg/ha to lb/acre	0.8921
kg/ha to cwt/acre	0.007966
kg/ha to tons/acre	0.0003983
tonnes/ha to tons/acre	0.3983
litre/ha to gal/acre	0.08902

Plant Nutrients

Plant nutrients are best stated in terms of amounts of the elements
(P, K, Na, Ca, Mg, S); the old 'oxide' terminology P_2O_5, K_2O, Na_2O,
CaO, MgO, SO_3) is still used in work involving fertilizers and lining
since Regulations require statements of P_2O_5, K_2O, etc.

For quick conversions

(Accurate to within 2%) the following factors may be used:

$2\frac{1}{3}$ x P = P_2O_5	3/7th x P_2O_5 = P
1 1/5th x K = K_2O	5/6th x K_2O = K
1 2/5th x Ca = CaO	7/10th x CaO = Ca
$1\frac{2}{3}$ x Mg = MgO	3/5th x MgO = Mg

For accurate conversions

To Convert	Multiply by	To Convert	Multiply by
P_2O_5 to P	014364	P to P_2O_5	2.2915
K_2O to K	0.8301	K to K_2O	1.2047
CaO to Ca	0.7146	Ca to CaO	1.3994
MgO to Mg	0.6031	Mg to MgO	1.6581

Conversion tables for British and Metric Weights and Measures

The figures in the central of the three columns in each table represents either one or the other of the two side columns, as required, e.g. 1 kg = 2.205 lb, 1 lb = 0.454 kg, 100 ha = 247.105 ac, 100 ac = 40.469 ha.

Kilograms	Weight kg or lb	Pounds	Hectares	Area ha or ac	Acres
0.454	1	2.205	0.405	1	2.471
0.907	2	4.409	0.809	2	4.942
1.361	3	6.614	1.214	3	7.413
1.814	4	8.819	1.619	4	9.884
2.268	5	11.023	2.023	5	12.355
2.722	6	13.228	2.428	6	14.826
3.175	7	15.432	2.833	7	17.297
3.629	8	17.637	3.237	8	19.769
4.082	9	19.842	3.642	9	22.240
4.536	10	22.046	4.047	10	24.711
9.072	20	44.092	8.094	20	49.421
13.608	30	66.139	12.140	30	74.132
18.144	40	88.185	16.187	40	98.842
22.680	50	110.231	20.234	50	123.553
27.216	60	132.277	24.281	60	148.263
31.752	70	154.324	28.328	70	172.794
36.287	80	176.370	32.375	80	197.684
40.823	90	198.416	36.422	90	222.395
45.369	100	220.462	40.469	100	247.105

1 lb = 16 ounces (oz)
1 hundredweight (cwt) = 112 lb
1 acre = 4840 sq yards

kg/ha	Weight/area kg/ha or lb/ac	lb/ac
1.121	1	0.892
2.242	2	1.784
3.363	3	2.677
4.484	4	3.569
5.605	5	4.461
6.726	6	5.353
7.848	7	6.245
8.969	8	7.138
10.090	9	8.030
11.211	10	8.922
22.421	20	17.844
33.632	30	26.766
44.843	40	35.688
56.054	50	44.609
67.265	60	53.531
78.486	70	62.453
89.696	80	71.374
100.907	90	80.296
112.108	100	89.218

Conversion tables for British and Metric Weights and Measures

The figures in the central of the three columns in each table represent either one or the other of the two side columns, as required, e.g. 1 cm = 0.394 in, 1 in = 2.540 cm, 1 m = 1.094 yd, 1 yd = 0.914m.

Length

Centi-metres	cm or in	Inches	Metres	m or yd	Yards
2.540	1	0.394	0.914	1	1.094
5.080	2	0.787	1.829	2	2.187
7.620	3	1.181	2.743	3	3.281
10.160	4	1.575	3.658	4	4.374
12.700	5	1.969	4.572	5	5.468
15.240	6	2.362	5.486	6	6.562
17.780	7	2.756	6.401	7	7.655
20.320	8	3.150	7.315	8	8.749
22.860	9	3.543	8.230	9	9.843
25.400	10	3.937	9.144	10	10.936
76.200	30	11.811	27.432	30	32.808
101.600	40	15.748	36.576	40	43.745
127.000	50	19.685	45.720	50	54.681
152.400	60	23.622	54.864	60	65.617
177.800	70	27.559	64.008	70	76.553
203.200	80	31.496	73.152	80	87.489
228.600	90	35.433	82.296	90	98.425
254.000	100	39.370	91.440	100	109.361

1 yd = 3 feet = 36 inches

Volume

Litres	litres or gal	Gallons
4.546	1	0.220
9.092	2	0.440
13.638	3	0.660
18.184	4	0.880
22.730	5	1.100
27.276	6	1.320
31.822	7	1.540
36.368	8	1.760
40.914	9	1.980
45.460	10	2.200
90.919	20	4.400
136.379	30	6.599
181.839	40	8.799
227.298	50	10.999
272.758	60	13.199
318.217	70	15.398
363.677	80	17.598
409.137	90	19.798
454.596	100	21.998

1 gal = 8 pints

Index